THE NEW BERGSON

MANCHESTER
UNIVERSITY PRESS

ANGELAKIHUMANITIES

Angelaki Humanities publishes works which address and probe broad and compelling issues in the theoretical humanities. The series favours path-breaking thought, promotes unjustly neglected figures, and grapples with established concerns. It believes in the possibility of blending, without compromising, the rigorous, the well-crafted, and the inventive. The series seeks to host ambitious writing from around the world.

Angelaki Humanities is the associated book series of
Angelaki – journal of the theoretical humanities.

ANGELAKIHUMANITIES

THE NEW BERGSON

edited by john mullarkey

MANCHESTER UNIVERSITY PRESS
MANCHESTER AND NEW YORK

distributed exclusively in the USA by St. Martin's Press

Copyright © Manchester University Press 1999

While copyright in the volume as a whole is vested in Manchester University Press, copyright in individual chapters belongs to their respective authors, and no chapter may be reproduced wholly or in part without the express permission in writing of both author and publisher.

Published by Manchester University Press
Oxford Road, Manchester M13 9NR, UK
and Room 400, 175 Fifth Avenue, New York, NY 10010, USA
http://www.man.ac.uk/mup

Distributed exclusively in the USA by
St. Martin's Press, Inc., 175 Fifth Avenue, New York,
NY 10010, USA

Distributed exclusively in Canada by
UBC Press, University of British Columbia, 6344 Memorial Road,
Vancouver, BC, Canada V6T 1Z2

British Library Cataloguing-in-Publication Data
A catalogue record for this book is available from the British Library

Library of Congress Cataloging-in-Publication Data applied for

ISBN   0 7190 5380 3 *hardback*
       0 7190 5553 9 *paperback*

First published 1999

05 04 03 02 01 00 99   10 9 8 7 6 5 4 3 2 1

GIFT OF NATHAN LYONS
2017

Typeset
by Northern Phototypesetting Co Ltd, Bolton
Printed in Great Britain
by Bookcraft (Bath) Ltd, Midsomer Norton

CONTENTS

FIGURES

CONTRIBUTORS

Keith Ansell Pearson is Professor of Philosophy and Director of Graduate Research in Philosophy at the University of Warwick. He has published numerous studies on Nietzsche, Deleuze and political philosophy.

Mark Antliff, Associate Professor of Art History at Duke University, North Carolina, is the author of *Inventing Bergson: Cultural Politics and the Parisian Avant-Garde* (1993) and co-editor, with Matthew Affron, of *Fascist Visions: Art and Ideology in France and Italy* (1997). A Guggenheim Fellow in 1995–96, he is currently completing a book-length study of the aesthetics of Georges Sorel and the impact of his cultural views on the development of fascism in France.

Garrett Barden has taught philosophy at the National University of Ireland, Cork (University College Cork), since 1972 and at various times in France, Iceland, Italy, Slovakia and the USA. He is the co-author of *Towards Self-Meaning* (1968) and the author of *After Principles* (1990). He is now finishing a book on justice. He was born in Dublin in 1939 and has studied in University College Dublin, Louvain, Heythrop College, Oxford University and the University of Western Australia.

Marie Cariou is Professor and Honorary Dean in the Faculty of Philosophy at Jean Moulin University in Lyon. She is also Vice-President of the University. Her publications include *Freud et le désir* (1973), *Bergson et le fait mystique* (1976), *Trois études sur l'atomisme* (1978), (in collaboration) *De la tyrannie au totalitarisme* (1986), *Lectures Bergsoniennes* (1990) and *Bergson et Bachelard* (1995).

Richard A. Cohen is Isaac Swift Distinguished Professor of Judaic Studies at the University of North Carolina at Charlotte. He studied philosophy at the Pennsylvania State University, the State University of New York at Stony Brook, and at the University of Paris–Sorbonne. He has translated and introduced several works by Emmanuel Levinas, published numerous articles on contemporary continental thought and is author of *Elevations: the Height of the Good in Rosenzweig and Levinas* (1994).

Gilles Deleuze was Professor of Philosophy at the University of Paris VIII until 1987. His publications include *Nietzsche et la philosophie* (1962), *Le Bergsonisme* (1966), *L'Anti-Oedipe*, and *Mille Plateaux*, with Félix Guattari (1972, 1980), and *Le Pli: Leibniz et le Baroque* (1988).

Paul Douglass is Professor of English and Chair of the English Department at San José State University. He is the author of *Bergson, Eliot, and American Literature* (1986), co-editor with Frederick Burwick of *The Crisis in Modernism: Bergson and the Vitalist Controversy* (1992), and is currently at work on a study of antiquities and modern literature and a biography of Lady Caroline Lamb.

Among Professor **P. A. Y. Gunter**'s publications are *Bergson and the Evolution of Physics* (1969), *Henri Bergson: a Bibliography* (2nd edn, 1986) and *Bergson and Modern Thought* (1987). An active environmentalist, his most recent publication is *Texas Land Ethics* (1997), with M. Oelschlaeger.

Ryu Jiseok is currently instructor in philosophy at the University of Chongju in South Korea and doctoral researcher at Charles de Gaulle University in Lille. His present interests include an exploration of various neglected aspects of Bergson's life and work based on those of his writings which are unpublished or published outside Œuvres and *Mélanges*. His own publications include 'Sur une lettre de Bergson à H. M. Kallen (1915)', *Revue Philosophique de la France et de l'Etranger* (1993).

Eric Matthews is a professor in the Department of Philosophy at the University of Aberdeen. Born and brought up in Liverpool, he received his university education (undergraduate and postgraduate) at Oxford, where he studied with Gilbert Ryle, A. J. Ayer and Paul Grice. He has been at Aberdeen since 1963, and has also held a visiting post at the University of New Orleans. Apart from articles in philosophical journals and collections, he has published *Twentieth-Century French Philosophy* (1996) and several translations of recent German philosophy.

F. C. T. Moore's supervisor, Gilbert Ryle, did not discourage his interest in French philosophy, and he learnt much from G. E. L. Owen about interpreting texts. His main posts (apart from numerous visiting positions in different parts of the world) have been at the universities of Birmingham (UK), Khartoum (on secondment) and Hong Kong, where he was appointed to the first chair of philosophy in 1979. He has published *Bergson: Thinking Backwards* (1996), *Sur les rapports du physique et du moral de l'homme par Maine de Biran*, édition critique (1984), *The Psychological Basis of Morality* (1978), *Wisdom from the Nile: a Collection of Folk Stories from Northern and Central Sudan* (1978), *The Psychology of Maine de Biran* (1970), and a translation of and introduction to *The Observation of Savage Peoples*, by J.-M. Degérando (1969).

John Mullarkey is a lecturer in philosophy at the University of Sunderland. His interests include process metaphysics and continental philosophy, and he has published papers on these areas in *Metaphilosophy*, *Philosophy Today*, *Process Studies* and *South Atlantic Quarterly*. He has written an introduction to Bergson for Edinburgh University Press entitled *Bergson and Philosophy*.

Timothy S. Murphy is a lecturer in the Department of English at the University of Oklahoma. He is the author of *Wising Up the Marks: the Amodern William Burroughs* (1997) and English translation co-ordinator for the Deleuze Web, an internet database of seminars given by Deleuze from 1971 to 1987.

Frédéric Worms is Maître de conférence de philosophie at the University of Lille III. He has written essays in both political philosophy and the history of philosophy, including a number devoted to Bergson. In 1997 he published a full-length study of *Matter and Memory* as well as a biography of Bergson in collaboration with Philippe Soulez.

institut français

The publication of this book is supported by the Cultural Service of the French Embassy in London

ACKNOWLEDGEMENTS

There are always more people involved in bringing a collection such as this to publication than simply those who have either edited or contributed to it. Those to whom I am particularly indebted are: Gerard Greenway at Angelaki for his advice, support, and general indefatigable determination in getting this project off the ground; Melissa McMahon and Pelagia Goulimari for their meticulous translations of the essays by Marie Cariou, Gilles Deleuze and Frédéric Worms; Matthew Frost and Stephanie Sloan at Manchester University Press for their diligent professionalism at all times; Pete Gunter and Tim Clark for their aid and advice at various crucial stages; and Ryu Jiseok, both for unearthing Bergson's correspondence with John Dewey and for providing such insightful annotations for it.

I must also thank the Presses Universitaires de France for granting permission to publish the essays by Gilles Deleuze and Frédéric Worms, and Annie Neuburger for permission to publish Bergson's letter to Dewey.

This book has been published with the help of a grant from the Bureau du Livre at the French Embassy in London. As editor, I personally benefited from a sabbatical granted to me by my colleagues at the University of Sunderland, for which I am also grateful.

Finally, I would like to thank Daniel Carey for hearing the right thing at the right time (and letting me know about it) and my wife Annalaura for her patience and support.

Copyright acknowledgements

Acknowledgement is due to the Presses Universitaries de France for permission to print Gilles Deleuze, 'Bergson's Conception of Difference', translated from 'La Conception de la différence chez Bergson', which first appeared in *Les Etudes*

Bergsoniennes, 4 (1956), pp. 77–112, and Frédéric Worms, '*Matter and Memory* on Mind and Body: Final Statements and New Perspectives', translated (with amendments) from the chapter 'Conclusions générales' in Frédéric Worms, *Introduction à* Matière et mémoire *de Bergson* (1997), pp. 265–8, 282–9, for both of which they hold the copyright.

ABBREVIATIONS

All the essays in this volume use these abbreviations of the works of Bergson in note references. The page references to the published English translation(s) are given first, followed by those to the French original in either *Œuvres* or *Mélanges* as appropriate.

CE   Henri Bergson, *Creative Evolution*, London, Macmillan, 1911, translated by Arthur Mitchell from *L'Evolution créatrice* (1907), in *Œuvres*, pp. 487–809. The pagination of the 1983 University Press of America edition is given after the Macmillan edition after a slash; the French pagination follows both.

CM   Henri Bergson, *The Creative Mind: an Introduction to Metaphysics*, New York, Philosophical Library, 1946, translated by Mabelle L. Andison from *La Pensée et le mouvant: essais et conférences* (1934), in *Œuvres*, pp. 1249–482. The paperback edition of this translation has a different pagination from the hardback and omits the endnotes. As it is more widely available than the hardback edition, references are given to both, the hardback's following the paperback's after a slash; the French pagination follows both.

DS   Henri Bergson, *Duration and Simultaneity, with Reference to Einstein's Theory*, Indianapolis, Bobbs-Merrill, 1965, translated by Leon Jacobsen, with an introduction by Herbert Dingle, from *Durée et simultanéité: à propos de la théorie d'Einstein* (1923), in *Mélanges*, pp. 57–244. The French pagination follows that of the English.

L   *Laughter: an Essay on the Meaning of the Comic*, London, Macmillan, 1911, translated by Cloudesley Brereton and Fred Rothwell from *Le Rire: essai sur la signification du comique* (1900), in *Œuvres*, pp. 381–485. The pagination of *Laughter* as it appears in the 1980 Johns Hopkins University Press book *Comedy*, edited by Wylie Sypher, is cited after the Macmillan edition after a slash; the French pagination follows both.

M   Henri Bergson, *Mélanges*, edited by André Robinet, Paris, Presses Universitaires de France, 1972.

ME   Henri Bergson, *Mind–Energy: Lectures and Essays*, Westport, Conn.,

Greenwood Press, 1975, translated by H. Wildon Carr from *L'Energie spirituelle: essais et conférences* (1919), in *Œuvres*, pp. 811–977. The French pagination follows that of the English.

MM   Henri Bergson, *Matter and Memory*, London, George Allen and Unwin, 1911, translated by Nancy Margaret Paul and W. Scott Palmer from *Matière et mémoire: essai sur la relation du corps avec l'esprit* (1896), in *Œuvres*, pp. 159–379. The pagination of the 1988 Zone books edition is cited after the Macmillan edition after a slash; the French pagination follows both.

MR   Henri Bergson, *The Two Sources of Morality and Religion*, Notre Dame, Ind., Notre Dame University Press, 1977, translated by R. Ashley Audra and Cloudesley Brereton, with the assistance of W. Horsfall Carter, from *Les Deux Sources de la morale et de la religion* (1932), in *Œuvres*, pp. 979–1247; the French pagination follows that of the English.

OE   Henri Bergson, *Œuvres*, edited by André Robinet, Paris, Presses Universitaires de France, 1959.

TFW   Henri Bergson, *Time and Free Will: an Essay on the Immediate Data of Consciousness*, London, George Allen and Unwin, 1910, translated by F. L. Pogson from *Essai sur les données immédiates de la conscience* (1889), in *Œuvres*, pp. 1–157; the French pagination follows that of the English.

INTRODUCTION

john mullarkey

LA PHILOSOPHIE NOUVELLE, OR CHANGE IN PHILOSOPHY

Few philosophers have been as influential on our age as Henri Bergson. At the threshold of the twentieth century, he reset the agenda of philosophy and its relationship with science, art and even life itself. Concerned with both examining and extolling the phenomena of time, change and difference, he was at one point held to be both 'the greatest thinker in the world' and 'the most dangerous man in the world'.[1] Yet fewer philosophers still have seen such a level of influence dissipate so quickly. The diffusion of his ideas was so extensive throughout intellectual Europe that, as a distinct and original body of thought, it was all but indiscernible by the 1920s. What excited many at the turn of this century, philosophers and non-philosophers alike, about this *'philosophie nouvelle'*[2] was its emphasis on organicism over logicism, the concrete over the abstract, and, ultimately, novelty itself over immutability. Such was its eventual ubiquity, however, that the originality of the Bergsonian world-view seemed to lose any distinctiveness as its ideas were incorporated (mostly without acknowledgement) into other movements – phenomenology, existentialism, structuralism – whose longevity was more secure. More than most philosophies, Bergsonism has the potential to be appropriated by a variety of philosophical traditions, and this was part of its downfall. None the less, the precise reasons for this disappearance are complex, and we will not try to retell the story of the rise and fall of Bergsonism here. Rather, it is in order to assess as well as contribute to the emergence of a *new Bergson* that this collection of essays has been commissioned.

Increasing interest in Bergsonian philosophy in the 1990s points to the fact that many now believe that the neglect of his work is both unfair to him and irresponsible to philosophy. The rising tide of essays, books, courses and conferences testifies to the new view that there is more to this philosopher than the numerous myths, prejudices and misreadings that have arisen around him since the high-point of his reputation. Without a doubt, the interest in Gilles Deleuze and what might be described as his contemporary implementation of Bergson's thought is partly responsible for this resurgence. Certainly, there is a real kinship between the method and results of Deleuze's 'philosophy of difference' and Bergson's 'intuition of *durée*', and references pointing to this fact are scattered through many of the essays within this volume. To allow the reader to judge the nature of this relationship first-hand, we have included Deleuze's 1956 essay, 'Bergson's Conception of Difference', which is published here in English for the first time. Yet the *actualité* of Bergson goes beyond a simple affinity with Deleuze. What is offered in this book is not a history of philosophical influence. Indeed, such comparative investigations of Bergson have appeared before, but as often as not, Bergson's ideas are placed in a purely historical context such that they only 'foreshadow', 'predate' or 'foresee' their complete realisation in another philosophy. Thus it is Whitehead, Heidegger or Merleau-Ponty who are allowed to forward the definitive version of the point being made, with *their* version alone being philosophically examined in terms of contemporary debate. It is precisely this habit of subsuming Bergson's arguments under a general heading that neglects the differences between his views and others which leads most often to Bergson's name being confined to a hundred opening paragraphs and a thousand lists of names (usually coming between Nietzsche and Scheler).

In contrast, this presentation of Bergson's work concentrates on the contemporary significance of *his* philosophy. With the emergence of such new areas as complexity theory and environmentalism, or the revitalisation of older issues concerning reductionism and materialism, there is probably no better time than now to progress from the usual strategy of gesturing towards the untapped fecundity of Bergson's ideas to a detailed examination of how they compare with work done by figures such as Stuart Kauffman (complexity theory/philosophy of biology), Garrett Hardin (environmentalism) and Thomas Nagel (philosophy of mind), to name but three.

A further key objective for this collection is the ability to maintain a bipartisan approach that places Bergson's work where it should be: between the concerns of the so-called 'continental' and 'analytic' (or 'Anglo-American') schools of philosophy. Traditionally, Bergson has been read by diverse figures: Martin Heidegger, Emmanuel Levinas and Walter Benjamin on the one side, Bertrand Russell, Hans Reichenbach and Adolf Grünbaum on the other. But this is no historical accident. Perhaps uniquely among twentieth-century thinkers, Bergson's writing lends itself to a cross-sectional interest in two ways. At the level of its content it addresses issues such as bodily intentionality, the multiplicity of the self and the radical indeterminacy of time that have continuously animated the researches of continental philosophers from Maurice Merleau-Ponty to Jacques Derrida. At the same time, however, it broaches such traditionally analytic subjects as the mind–body problem, relativity physics and the philosophy of biology. Bergsonism is no less Janus-faced at its formal level either. While his arguments continuously aspired to keep track of the sciences in a thoroughly Anglo-American fashion, he none the less endeavoured to embed this scientism within a consciously stylised writing that is more evocative of contemporary French philosophy than the writings of Paul Churchland or Daniel Dennett. Each of his books, as Bernard Gilson once wrote, was 'conceived at once as a scientific work and as a work of art'.[3] Reflecting this 'double life' of Bergson's philosophy, therefore, are the authors contributing to this book themselves, whose diversity of backgrounds and chosen fields of enquiry range across the current divisions within philosophy.

Irrespective of their particular philosophical allegiances, however, central to each essay found here is an acknowledgement of the need to return to the ideas of Bergson himself, separating his own arguments from the multitude of impressions that have attached themselves to the term 'Bergsonism'. In retrieving his thought from such philosophical ghettos as 'vitalism', 'spiritualism' and 'psychologism', the authors in this collection argue for an alternative image of Bergson, an image that has only begun to emerge in recent years.

Yet one should not think that there is a *single* contemporary image of Bergson at which one might arrive. The interpretations of Bergson are as multifarious as are his own writings, and this is no less true here than anywhere else. *The New Bergson* could just as well have been retitled *The New Bergsons*, for the fertility of his ideas has spawned numerous readings. Indeed, this is a point well worth dwelling on in terms of Bergson's attitude towards philosophy itself. Near the beginning of his 1911 lecture, 'Philosophical Intuition', Bergson says that in each philosophical system there is usually only one 'infinitely simple' insight which is central to the philosophy. But the insight itself is barely expressed, and the philosopher must continuously reformulate his or her work in the effort to express it adequately.[4] It is these reformulations which comprise the many faces of a philosophy. Should we look, then, for the definitive philosophy of Bergsonism, we embark upon a problematic project. Indeed, one recent commentator has reminded us that 'we must always ask which image of Bergson is under consideration'.[5] To think that there is just one version of Bergsonism, be it positivist or metaphysical, speculative or critical, testifies as much to one's own manner of reading as it does to his work itself.

3

But this is not to argue for relativism or that one reading of Bergson is as good as another. Though we might agree with his own view that each philosophy involves only one insight at its origin, that is not also to say that one cannot see certain patterns in the repeated formulations of that philosophical idea. Bergsonism is not a chaotic mess: just as his own philosophy replaces the idea of an absolute and original disorder with a theory of different types of order, so there are varieties of order that are recognisably Bergsonian. It is these patterns or orders one thinks of when referring to 'his philosophy'.

Notwithstanding this last fact, however, we must admit that any examination of a philosopher's work brings with it some simplification and even misrepresentation. In one of his earliest writings, Bergson himself said that even the best expositions of a philosophy are unfaithful; by being inevitably more systematic and abstract, they lose what is personal and profound in the philosopher's original vision.[6] So how can such a work be examined without at once having its content corrupted and its spirit betrayed? The answer may lie in what Bergson means by what is 'personal and profound' in any thought, namely its *movement*. What is true of Bergson's philosophical vision of the universe – that it grows, develops, endures – is no less true of philosophical thought, and for strictly *logical* reasons.

I

H. Wildon Carr, an early and influential advocate of Bergson's work in Britain, provides a clue to this logic in his study of Bergson from 1919, *Henri Bergson: the Philosophy of Change*. He begins his examination with the assertion that 'the philosophy of Bergson is not a *system* ... one of its most important conclusions is that the universe is not a completed system of reality'.[7] Carr makes an interesting connection here between a philosophy – in this case Bergson's non-systematic thought – and the *subject* of that thought, to wit, an incomplete universe. It is significant in that it implies a link between cosmic incompleteness and the fragmentation of any theory concerning that incompleteness. The alternative, quite rational, possibility of a systematic presentation of a non-systematic subject-matter is bypassed. Yet, in fact, Carr expresses a profound insight into Bergson's work that is too little appreciated.

Bergson's writings are replete, of course, with classic formulations of a non-systematic philosophy. Our perennial temptation to think that physical laws are eternal, for example, is traced back by him to the mistaken view that the universe must be 'coherent'.[8] But incoherence also plays a role in the presentational form of Bergson's work, demanding, he argues, the perpetual sacrifice of his firmest convictions and best explanations in order to preserve himself from what he calls 'intellectual automatism'.[9] Hence, when Bergson proclaims 'Je n'ai pas de système', there is no tone of apology in his voice.[10] As a consequence, he openly acknowledged that his works were not coherent among themselves.[11] The changes in emphasis as regards the prime location of 'duration' – in the continuous present for *Time and Free Will*, in the eternal past for *Matter and Memory* – are just one testament to that fact. Bergson's ambivalence towards instinct – at times closer to life, at other times closer to death – is another. Indeed, Bergson stated that he never began a new work without also forgetting his previous positions and demanding a new effort of research.[12] Others, however, might not approach such incoherence so positively. Isaiah Berlin, for example, accused Bergson of being the one living thinker mainly responsible for the 'abandonment of rigorous critical standards and the substitution in their place of casual emotional responses' in contemporary thought.[13]

Yet this casualness or incoherence may have more philosophical import than is usually imagined. Bergson is remembered mostly as a 'philosopher of change', a 'process philosopher', but rarely has this mobility been examined at the metathematic level of philosophical form itself. Readings of Bergson have mostly focused on a certain philosophy of mind and nature, and quite rightly so. None the less, a hint at a higher-order instance of process can also be researched, as can be seen in the following quotation from Bergson's last major works, *The Two Sources of Morality and Religion*: 'action on the move creates its own route, *creates to a very great extent the conditions under which it is to be fulfilled*, and thus baffles all calculation'.[14] The point being made about the conditions of possibility could be taken as merely a question of physical possibility, the removal of an obstacle, for example, rather than a reference to logical possibility. Two facts conspire against this natural interpretation, however. The first is that Bergson saw no qualitative distinction between the physical and the logical. In *Creative Evolution*, Bergson claims that logic *is*, in fact, physical in its origins: 'our logic', he writes, 'is, pre-eminently, the logic of solids'. The 'all or nothing' bivalent logic of what Bergson calls 'materialistic realism'[15] is an abstract from space, the objective space of solid impenetrable bodies, where no two objects can simultaneously occupy the same location.[16] Yet this is not the only type of logic because it is derived from just one type of space. According to Bergson there are 'degrees in spatiality',[17] a view which, if seemingly counter-intuitive, is actually no more revolutionary than the contemporary theory of 'fuzzy sets', which is based on an even more paradoxical view of 'different degrees of class-membership'.[18] Fuzzy logic – no less than any other logic – has more to do with alternative physical states than most logicians may be willing to admit.

The second fact is that Bergson thought of abstraction itself as a physical process in its actual operation and not just its origins. In his excellent study of process philosophy, Nicholas Rescher makes a remarkable point when describing Bergson's work which helps to underline this: 'Everything in the world is caught up in a change of some sort, so that it is accurate rather than paradoxical to say that what is changing is change itself.'[19] He then adds that it would be unfaithful to the spirit of process philosophy to set any ontological categories which would imply concepts and positions which a process philosophy must permanently reject.[20] But what, we might ask, would this process philosophy be if not a changing philosophy that must countenance the possibility of permanent transformation, even for itself? Probably to avoid such seeming nonsense, Rescher does add that, 'at the most abstract level', all true philosophical positions must be the same, even for process thought.[21] For a Bergsonian, though, this means of escape from paradox is of no help, because there is no point which can be called the highest level of abstraction, as Bergson believes that abstraction is an ongoing physical process, with no highest or lowest levels.

To look at what Bergson understands by the process of abstraction or concept formation, one must turn to the notion of movement that lies at the heart of his metaphysics. The individuality of movement *is* its metaphysical status. What makes a movement individual is the rich particularity of the situation in, or rather, with which it unfolds. When represented, however, this movement has each of its various dynamic properties 'extracted' as a concept, leaving a bare, formless and static object behind. Abstraction for Bergson is always extraction.[22]

This subjectivisation of movement and concomitant immobilisation of the world (the Kantian view of time is one of Bergson's targets here) is facilitated through what we might term 'inattentiveness'. We can only isolate a moving object from its supposedly static world by ignoring the specific moment that individuates that world as the one belonging exclusively to the object. Indeed, prior to our inattention, there was no 'object plus world' at all. For the purely pragmatic need to control (and intellect has its roots in praxis for Bergson), we cut the 'object' out as a figure against a background. It is precisely when we abstract (or extract) our regard from 'them' in favour of an overview that the two are separated: 'the concept generalizes at the same time that it abstracts'.[23] In this respect, Bergson's critique of abstraction is close to Berkeley's: there is no real process of abstraction that would result in a genuinely new and purely formal image, but only one image that is employed generally to stand for another set of images.[24] It is a matter of ignorance and blindness towards differences rather than the lucid perception of real identities.[25] By immobilising inhabitant and place, one ignores what is specific to them at each moment, and so they dissociate into a relation of container and contained.[26]

At a higher level of abstraction again, materialism and idealism have, in their respective ways, continued to effect this dissociation concluding with a total bifurcation between an inert, homogeneous and objective 'outside' and a living, heterogeneous and subjective 'inside':[27] 'formless matter' and 'matterless thought', as Bergson puts it.[28] As '-isms', we would normally deem philosophical views such as these physically impotent, yet, for Bergson, they are part of the physical process of abstraction–extraction.

One commentator has described the Bergsonian picture of intellectuality as the mobility of mobility, that is, the dissociation of one type of movement, action, into another type of movement – a type of meta-mobility.[29] Hence, in *Creative Evolution* two types of sign are described: the *'instinctive sign'* which 'is adherent', and the *'intelligent sign'* which 'is mobile' and 'free'.[30] Yet the intelligent sign's freedom is literally abstract, a free-floating form without content, a frame for thought rather than a genuine intuitive thought. That is why, for Bergson, intellect does not merely dissociate form from content, it *is* form dissociated from content. Intellect is less a faculty for such dissociation than a process of dissociation, both produced and producing at one and the same time. What we term the intention of a thought-object is only the amplification of the process of abstraction–extraction producing further meta-level extractions which are more and more free-floating. Another name for this process might be the subjectivisation of movement or time.

Of course, one might still ask why this should be called a physical event. The answer lies in the Bergsonian picture of the external world itself. In *Matter and Memory* the opening passage fixes reality between idealism and materialism, in what Bergson calls 'partial realism':[31]

> We will assume for the moment that we know nothing of theories of matter and theories of spirit, nothing of the discussions as to the reality or ideality of the external world. Here I am in the presence of images, in the *vaguest* sense of the word, images perceived when my senses are opened to them, unperceived when they are closed.[32]

Bergson's choice of the term 'image' here might be deemed part of a covert preference for idealism, but it can equally be read as a form of 'ultra-externalism', founding mind wholly on matter.[33] What is really significant is that it is neither, for these Bergsonian images pre-exist any bifurcation between inside and outside, subject and object.

Within this menagerie, each image can be impoverished to become a percept-image and further again to become a concept-image, as types of image build upon each other into a system of ever more rarefied strata.

That is why Bergson defines the concept as an image *of* an image, though he never explains the 'of' here in terms of reference, but simply asserts the existence of an imagery from the outset that is subsequently more and more decontextualised.[34] This impoverishment of a given type of image is itself a process, the process of abstraction which is simultaneously the process of inattention to specificity. However, this inattention is ultimately described as a process of immobilisation. That is why it concerns the physical, because it concerns time. Each level of imagery is also a context, a world, that can be immobilised to become a container for some 'new' content-meaning. Hence, what novelty the concept or 'intelligent sign' has is born from a reduction or immobilisation of its context such that the former can stand out as something new against a static background. So where I spoke earlier of inattention as the agent of abstraction, one should not read that as a psychological process so much as a physical one.

Taking on board, then, what Bergson writes about concept-formation as well as logic, one understands why the changing form of Bergson's philosophy is tied to its changing content, and that Bergson's process philosophy cannot be separated from questions of metaphilosophy: what one understands philosophy to be and how one goes about creating, studying and representing it. From the Bergsonian perspective metaphilosophy, as its etymology would suggest, simply means change in philosophy. No less than a process meta-physics designates change and transformation in *physis*, so meta-philosophy designates the transformation of *philosophia*. But we must be mindful not to think of this as the tracing of such changes (that would simply be the history of philosophy), so much as the change itself, what Bergson regards as the necessary 'movement' of thought. This movement is also named by him 'thinking in duration', which Bergson explains as the inevitability that a philosophical terminology – including his own jargon of 'durée', 'multiplicity', and so on – will lose its force and have to be replaced with a new language if that philosophy is to remain vital.[35] Such linguistic supersession is not simply a question of avoiding a fall into platitudes and rigid associations; rather, it is essential, he says, that we continually create new concepts and not just new names for old concepts. These novel concepts will appear vague, confused and even paradoxical at first – he often cites the example of 'unconsciousness' as it was received in the nineteenth century[36] – but such concepts will eventually, as he puts it, 'become clear' because conceptual clarity is itself a process too.[37] Hence, a certain fidelity to one's philosophy may actually require a systematic inconsistency, so to speak, perpetual contradiction, or, if you prefer, 'casualness'. Most fascinating for us is what follows from this in relation to the Bergsonian attitude towards other philosophies, be it their form or their content.

II

Lacking the virtues of a system is endemic to Bergson's philosophy, it is said, because it is itself 'an analysis against analysis', and as such one that can ultimately only suggest rather than demonstrate its truth.[38] Consequently, it has also been argued that Bergsonism is indefensible simply by virtue of the fact that Bergson cannot 'account' for his ideas. The real target of these attacks is Bergsonian intuition. The intuition of *durée* is described by Bergson as a means of 'grasping' the movement of change immediately, 'over and above all expression, translation or symbolic representation'.[39] It is not surprising that an immediate grasp of the temporal, which is itself inexpressible, should strike some as a poor place to begin one's philosophy.

And yet this dichotomy of symbolic and non-symbolic is not wholly faithful to Bergson's thinking. It is only the bivalent realism found in certain forms of imperious representationalism which worries Bergson.[40] In its place he offers a range of alternative forms of representation.[41] A metaphor, for example, is described as a fluid concept with boundaries not yet fixed. As such, it possesses a movement which can imitate the ongoing dynamism of nature.[42] Such fluid imagery as Bergson uses to describe *durée* may appear metaphorical to some, yet it is, he says, the only precise manner in which he can express himself. They are precise in virtue of the fact that they instantiate what they are supposedly trying to represent. In a sense, then, Bergson is really against metaphor altogether. The so-called 'clear and distinct' concepts of scientific realism (read 'materialism'), and the vague and indistinct concepts of duration, are both literally true when applied in their own categories, and only metaphorical when placed in the wrong category. Hence, it is no less figurative to speak of consciousness as a mechanical process than it is to think of matter as a form or symbol of spirit. Both materialism and idealism are equally wrong because they are equally totalising in their attempt to subsume all reality under one homogeneous explanation. From this perspective Bergson is thoroughly classical, with a realist view of truth as correspondence.[43] The difference is that Bergson advocates different types of reality (static and mobile) and so different types of concept to correspond with these realities.

Bergson's strategy here in avoiding the dichotomy of woolly metaphor and clear concept is to divide and conquer: throughout his work he multiplies the number of variables at play on both sides of a divide. We have seen that there can be two forms of correspondence. There are also, for example, two types of clarity, the first instantaneous and deductive, the second a generative '*becoming* clear' which, while comparatively slow to emerge, is all the more enduring as a result.[44] He also speaks of types of simplicity – the one based on experienced immediacy, the other on logical implication – and similarly one encounters types of unity, multiplicity and even of alterity and sameness.[45] In each case of this multiplication, a vital changing variety is contrasted with a rigid inert one.

Yet it would also be wrong to think that Bergson has placed all rigidity on the side of the logical and all fluidity and transience on the side of the alogical. There are types of logic for Bergson too. Such being the case, his remedial work in philosophy will concern conceptual content no less than the formal expression of that content, as we have seen. As regards the content of contrasting philosophies on the other hand, the fact that materialism and idealism are both wrong because they are both totalising discourses is worth reiterating.

A dominant distinction within current philosophy is that between monism and dualism, with materialist monism often being deemed the only viable position in many circles. But we might add to this opposition a further third category of metaphilosophical dualism or dualisation, which is peculiar to Bergson's own view. What he writes about reductionism in the specific areas of biology, psychology or physics, he also regards as valid for metaphilosophy. Totalising philosophies lack explanatory power, for in claiming that everything is (directly or indirectly) x, y or z (physics is fundamental to all knowledge, metaphysics reduces to logic, ethics is first philosophy, and so on), they lose the ability to account for contrary views, even as derivative illusions or errors.[46] The 'firstness' of a philosophy – be it materialism, empiricism, idealism or whatever – enters it into a relationship of reduction, elimination or separation with its rivals. But in each case it can be asked whether there is any remainder left of the rival, and if so, of what type, and how. What is at issue here is the self-sufficiency or identity of the monism. A case in point, for instance, is the following critique Bergson makes of idealism:

> To say that an image of the surrounding world issues from this image of a dance of atoms [of the brain], or that the image of the one expresses the image of the other … is self-contradictory, since these two images – the external world and the intra-cerebral movement – have been assumed to be of like nature.[47]

Notions of expression or issuance imply a duality, whereas being of 'like nature' invokes a monism. Monisms attempt to assert that 'everything is x', yet, despite themselves, they usually end up having to show how some x influences, causes, symbolises, expresses, issues or produces some other y, even if this y is an illusion – the illusion of dualism, for example. It is this totalisation which is precisely where they err, for Bergson's famed critique of nothingness and negation marks the attempt to show that all thought, even 'erroneous' thought, stands for something: 'Error itself', Bergson writes, 'is a source of truth';[48] '*Yes* and *no* are sterile in philosophy. What is interesting ... is *in what measure?*'[49] Perhaps the only error which is not instructive is the one that denies the existence of something absolutely; the correct way can only be a question of fixing something's just place in the whole.[50] Cartesian dualism may be 'dead in the water' in contemporary philosophical terms, but neither can materialism pretend to ignore its own inability to explain away the abundantly vital metaphilosophical duality of materialism and dualism. And, having rejected any recourse (in defence of monism) to a theory of 'error' or 'misrepresentation' through his critique of negation, it is this metaphilosophical weakness that Bergson can use to subvert all monisms.

The ultimate crime of any monistic philosophy, for Bergson, is that it is static whereas his own dualistic thought is dynamic. Most of the critical examinations of Bergson agree on this: his thought embraces a 'dynamic monism' allowing for 'qualitative diversity;'[51] he is neither a monist nor a dualist alone, the 'infrastructure' of his philosophy is at once 'dualist and unitary'.[52] H. Wildon Carr himself mentions 'divergent tendencies' in Bergsonism rather than any dualism,[53] but whatever the formulation, in each case it is a question of a process of dualisation over either static dualism or monism.

What Bergson advocates are dualities according to his own 'law of dichotomy'.[54] By this, he understands a universal principle of bifurcation which explains how every unity is provisional or practical, being destined to fragment for the simple reason that life (and life, existence and time are interchangeable terms for Bergson) is beyond the 'one and [the] many', being instead a 'reciprocal interpenetration' of opposed forces held together in tension.[55] This constant dichotomisation (without subsequent Hegelian mediation, I might add) is the driving force of reality, which is, of course, wholly movement and force anyway.

In Bergson's most famous work, *Creative Evolution*, he asserts that 'it is no longer then of the universe in its totality that we must speak ... for the universe is not made, but is being made continually'.[56] The point here is not a quantitative one concerning an expanding, condensing or dying universe, but concerns the qualitative emergence of radical and unforeseeable novelty. And, just as H. Wildon Carr indicated in 1919, this novelty concerns our thoughts in and about philosophy. In philosophy, because Bergson believes that the secret of remedying our overly rigid thinking is by thinking in duration, and so he commends the use of fluid concepts and permanently mutating philosophical schemes. Metaphysics, he writes, must 'remodel' itself on the processes of reality.[57] But then this begins to merge with the process of philosophy as such, where thoughts can proceed to dichotomise into new, apparently opposed forms. The highest-order descriptions must themselves transform, these transformations being one aspect of the processes of reality.

Bergson once wrote that thought about time inevitably becomes 'lodged in concepts such as duration, qualitative or heterogeneous multiplicity, unconsciousness – even differentiation'.[58] It is significant that the concepts he lists here, 'duration', 'differentiation', and so on, are the ones peculiar to the Bergsonian philosophy of time. For Bergson, philosophy is not about discovering the right expression to represent reality – be that reality a process one or not – but rather, because logical essences themselves mutate, philosophy is about creating the right expression. As Bergson puts it, philosophers need not 'determine ... the categories of thought ... [they] must engender them'.[59] Admittedly, he adds, 'the idea that for a new object we might have to create a new concept, perhaps a new method of thinking, is deeply repugnant to us',[60] yet the task of philosophy must be to perpetrate this continual 'violence' to the mind's natural orientation.[61]

III

Be it termed 'inconsistency' or 'casualness', be it analysed in terms of the formation of concepts or the origins of logic, when viewed negatively each of these areas has contributed in some way or other to the picture of Bergson's work as irredeemably inconsistent and so of negligible value. That there are so many images of Bergsonism is regarded as a fault. But in attempting to readdress the value of Bergson's philosophy the essays gathered for this collection do not try to reduce Bergsonism to one all-embracing image, to one system. This Introduction itself, for instance, is but one possible interpretation that seeks to embrace one type of incoherence in preference to an impoverished view of philosophical clarity, logic and consistency. Yet this is just one way in which we might retrieve Bergson from the philosophical ghettos: the other contributors all follow their own strategy in re-establishing the validity of Bergson's work.

For the most part, this takes the form of showing the means by which we might read Bergson anew as a contemporary philosopher rather than a historical curiosity. Consequently, the essays aim to contextualise Bergson's ideas in areas significant to current debate in philosophy. We have divided these strands of investigation into five sections – 'History and Method', 'Ontology', 'Mind', 'Life' and 'Art' – usually with two essays in each section. The first focuses on Bergson's place in philosophical history (Richard Cohen), with particular emphasis being given to his methodology (Garrett Barden). The second section on ontology is both theoretical – looking at Bergson as a philosopher of difference (Gilles Deleuze) – and applied – comparing the Bergsonian metaphysics of space and time to that of David Bohm and relativity theory (Timothy Murphy).

The middle section on the philosophy of mind is unusual in having five contributions, but this reflects its focus, *Matter and Memory*, long considered the 'bed-rock of Bergsonism', being at once the most 'learned', 'rich' and 'difficult' of his works.[62] The first two essays here comprise detailed examinations of *Matter and Memory* from the perspective of the ultimate significance of its dualism (Frédéric Worms) and its method in analysing memory (Marie Cariou). The second pair utilise Bergson's theory of mind in an examination of subjectivity (Eric Matthews) and the Bergsonian analysis of magic and magical consciousness found in his last major work *The Two Sources of Morality and Religion* (Tim Moore). These four are prefaced by a letter from Bergson to John Dewey dating from 1913 and published here for the first time. Though brief, it is of immense significance for readers of *Matter and Memory*, casting new light on Bergson's theory there of the 'image' and dubbing the book's method as a whole with the title 'partial realism'.

The penultimate section focuses on *Creative Evolution*, by far the most widely read of Bergson's books, and the one which has undoubtedly fixed his popular image as a 'philosopher of life'. The two essays here respectively examine the relevance of creative evolution for current philosophy of biology (Keith Ansell-Pearson) and, from the ethical perspective of modern-day environmentalism, Bergson's philosophy of nature in general (Pete Gunter). The fifth and final section turns to what has always remained a fertile area of research: Bergsonian aesthetics. Mark Antliff's essay reaffirms the enormous influence Bergson has had on French art and culture, in this particular case elucidating the intimate connection between Matisse's artwork and Bergson's theory of *durée*. In the last essay in this volume, Paul Douglass provides an exhaustive analysis of the significance of cinema to Bergson, showing why he described the early twentieth-century cinematographical method as analogous with perception, and where that analogy remains apt in terms of contemporary cinema and film semiotics.

For too long, Bergson has remained hermetically sealed to the uninitiated reader who has had no way of sorting out the merits of Bergsonism from the prejudices of partisan presentations. We hope that this collection can act as an access-point for those who are attracted to the Bergsonian world-view but who as yet have not had the necessary resources to begin an engagement with it. Hence, the five sections of this book have been chosen to reflect the contributors' own expertise as well as the timeliness of Bergson's thought. Each in its own way, they establish a set of conceptual tools such that those who see the relevance that Bergson has for their own ideas can find the appropriate entry-point into it.

john mullarkey

Notes

1 Frédérick LeFevre, 'Une heure avec Maurice Maeterlinck', *Les Nouvelles Littéraires* (7 April 1928), p. 8, cited in R. C. Grogin, *The Bergsonian Controversy in France 1900–1914* (Calgary, The University of Calgary Press, 1988), p. 61; W. Lippman, 'The Most Dangerous Man in the World', *Everybody's Magazine*, 27 (1912), pp. 100–1.

2 Edouard Le Roy, 'Une Philosophie nouvelle: M. Henri Bergson: I. La Méthode. II. La Doctrine', in *Revue des Deux Mondes*, vol. 7 (1912), translated by Vincent Benson as *A New Philosophy: Henri Bergson* (London, Williams and Norgate, 1913).

3 Bernard Gilson, *L'Individualité dans la philosophie de Bergson* (Paris, Librairie Philosophique J. Vrin, 1978), p. 64.

4 CM, pp. 108–9/127–9; OE, pp. 1346–7.

5 Sanford Schwartz, 'Bergson and the Politics of Vitalism', in Frederick Burwick and Paul Douglass (eds), *The Crisis in Modernism: Bergson and the Vitalist Controversy* (Cambridge, Cambridge University Press, 1992), pp. 277–305: p. 303.

6 See M, p. 370.

7 H. Wildon Carr, *Henri Bergson: the Philosophy of Change* (London and Edinburgh, T. C. and E. C. Jack, 1919), p. 14.

8 CM, p. 214/254; OE, p. 1445.

9 M, p. 362.

10 M, p. 940.

11 See Jean de La Harpe, 'Souvenirs personnels d'un entretien avec Bergson', in Albert Béguin and Pierre Thévanez (eds), *Henri Bergson: essais et témoignages* (Neuchâtel, Editions de la Baconnière, 1943), pp. 357–64: p. 360.

12 *Ibid.*: 'I have produced each of my books in forgetting all the others'; see also M, p. 798.

13 Isaiah Berlin, 'Impressionist Philosophy', *London Mercury*, 32 (191) (1935), pp. 489–90, cited in P. A. Y. Gunter, *Henri Bergson: a Bibliography*, 2nd edn (Bowling Green, Ohio, Philosophy Documentation Center, Bowling Green State University, 1986), p. 232; see also P. A. Y. Gunter, 'Bergson's Philosophy of Education', *Educational Theory*, 45 (3) (1995), pp. 379–94: p. 380.

14 MR, p. 296; OE, p. 1227, emphasis added.

15 MM, p. 14/26; OE, p. 177.

16 CE, p. ix/ix; OE, p. 489.

17 CE, p. 216/205; OE, p. 669.

18 Milič Čapek, 'Bergson's Theory of the Mind–Brain Relation', in A. C. Papanicolaou and P. A. Y. Gunter (eds), *Bergson and Modern Thought: Towards a Unified Science* (Chur, Switzerland, Harwood Academic Press, 1987), pp. 129–48: p. 145.

19 Nicholas Rescher, *Process Metaphysics: an Introduction to Process Philosophy* (New York, State University of New York Press, 1996), p. 17.

20 *Ibid.*, p. 36.

21 *Ibid.*

22 CM, pp. 167/196–7, 116/137; OE, pp. 1401, 1354; MR, p. 180; OE, p. 1128.

23 CM, p.167/196; OE, p. 1400.

24 Intellectual form is empty of all concrete imagery for Bergson; see CE, pp. 157–9/149–51; OE, pp. 621–3.

25 See CM, pp. 116/136–7 for Bergson on Berkeley's ideas.

26 See MM, pp. 277–8/208–10; OE, pp. 343–4. The intimacy between inhabitant and place inhabited is only restored as our attention to life and movement fixes on their coexistence at each moment. In contrast to this impoverishment of perception into

conception (and thereafter of conception into more and more abstraction), when we describe this movement adequately, our necessarily 'thick' or 'metaphysical' description will appear to be a *projection* on the part of the subject. In fact, it will be a projection, but only of that metaphysical depth which belonged to it indigenously and which was first extracted precisely by our abstract representation of it.

27 On this idea of 'inner' and 'outer' see A. D. Lindsay, *The Philosophy of Bergson* (London, J. M. Dent, 1911), pp. 5, 91–2, 156–7, 168–9.
28 MM, p. 9/23; OE, p. 174.
29 See Paul Miquel, 'Animalité et humanité dans *L'Evolution créatrice*', in Alain Niderst (ed.), *L'Animalité: hommes et animaux dans la littérature française* (Tübingen, Gunter Narr Verlag, 1994), pp. 201–11: p. 209: 'la connaissance se dissocie de l'action'.
30 CE, p. 167/159; OE, p. 629.
31 See Bergson's letter to John Dewey of 3 January 1913 (chapter five).
32 MM, p. 1/17; OE, p. 169.
33 See F. C. T. Moore, *Bergson: Thinking Backwards* (Cambridge, Cambridge University Press, 1996), pp. 31–2.
34 See for the following, CE, pp. 167 ff./158 ff.; OE, pp. 629 ff.
35 CM, p. 35/39; OE, pp. 1275–6.
36 See M, pp. 1062–4; MM, p. 183/142; OE, p. 284.
37 See M, p. 1064; CM, pp. 35–6/39–41; OE, pp. 1276–7.
38 V. Delbos, 'Matière et mémoire: revue critique', *Revue de Métaphysique et de Morale* (1897), p. 373, quoted in François Heidsieck, *Henri Bergson et la notion d'espace* (Paris, Le Circle du Livre, 1957), p. 90; see also Heidsieck, *Henri Bergson*, p. 175.
39 CM, p. 162/191; OE, p. 1396.
40 See CM, p. 168/198; OE, pp. 1401–2, where Bergson speaks of metaphysics being itself, not when it dispenses with concepts, but when it 'frees itself of the inflexible and ready-made concepts and creates others very different from those we usually handle, I mean flexible, mobile, almost fluid representations.'
41 For a fuller account of this area in Bergson's philosophy, see J. Mullarkey, 'Bergson and the Language of Process', *Process Studies*, 24 (1995), pp. 44–58.
42 See M, p. 501.
43 Hence, Bergson none the less exhorts us to 'use metaphors seriously' (M, p. 980). Note, though, that the forms of correspondence would not be the same, the movement of the metaphor being to the moving reality it suggests as part is to whole rather than sign is to referent.
44 M, p. 1064.
45 See TFW, pp. 141–2, 83, 87, 121–2; OE, pp. 93–4, 57, 59, 81.
46 ME, p. 246; OE, p. 969. Every type of monism, he writes (ME, p. 237; OE, p. 963), involves an illegitimate movement between two 'notation-systems', the one idealist, the other materialist. If we were to try to follow its reasoning we would find that 'we pass instantly from realism [materialism] to idealism and from idealism to realism, showing ourselves in the one at the very moment when we are going to be caught in the act of self-contradiction in the other'.
47 ME, p. 238; OE, p. 964.
48 M, p. 331.
49 M, p. 477.
50 See Simon Frank, 'L'Intuition fondamentale de Bergson', in Béguin and Thévanez, *Henri Bergson*, pp. 187–95: p. 193.
51 Milič Čapek, *Bergson and Modern Physics: a Reinterpretation and Re-evaluation* (Dordrecht, D. Reidel, 1971), p. 193; Čapek, 'Bergson's Theory of the Mind–Brain

Relation', p. 132.

52 See Georges Mourélos, *Bergson et les niveaux de réalité* (Paris, Presses Universitaires de France, 1964), p. 90.

53 Carr, *Henri Bergson*, p. vii.

54 See MR, pp. 296 ff.; OE, pp. 1227 ff. The place of dichotomy in Bergson's metaphilosophy and thought in general is explored further in John Mullarkey, *Bergson and Philosophy* (Edinburgh, Edinburgh University Press, 1999).

55 CE, p. 187/177–8; OE, p. 646.

56 CE, p. 254/241; OE, p. 670.

57 ME, p. 77; OE, p. 862.

58 CM, p. 35/39; OE, p. 1275.

59 CE, p. 218/207; OE, p. 671.

60 CE, p. 51/48; OE, p. 535.

61 CE, p. 31/30; OE, p. 519.

62 Ian Alexander, *Bergson: Philosopher of Reflection* (London, Bowes and Bowes, 1957), p. 30; Leszek Kolakowski, *Bergson* (Oxford, Oxford University Press, 1985), pp. 37–8; A. E. Pilkington, *Bergson and his Influence: a Reassessment* (Cambridge, Cambridge University Press, 1976), p. 7.

HISTORY AND METHOD

|

richard a. cohen

PHILO, SPINOZA, BERGSON: THE RISE OF AN ECOLOGICAL AGE

What is the proper stature of Bergson's thought? Was it only the myopia of temporal proximity and discipleship that led Edouard Le Roy in 1913 to claim for the philosophical revolution effected by Bergson equity with those of Kant and Socrates?[1] Are we to believe that similar distortions account for Bergson's election to the Collège de France in 1900, the French Academy in 1914 and his Nobel Prize of 1927? Did John Dewey simply lose perspective when he wrote that 'No philosophic problem will ever exhibit just the same face and aspect that it presented before Professor Bergson',[2] or when William James in 1907 wrote that Bergson's book *Creative Evolution* 'is a true miracle in the history of philosophy and as far as the content is concerned it marks ... The beginning of a new era'?[3] Must we write off to the exaggerated homage typical of centennial celebrations Maurice Merleau-Ponty's words of 1959, when he spoke of 'Bergson's great books', singling out *Matter and Memory*,[4] or Jean Wahl's declaration on the same occasion that 'if one had to name the four great philosophers one could say: Socrates, Plato – taking them together – Descartes, Kant and Bergson'?[5] But even if proximity and eulogy deluded everyone, and it exceeds our credulity to think so, then we would still have to account for the words of Emmanuel Levinas, who in a Paris radio interview in February 1981 ranked Bergson's doctoral dissertation, *Time and Free Will*, as one of the 'four or five ... finest books in the history of philosophy', alongside Plato, Kant, Hegel and Heidegger.[6] Can this Bergson be the same Bergson who is almost forgotten today, as he was already almost forgotten in pre-World War II France? What is Bergson's proper place in the history of the Western spirit? What did he accomplish?

To anyone familiar with the history of Western philosophy, or with histories – philosophical or otherwise – of that history, what is striking about the above claims regarding the who's who of philosophical greatness is not the appearance of such names as Socrates, Plato, Kant, Descartes, Hegel or Heidegger, who are 'regulars' in such estimates, but rather the appearance of Bergson, who is not. It is not that anyone would deny the conceptual rigour, the intellectual penetration or the literary elegance of Bergson's works. Rather it is that, with the exception of Levinas,[7] hardly a leading thinker in the final third of the twentieth century has placed Bergson's philosophical genius at the highest level in the elite pantheon of great thinkers. With time, the light of his sun seems to have set, or perhaps it was only a meteor's flash in the first place? I don't think so. I would rather say that while Bergson's reputation may have eclipsed, his sun shines as brightly as ever – and it shines brightly indeed. The object of this essay is to show how and why the estimation of Levinas and Bergson's earlier admirers is right and that the philosophy of Bergson is not only of continued importance, but that its greatness is of the highest rank because it represents nothing less than one of the three seminal turning-points of Western thought.[8]

Oddly enough, however, in order to show how and why Bergson merits standing in the very first rank of philosophers, we must turn away from the standard histories of philosophy, especially those propagated by Hegel and Heidegger. We must turn instead to a lesser-known history, that elaborated by the Harvard scholar Harry Austryn Wolfson (1887–1974). Here the fulcrum of Western thought turns not upon Socrates, Plato, Descartes, Kant, Hegel or Heidegger, but rather upon two thinkers who do not appear in this list and who are rarely highlighted in histories of philosophy: Philo of Alexandria (c. 20 BCE–50 CE) and Baruch Spinoza (1632–77). The standard histories pass swiftly over the former, and while recognising the greatness of the latter, cast Spinoza in the shadows of Descartes, Kant, Hegel and sometimes even Leibniz. None the less, it is by grasping how and why these two thinkers, Philo and Spinoza, are the two major pivots, the two decisive turning-points in the history of Western spirit, that we shall then be able to see how and why Bergson's contribution, like theirs, is of the highest order. My thesis is that the novelty, profundity and comprehensiveness of Bergson's work is as radical and revolutionary as that of Philo and Spinoza, and that as the third and most recent figure in a trinity of momentous turning-points which determine the history of Western spirit, his is nothing less than the core inspiration and guiding spirit of our time.

The account wherein Philo and Spinoza serve as the two major axes in the development of Western spirit is that elaborated by Wolfson in the course of two major studies: *The Philosophy of Spinoza* (1934)[9] and *Philo: Foundations of Religious Philosophy in Judaism, Christianity and Islam*

(1947).[10] The thesis of this essay, that Bergson's is a philosophy of the highest rank because it represents a third no less decisive turning-point than those represented by Philo and Spinoza, can thus be seen as a supplement to, and, as we shall see, a revision of Wolfson's original thesis. Hence to appreciate the full nature and the grandeur of Bergson's philosophical accomplishment, we must first turn to Wolfson.[11]

Wolfson's account follows standard accounts in dividing Western spiritual history into three periods: the ancient, the medieval and the modern. It deviates, however, in placing Philo and Spinoza at the two great divides in this tripartite history. Philo stands between the ancient and medieval periods. He is the first medieval, with all subsequent medievalism in some sense 'Philonic'. Spinoza stands between the medieval and modern periods. He is the first modern, with all subsequent modernity in some sense 'Spinozist'. The standard philosophical histories, in contrast, begin the medieval period later, usually with Neoplatonism, and begin the modern period earlier, with Machiavelli, Francis Bacon or more usually Descartes.

To grasp how and why pride of place must be accorded to Philo and Spinoza, however, we must first understand the principal question or issue that in Wolfson's estimation drives Western history and marks its specific character. It is not hard to discover. In contrast to the philosophical histories of Hegel and Heidegger, who in typical post-Renaissance fashion present a Western spiritual history revolving around the epistemological conflict inaugurated by the difference between Parmenides and Heraclitus, that is, between the relative weight and roles assigned to being and becoming in the constitution of truth, what defines and drives Western spiritual history for Wolfson is the larger and more complex question of the proper relation between reason (stretched between being and becoming) and revelation. That is to say, what is central and decisive for Wolfson is the Athens–Jerusalem question.[12] Not being and becoming, but rather reason and revelation would thus stand as the two genuine absolutes whose contention – within and between one another – defines Western spiritual development. The concrete accommodations worked out between these two comprehensive and fundamentally different world-views, worked out by and through individuals, beliefs, literatures, peoples, traditions, institutions, cultures and philosophies, would thus constitute nothing less than the meaning of the history of Western spirit.

The logical permutations of the relation linking the spheres of reason and revelation are fourfold: separation, domination of revelation over reason, domination of reason over revelation, and harmony. Wolfson, however, identifies only three of these four possibilities in his actual history. In his account, the ancient period is that epoch in which reason and revelation were separate; the medieval period, inaugurated by Philo, is that epoch in which reason and revelation were in harmony; and the modern period, which he sees as our period, inaugurated by Spinoza, is that epoch in which reason dominates revelation. Without challenging its underlying principle, that of the primacy of the Athens–Jerusalem question over the Parmenides–Heraclitus debate, my thesis none the less requires a twofold revision of Wolfson's account. First, my claim is that Bergson represents the inauguration of a *fourth* period, our epoch, which, following philosophical convention, I call the 'contemporary' period. Second, my claim is that the contemporary period inaugurated by Bergson, and not the medieval period inaugurated by Philo, represents the genuine harmonisation, or more accurately the task of the harmonisation, of reason and revelation.

For Wolfson, as I have indicated, the medieval period initiated by Philo of Alexandria represents the harmonisation of reason and revelation which were separate (and hostile when in contact) in the ancient period. Hence for Wolfson the modern period initiated by Spinoza represents a disturbing upset of the medieval harmony, whereby reason no longer accepts a complementary place alongside revelation but aims rather to subjugate and rule it. Regarding the relation of reason and revelation in the modern period, I agree with Wolfson. Spinoza and the modern period indeed represent the effort of reason to dominate revelation. What I challenge, however, in the name of Bergson, is the claim that what the modern period overcame was a medieval harmonisation of reason and revelation. Indeed, it is precisely because Wolfson did not appreciate Bergson's genuine harmonisation of reason and revelation that he could mistake the medieval accommodation of reason and revelation for that harmonisation (and mistake the modern period for our own).[13] In the face of Bergson's thought, however, it becomes evident that the medieval period represents not the harmonisation, but rather the domination of revelation over reason.

That the medievals saw themselves as harmonising reason and revelation in no way upsets this thesis. Spinoza, too, after all, makes the same claim – of proper harmony – for his own thought, which is quite obviously biased in favour of reason as against revelation. It is because the modern period and the medieval period are not simply different, one a harmony, the other a domination, but rather are diametrically opposed forms of domination, one in which reason sets out to dominate revelation and the other in which revelation sets out to dominate reason, that we can understand the fierce intensity of the life-and-death struggle by which modernity overcame medievalism and with which medievalism unsuccessfully resisted modernity. Hence Spinoza, for instance, speaks harshly against Maimonides,[14] one of the greatest of the medieval synthesisers, and contemporary 'medievalists', e.g. Thomists and Talmudists, are so often sceptical if not quite disdainful of claims (often indeed exaggerated) made on behalf of modern science. Spinoza saw that the reason allegedly harmonised with revelation in the medieval period was precisely reason subjugated to revelation, that is to say, reason teleologically glossed. A non-teleological reason, reason reduced to efficient causality and deductive implication, which for Spinoza is the only genuine or scientific form reason can take, finds any inner accommodation with revelation intolerable. The medieval accommodation of reason and revelation was not, then, as Wolfson thought, based on a genuine harmonisation of reason and revelation, but rather on a harmonisation with reason teleologically understood. But the modern period, inaugurated by Spinoza, is precisely the insistence that teleology is the province solely of revelation and the concomitant claim that non-teleological reason is alone genuine reason and as such the sole and rightful guide to truth, and as such ruler over revelation.

In view of the above twofold revision of Wolfson, we can now properly grasp the significance of Bergson's overcoming of the modern period, for it represents an unprecedented harmonisation of reason and revelation in contrast to their ancient separation, the medieval rule of revelation and the modern rule of reason. Thus, to restate my thesis in a revised Wolfsonian context: just as Philo is the first medieval because he brought reason and revelation together by making reason the handmaid of revelation and Spinoza is the first modern because he reversed this relation, making revelation the handmaid of reason, Bergson is the first contemporary, and our epoch is Bergsonian, because he brings reason and revelation into harmony.

But what more specifically did Spinoza accomplish that Bergson overcame? Before Spinoza, Philo brought Athens and Jerusalem, reason and revelation, together by means of allegory. The Bible, revelation, would henceforth be interpreted, to the limits of human understanding and inventiveness, as an allegory of reason. The Bible would be reason cut to the measure of human imagination. While Philo's allegories often seem forced today, the complex and sophisticated philosophies of Maimonides and Aquinas, at the high-point of medieval thought, remain no less bound to biblical parameters. When Maimonides, for instance, in his *Guide for the Perplexed*, follows Aristotle and reason by prizing active intellect above imagination, he will at the same time remain loyal to Philo and revelation by presenting this hierarchy as (or as if it were) a gloss on the story of Adam's fall. This framing, with its theological assumption that reason can fully blossom as reason while serving as handmaid to revelation, annoys Spinoza to no end. Spinoza, rebelling from the medieval spirit, throws off the biblical scaffold of truth, which in his hands, that is to say, within the architecture of a new conception of reason, has become no more than an empty shell, dead letters appropriate perhaps for political purposes for the masses in their ignorance, but of no intrinsic value to the knowing few, who are scientists and hence modern to the core. What transforms the revelatory biblical narrative, the medieval allegory, from authoritative parameter to prudential but ultimately empty and discardable shell is, as has been indicated, an altered conception of reason, a thoroughly and exclusively modern conception of what counts as scientific knowledge: knowledge of necessary efficient causality and knowledge as necessary deductive implication. This new modern conception of reason – reason stripped of final causality – is fatal to Aristotelian reason, and hence fatal to the Philonic correlation of (Aristotelian) reason and revelation through allegory. The medieval compromise is now seen for what it always was, the surreptitious victory of revelation over a reason bridled by the restraints of revelation in the first place. Hence Spinoza's polemic against the Bible and revelation, against Maimonides and the medieval spirit, is at bottom an attack by modern science against Aristotelian reason as well.

In the final chapter, entitled 'What is New in Spinoza', of his great work on Spinoza, Wolfson distinguishes four dimensions, four 'acts of daring',[15] by means of which Spinoza overturns the medieval world-view – reason subservient to revelation – and replaces it with a modern one – revelation subservient to reason. In each case two incommensurable realms, the divine and the mundane, one above the other, are reduced to one realm of uniform and homogeneous nature.[16]

> By declaring that God has the attribute of extension as well as of thought, Spinoza has thus removed the break in the principle of the homogeneity of nature. This is his first act of daring.
>
> ...
>
> By denying design and purpose in God Spinoza has thus removed the break in the principle of the uniformity of the laws of nature. This is his second act of daring.
>
> ...
>
> Spinoza's insistence upon the complete inseparability of the soul from body has thus removed another break in the homogeneity of nature. This is his third act of daring.
>
> ...
>
> Spinoza's insistence upon the elimination of freedom of the will from human actions has thus removed another break in the uniformity of the laws of nature. This is his fourth act of daring.[17]

In Spinoza's paradigm-shift from the medieval to the modern, we must distinguish two closely related but different reorientations: homogeneity and uniformity. Reversing the ancient and medieval efforts which consisted in distinguishing and grasping a lower realm (dependent creation or *physis*, 'nature') in terms of a higher one (independent thought, purpose, soul, will), Spinoza *homogenises* the two. He homogenises them by *reducing* the higher to the lower, a move which has the initial effect of eliminating the higher realm, but the ultimate effect, as Nietzsche emphatically points out, of levelling all ranks and thus eliminating the notion of rank altogether. Spinoza does this because he understands the lower realm, the mundane, in terms of a specific and narrow interpretation of matter. It is not as simple as saying that he naturalises spirit. Rather, in keeping with the mechanist model of physics dominant in early modern science, he mechanises spirit. Materialists like de la Mettrie make clear in a language and thought perhaps simpler but following the basic contours of Spinoza's, that 'man is a machine' not only because the human is an integral part of nature, but more profoundly because that nature of which the human is an integral part is itself a machine. Like the medievals, who saw the will of God in all things, Spinoza reduces everything to order, but unlike the medievals he reduces all order not to will but to the *uniformity* of efficient causality in extension and deductive implication in intellection, a *mathesis universalis*. Based on this new interpretation of order as uniformity, and uniformity as strict causality and implication, Spinoza's four 'acts of daring' follow from the homogenisation or levelling of higher and lower, that is to say, from the scientific conception of a *universe*: intellection is the mirror of extension, freedom is nothing other than necessity, the soul is conflated with body and purpose is banished altogether from science to politics. Spinoza homogenises higher and lower by reducing everything to the uniformity of universal and necessary relations. This reduction occurs despite, or perhaps in view of Spinoza's *metaphysical* account of the universe in terms of substance, which he distinguishes from its two known 'modes', duration and quantity (which are further distinguished in an almost Bergsonian fashion, it is interesting to note, from time and measure respectively).[18]

Wolfson has shown us that both Philo and Spinoza bring together Athens and Jerusalem, and do so through a relation of subordination. The medieval world inaugurated by Philo, which makes reason subordinate to revelation through more or less sophisticated allegories, is based ultimately on the *will* of God. It is thus in the final account a theo-logical world, a world of providence, however knowable or mysterious. The modern world inaugurated by Spinoza, in contrast, which makes revelation subordinate to reason through a universal and necessary uniformity, *mathesis universalis*, is based ultimately on necessary *causality*. It is thus in the final account a rationalist world, whether necessary or statistically probable.

What Bergson does is also to bring together Athens and Jerusalem. But instead of doing so by subordinating one to the other, making reason conform to will or will conform to reason, and thus misreading both, he rad-ically alters and deepens our understanding of both will and cause, revelation and reason, by uniting them in the biological notion of *growth*.[19] Reality is no longer conceived either on the model of inorganic matter, conceptually reconstructed from elements taken from one periodic table or another, joined together by uniform forces, as it was by modern ratio-nalism, or on the model of human will and generations, as it was in ancient mythology and cosmology, and in absolutised form in biblical and medieval theology too. Rather, both *physis* and will, reality and desire, order and inspiration, come together for Bergson in the unitary notion of organic development, cumulative progress, inner growth. In contrast to the theo-logical and onto-logical visions of earlier periods, it is Bergson who launches an *eco-logical* vision of the contemporary world, the world grasped as an integral developing interrelationship of matter and spirit, mind and body. And not merely interrelationship, as if mind and body, spirit and matter, and so on, were first separate and then related, as if so-called 'secondary' qualities could be added to 'primary' qualities. Rather, Bergson *begins* with the inextricable intertwining, the integral unity of what previous thought had separated. Reality conceived in its original character as creative evolution thus requires grasping man and world not in the mediated terms of a scientific reconstruction, which for Bergson is a second-order explanation motivated by unacknowledged practical inter-ests, but rather in the immediate, intuited by the philosopher in terms of *durée* and *zoe*, duration and vitality, both manifesting a universal *élan vital*, a vital energy driving and contained in all things each in its own way. Berg-son's fundamental distinction between static quantification and moving dynamism, where the former is derived from the latter, and the latter is the true object of philosophical enquiry, whether this distinction is charac-terised in terms of discontinuity and continuity, spatialised time and dura-tion, representation and memory, closed and open society, or in other forms and registers of meaning, runs as a central theme through all his work from *Time and Free Will*, *Matter and Memory* and *Creative Evolution* to *The Two Sources of Morality and Religion*. In every instance Bergson shifts from a static and conceptual compartmentalisation, serving practical purposes, to an immediate reality, grasped in terms of (1) interpenetrating flow, (2) cumulative growth and (3) unpredictable future. From the begin-ning to the end of his thought, then, by means of an integral organic model Bergson overcomes the dualisms which plagued philosophy and haunted theology hitherto.

Now one might be tempted to think that the Hegelian dialectic had already accomplished and must be credited with the conception of an inte-gral developmental unity, the organic movement that I am ascribing to

Bergsonian thought. But this would be mistaken. It is true that Hegel *homogenises* the dualisms which run through philosophy and theology up to Kant, bringing the 'other' into the purview of the 'same'. But his means, the famous 'negation of the negation', remains bound to the very representational logic it strives to overcome. Not only does the 'negation of the negation' blindly fail to appreciate an originary and original positivity prior to representational thought, its alleged movement is in truth but a calculus, a reconstruction of movement, but not movement itself. It re-creates, but now in an even more disguised form, as a calculus, precisely the discontinuity it claims to overcome. Hence its claims are rhetorical, in the bad sense of empty rhetoric. It was, after all, precisely to preserve the truth of judgement from certain *aporiai* that Kant was forced to distinguish noumena from phenomena, and it is precisely to preserve the same propositional truth – now called 'the Concept' – that Hegel conflates Kant's distinction. This unacknowledged loyalty to modern thought hidden in the alleged novelty of a positivity found through double negation, and the artificiality of the vast claims made in the name of this ostensively new positivity to 'surpass' the *aporia* of 'simple' affirmations and negations, is surely what so irked Schopenhauer in his polemics against the legerdemain of Hegel. But we must agree both with the content and with the tone of Schopenhauer's anti-Hegelianism (though not with his – or Nietzsche's for that matter – return to Kant). By interpreting the stilted activity of negation as genuine movement, even though negativity remains bound to classical logic, and interpreting the world and history in terms of this allegedly new movement, which is in truth only judgemental activity, Hegel constructs a simulacrum, an artificial version of the genuine movement found in the biological model that Bergson later introduced. The charge of artifice would also be Bergson's complaint against Spencerian mechanism.

Nor should we think that the respect for the biological ostensively expressed in Aristotle's notion of finality and the movement it implies[20] captured what Bergson would later express. Bergson does not argue, in contrast to Aristotle, that all things tend towards a *telos*, an end, but rather that they manifest, indeed are manifestations of an internal finality, if one may use this expression, an 'impulsion' rather than an aspiration. The interpenetrating qualities and cumulative movement Bergson sees in duration, memory and life ceaselessly grow not because they approach ever more closely to a pre-set goal, but because they ever-increasingly build upon themselves, constantly grow upon their own growth, and do so unpredictably, hence 'creatively'. 'Life', Bergson writes in *Creative Evolution*, 'transcends finality ... It is essentially a current sent through matter, drawing from it what it can. There has not, therefore, properly speaking, been any project or plan.'[21] The tendency in all things – the *élan vital* –

unfolds, but does so unpredictably, creatively, rather than aiming deliberately at a pre-established goal.

Because the integral unity of Bergson's conception is driven neither as a mechanism nor by a finality, but internally, feeding upon itself, it works quite otherwise than do the unitary visions of Hegel and Aristotle. If the *élan vital* may be said to be progressive, it is not because it is mechanically driven forwards or hypnotically drawn upwards, both by prearranged order, but rather because Bergson notices that with the emergence of conscious memory in human life not only is there an accumulation of the past, as there is with inorganic matter and organic life, each after their own fashion, but there also arises the new possibility, by means of deliberate reflection, of an awareness of that accumulation, and hence a doubling of the progressive development of all things with a progressively developing awareness of that development. In a word, Bergson's famous intuition,[22] by going against the grain of simple or direct development, that is to say, in the case of the human, by going against the ingrained habit of practical or utilitarian concerns, opens the possibility of a pure or philosophical awareness of instinct and common sense, and hence represents *élan vital* become conscious of itself.

The true ally of Bergson is of course neither Aristotle nor Hegel before him, but Merleau-Ponty after him. It is no mere coincidence, then, that Merleau-Ponty succeeded to Bergson's chair of Modern Philosophy at the Collège de France.[23] It is because he succeeds his thought. We have already heard Merleau-Ponty's admiration for *Matter and Memory*, which is no wonder, since there, on the plane of perception so dear to Merleau-Ponty, Bergson repudiates the dualisms of both materialism and idealism and offers a third alternative, the sense of which Merleau-Ponty's entire work is devoted to extending. The whole of his posthumous work *The Visible and the Invisible*,[24] published in 1964, for instance, is a working-out, an elaboration and development of fundamental Bergsonian themes, the intertwining of sense and significance, mind and body, spirit and matter. Perhaps Merleau-Ponty's 'phenomenological' method, too, owes as much to Bergson as to Husserl, of whom Merleau-Ponty is so critical, and for Bergsonian reasons. The Husserlian 'intuition of essences' serves for Merleau-Ponty not to alter or deepen but to refine Bergson's method of 'intuition' – and for the considerable development and articulation of Bergsonian themes due to this refinement we must be grateful indeed.[25]

When in *Matter and Memory* Bergson declares that his 'problem is no less than that of the union of soul and body', and resolves it, against materialism and idealism (which Merleau-Ponty will call 'empiricism' and 'intellectualism'), with the following discovery: 'It is in very truth within matter that pure perception places us, and it is really into spirit that we penetrate by means of memory',[26] these words could be placed verbatim into the most central positive sections of either of Merleau-Ponty's two major works, the *Phenomenology of Perception*[27] or *The Visible and the Invisible*, without disruption or discontinuity to their philosophical arguments and themes (or style, for that matter). If one were to read the following without reference being given: 'our perception being a part of things, things participate in the nature of our perception', who could tell, without checking, whether the words were Bergson's or Merleau-Ponty's? They are Bergson's.[28] 'Every focus is always a focus on something which presents itself as to be focused upon' (Merleau-Ponty).[29] 'Perceiving is pinning one's faith, at a stroke, in a whole future of experiences, and doing so in a present which never strictly guarantees the future' (Merleau-Ponty).[30] 'But we must not confound the data of the senses, which perceive the movement, with the artifice of the mind, which recomposes it. The senses, left to themselves, present to us the real movement, between two real halts, as a solid and undivided whole' (Bergson).[31]

Of course Merleau-Ponty, who like Bergson believes not only in the interpenetration of past and present but in the genuinely *creative* character of reality, its unpredictable futurity, will give up Bergson's gloss that the ongoing amplification of matter, memory and life must be understood as a progressive creative *evolution*.[32] And one wonders whether Bergson has not indeed succumbed to an Aristotelian notion of finality when he interprets cumulative growth as progressive growth. Though Merleau-Ponty will support the philosophical life of self-consciousness, of conscious awareness of the interactive intertwining character of sense and significance, and will even propose a politics consistent with such self-awareness, he will not follow Bergson, who in his later work projected his own optimistic evaluation of this awareness as a developmental progress on to the universe at large. Who is right and who is wrong regarding a large question such as this, how far or how broadly the intertwining of sense and significance can be taken, is not, however, a matter for this essay to decide.

The point of this essay is not even to show that Merleau-Ponty is Bergson's sole heir, though he is perhaps Bergson's most faithful and original successor. The point, rather, is much broader. It is to show that the integral and dynamic unity of mind and body, matter and spirit, past and present – elaborated by Bergson in many writings through the notions of growth and creative evolution, borrowed from and reflecting the organic world – inaugurates a new epoch of the Western spirit – our epoch. In contrast to the ancient period where reason and revelation stood apart from one another, or the medieval period inaugurated by Philo where reason was handmaid to revelation, or the modern period inaugurated by Spinoza where revelation was handmaid to reason, the contemporary period inaugurated by

Bergson is one in which reason and revelation are brought into integral harmony. In contrast to medieval theology and modern ontology, our period is the epoch of *ecology*, where spirit and matter, mind and body, sense and significance, and so on, are understood in terms of their integral harmony and inner dynamic. Whether that integral harmony and inner dynamic be determined in *aesthetic* terms, in terms of creativity, in the manner of Bergson himself, or of Nietzsche, Bataille, Heidegger, Merleau-Ponty and others after him, or in *epistemological* terms, in the manner of Husserl, Gadamer, Jonas, Polanyi and others, or in *ethical* terms, in the manner of Levinas, Habermas, Marion and others, contemporary spirit – philosophical and otherwise – remains under the sign of Bergson. Such is his greatness.

Notes

1 Reported by Edouard Morot-Sir in 'What Bergson Means to Us Today', in Thomas Hanna (ed.), *The Bergsonian Heritage* (New York, Columbia University Press, 1962), p. 37; the reference is most probably to Edouard Le Roy's *The New Philosophy of Henri Bergson* (New York, Henry Holt, 1913).
2 John Dewey, 'Preface', *A Contribution to a Bibliography of Henri Bergson* (New York, Columbia University Press, 1912), p. xii, cited in Robert C. Grogin, *The Bergsonian Controversy in France 1900–1914* (Calgary, The University of Calgary Press, 1988), p. 206.
3 Cited in Joseph Chiari, *Twentieth-Century French Thought: from Bergson to Lévi-Strauss* (New York, Gordian Press, 1975), p. 32.
4 Hanna, *The Bergsonian Heritage*, p. 137. See also Merleau-Ponty's inaugural lecture of January 1953 at the College of France: Maurice Merleau-Ponty, *In Praise of Philosophy*, trans. John Wild and James M. Edie (Evanston, Northwestern University Press, 1963), especially his remarks on Bergson, pp. 9–33.
5 Hanna, *The Bergsonian Heritage*, p. 153.
6 Emmanuel Levinas, *Ethics and Infinity*, trans. Richard A. Cohen (Pittsburgh, Duquesne University Press, 1985), p. 37. The other four books named by Levinas are: Plato's *Phaedrus*, Kant's *Critique of Pure Reason*, Hegel's *Phenomenology of Mind* and Heidegger's *Being and Time*.
7 Another exception is Gilles Deleuze, author of *Le Bergsonisme* (Paris, Presses Universitaires de France, 1966).
8 My claim for Bergson's contemporary significance is thus much larger than that of Robert C. Grogin, who, while greatly appreciating Bergson's past and present contribution, ends by limiting his importance to the religious sphere. See Grogin, *The Bergsonian Controversy*, pp. 206–7.
9 Harry Austryn Wolfson, *The Philosophy of Spinoza*, 2 vols (Cambridge, Mass., Harvard University Press, 1934).
10 Harry Austryn Wolfson, *Philo: Foundations of Religious Philosophy in Judaism, Christianity and Islam*, 2 vols (Cambridge, Mass., Harvard University Press, 1948). Wolfson's thesis regarding the periodicity of Western spiritual history is also found in his *Philosophy of the Church Fathers* (Cambridge, Mass., Harvard University Press, 1956).

11 We can speculate that Levinas's assessment may have actually been influenced by Wolfson, in so far as already in 1937 Levinas had published a review of Wolfson's *The Philosophy of Spinoza* in the *Revue des Etudes Juives* ('Spinoza, philosophe médiéval', January–June issue, pp. 114–19). As far as I know, Levinas never mentions Wolfson after this review.

12 Wolfson was certainly not alone in highlighting the centrality of the Athens–Jerusalem question. One thinks perhaps, in the first instance, of his contemporary, the University of Chicago scholar Leo Strauss (1899–1973), who also wrote extensively on Spinoza, whom he considered 'the most extreme, certainly of the modern critics of revelation, not necessarily in his thought but certainly in the expression of his thought'; in 'Progress and Return', in Leo Strauss, *Jewish Philosophy and the Crisis of Modernity: Essays and Lectures in Modern Jewish Thought*, ed. Kenneth Hart Green (Albany, NY, SUNY Press, 1997), p. 130.

13 Such an attachment and bias is of course hardly surprising coming from a Jew, especially a Jew of Wolfson's deep *Jewish* learning. Jews have long considered the material and spiritual flourishing of the Jewish communities of eleventh- to thirteenth-century Moorish Spain to have been the 'Golden Age' of Judaism, as it is called. In a short article entitled 'Hebraism and Western Philosophy in H. A. Wolfson's Theory of History' (English translation in *Immanuel*, 14 (1982), pp. 77–85), Professor Warren Zev Harvey (of the Hebrew University of Jerusalem) points out that in a youthful essay of 1912, entitled 'Maimonides and Halevi, A Study in Typical Jewish Attitudes towards Greek Philosophy in the Middle Ages' (reprinted in Wolfson, *Studies in the History of Philosophy and Religion*, vol. 2, pp. 120–60 (Cambridge, Mass., Harvard University Press, 1973–77)), Wolfson had not yet settled into his later estimation of the medieval period as the harmonisation of reason and revelation. Oddly enough, instead of understanding it as harmonisation, or even as the victory of Hebraism, as I argue, the young Wolfson saw in medieval philosophy the victory of Hellenisation. I would argue that both of these mistaken views, Wolfson's mature view that medieval Jewish thought represents a harmonisation of reason and revelation, and his youthful view that it represents the domination of reason over revelation, result from his lack of appreciation for Bergson's philosophical contribution.

14 In chapter seven of the *Tractatus Theologico-Politicus* Spinoza writes of Maimonides and his method: 'he assumes that it is legitimate for us to explain away and distort the words of Scripture to accord with our preconceived opinions, to deny its literal meaning and change it into something else even when it is perfectly plain and absolutely clear. Such licence, apart from being diametrically opposed to the proofs advanced in this chapter and elsewhere, must strike everyone as excessive and rash'; Baruch Spinoza, *Tractatus Theologico-Politicus*, trans. Samuel Shirley (Leiden, E. J. Brill, 1991), p. 158.

15 Wolfson, *The Philosophy of Spinoza*, vol. II, p. 332.

16 Alexandre Koyre, in his famous study, *From the Closed World to the Infinite Universe* (Baltimore, Johns Hopkins University Press, 1957), also describes this modern displacement, occurring in the sixteenth and seventeenth centuries, of ancient and medieval dualisms, 'the replacement of the Aristotelian conception of space – a differentiated set of inner worldly places – by that of Euclidean geometry – an essentially infinite and homogenous extension' (p. viii).

17 Wolfson, *The Philosophy of Spinoza*, vol. II, pp. 333, 335, 336, 339.

18 See letter no. 12, 20 April 1663, in Baruch Spinoza, *The Letters*, trans. Samuel Shirley (Indianapolis, Hackett Publishing Co., 1995), pp. 101–7.

19 'The empirical experience upon which truth rests, is no longer mathematical, but

biological, conforming with the fluctuations of life apprehended by consciousness',
writes Joseph Chiari of the revolution effected by Bergson (*Twentieth-Century
French Thought*, p. 27).

20 For a biological reading of Aristotle, see Marjorie Grene, *A Portrait of Aristotle* (London, Faber & Faber, 1963). Perhaps Grene's reading reflects rather than offers an alternative to Bergson.

21 CE, pp. 279–80/265; OE, p. 720.

22 Though it is beyond the scope of this essay to elaborate the precise manner in which Bergsonian 'intuition' and 'intellect' surpass and function otherwise than faith and reason, traditionally conceived, there can be no doubt that both of the latter must be thoroughly reconceived – with a view to their integration – within the Bergsonian model.

23 Prior to Merleau-Ponty's election in 1953, two professors held Bergson's chair at the Collège de France: Edouard Le Roy (1870–1954), cited at the beginning of this essay, who substituted for Bergson from 1914 to 1921, when he was elected in his own right, and Louis Lavelle (1883–1951), elected in 1941. Etienne Gilson, a neo-Thomist, held the chair of the History of Medieval Philosophy from 1932–50.

24 Maurice Merleau-Ponty, *The Visible and the Invisible*, ed. Claude Lefort, trans. Alphonso Lingis (Evanston, Northwestern University Press, 1968).

25 Merleau-Ponty writes, for example: 'The return to the immediate data, the deepening of experience on the spot, are certainly the hallmark of philosophy by opposition to naive cognitions. But the past and the present, the essence and the fact, space and time, are not *given* in the same sense, and none of them is given in the sense of coincidence'; Merleau-Ponty, *The Visible and the Invisible*, p. 124.

26 MM, p. 235/180; OE, p. 317.

27 Maurice Merleau-Ponty, *Phenomenology of Perception*, trans. Colin Smith (London, Routledge & Kegan Paul, 1962).

28 MM, p. 237/182; OE, p. 318.

29 Merleau-Ponty, *Phenomenology of Perception*, p. 264.

30 *Ibid.*, p. 297.

31 MM, pp. 247–8/189; OE, p. 325.

32 Merleau-Ponty will also accuse Bergson of not having developed a theory of history (see Hanna, *The Bergsonian Heritage*, p. 142), but I think on this question Emile Bréhier is more to the point, finding a philosophy of history in Bergson's philosophy of religion elaborated in *The Two Sources of Morality and Religion* (1932); see Emile Bréhier, *The History of Philosophy*, vol. VII: *Contemporary Philosophy since 1850*, trans. Wade Baskin (Chicago, University of Chicago Press, 1973), p. 128.

garrett barden

METHOD IN PHILOSOPHY

A method is a practice that envisages a result. Intellectual method is a practice that necessarily precedes reflection upon it, which reflection necessarily is an instance of the method.

Basic intellectual method is a movement from ignorance, through question, suggestion and consideration of evidence to more or less tentative, more or less provisional, conclusion.[1] Method in a particular discipline is a specification of basic method invented for that discipline and without which the discipline would not exist. The object of physics is matter in motion and the approach is the spatio-temporal measurement and correlation of motions. The object of economics is the set of transactions called 'the market' and the approach is the correlation of these transactions.[2] Significantly, method in particular disciplines may be, and commonly is, specified without adverting to basic method which is taken, operatively, for granted.

The purpose of this essay is not to provide an historical account of Bergson's method – neither of his practice nor of his theory of method[3] – but to get from a reading of Bergson some greater precision on the nature of basic method.

Because *la durée* – duration – is crucial to any account of Bergson's method and because he spent a considerable effort in discussion with Einstein, it is important to recognise that his intuition is not of time in physics. In the first part of the introduction to *The Creative Mind*, he writes that when we speak of time 'we are thinking of the measurement of duration and not of duration itself'.[4] Whatever one may think of the argument between Einstein and Bergson, it remains that time and space in physics are measures of physical objects in their spatio-temporal relations and that Bergsonian duration is not this.[5] He asks how duration appears 'to a consciousness that would see it without measuring it, that would grasp it without bringing it to a halt, that would take itself as the object of enquiry and that, at once spectator and actor, at once spontaneous and reflective, would bring into coincidence the attentiveness that focuses itself and the time that flies?'[6]

The duration that appears to consciousness is the duration of that consciousness itself. The object of enquiry, the object from which enquiry begins, is the enquiring consciousness itself; that enquiring consciousness is durational and the object towards which enquiry tends is the nature or character of that durational consciousness. The first moment in philosophic investigation is to notice this durational consciousness. Consciousness takes itself as its object, attends to itself: 'Bergson's is a philosophy of attention: intuition is the attention of mind to its object and, if the proper object of philosophy is mind, the attention of the mind to itself.'[7] The attentiveness of mind (esprit) to itself requires, as Lacroix writes in the same paper, a withdrawal from the ordinary, everyday, good and necessary concerns of human living. Such preparatory withdrawal is not peculiar to philosophy. However, the proportionate object of human intellect is not itself but, in Aquinas's account and Aristotle's phrase, 'form in matter' or, in modern terminology, the data of sense. To reflect upon itself is a more unusual and difficult undertaking.[8]

How is the intellect to reflect upon itself? My enquiring is present to me only when I am enquiring; my understanding when I am understanding; my judging only when I am judging; my deciding only when I am deciding. The mind catches itself in the act. 'The mind does not know itself truly and does not grasp itself except in its effort to discover a precise solution to a particular problem.'[9]

The mind's attention to itself is one's attention to one's own conscious activity, for one is intellectually present to oneself only when thinking, and Bergson repeatedly writes of the task of the philosopher as teacher as being to bring the student to perform the experiment; not to talk about attentiveness but to lead the student to attend: 'The sole task of the philosopher here [when bringing the student to have the intuition] is to provoke a certain work which, in most people, the habits more adapted to ordinary living tend to block.'[10] Aquinas writes of adjusting the phantasm or pedagogic image (for example, manipulating the diagram) to bring about understanding in the student – that the student may, so to say, grasp, see, understand the form in the image. Bergson shared this conviction: the only way to teach a student a mathematical proof is to assist the student genuinely to repeat the proof for himself; we cannot follow a proof in mathematics without resolving the problem for ourselves: 'From the visual and aural images we leap to the abstract representation of relations.'[11]

Attention to his conscious activity, attention to himself as consciously enquiring, yielded Bergson the basic insight that may initially be expressed as: 'I endure', 'I am a being that endures.' By attending to one's conscious activity, one may understand oneself as an enduring subject, as a subject whose essence is becoming. Attention and understanding are not identical. One may attend without the attentiveness yielding that particular intuition or insight; attentiveness may yield some other intuition or none. Much of Bergson's writing is concerned to explore, express and enlarge upon this intuition of duration but, to be read fruitfully, requires the reader to have repeated that intuition in himself or herself.

That Bergson noticed the distinction between attention and understanding has been denied, and the idea of his anti-intellectualism rests on the idea that he fails to make this distinction. The quotation above about mathematical proof is, however, a clear example of the importance he gives to it.

Attention and understanding are not identical. Without attention there will not be understanding, but attention does not guarantee understanding. The understanding incompletely expressed in the sentence 'I am an enduring subject' arises from attentiveness to one's own consciousness but is not simply that attentiveness. Bergson's pedagogical method is to lead the reader to the appropriate attentiveness in the hope that understanding will emerge. He fears the overweening dominance of language, of conversation; he warns against the temptation to manipulate – however 'intelligently' or 'rationally' – already available concepts or expressions. Unless there is a personal attentiveness to one's own consciousness from which a personal understanding genuinely arises, philosophy becomes no more than a clever juggling of verbally mastered signs.[12] Thus, philosophy is an empirical enquiry and one task assigned to philosophical writing is that of assisting the reader to perform the experiment. To do philosophy guided by Bergson is not to read and believe but to repeat the experiment.

Bergson has been found cloudy, metaphorical and verbose. And yet to become lost in moribund discourse from which genuine understanding of the object has disappeared is what he greatly fears. It is, then, worth examining the function of an important recurrent image: the piece of music. The experience of listening to a piece of music appears already in *Time and Free Will* and reappears in later writings.[13]

The piece of music is heard and understood as a whole. It is not simply one noise after another – although to someone entirely tone- or tune-deaf it appears to be just that. It is a single whole – in some respects a 'substance' – but the substance does not underlie the appearances.[14] The image of the tune or piece of music is used to extirpate the metaphor – so hoary that it hardly appears as metaphor – of the concealed, underlying, unchanging substance beneath the apparent, changing accidents. The substance of the tune is the interrelated parts. The tune-deaf listener hears the individual notes but fails to hear them as related other than sequentially to one another. The substance or form of the tune does not underlie the audible notes, it is the interrelated notes and so is temporal or enduring. But the listeners who attend to the piece of music and grasp the enduring or temporal form are themselves temporal and enduring. Here again there is no eternal, completed, underlying 'substantial' subject to whom these events occur; the subject is the endlessly complex set of temporal interrelations between the events of a life that make those events the life of a single subject as the discrete notes of the tune form a single temporal tune.[15]

Bergson did not intend 'to dispense with the notion of substance. On the contrary, we affirm the persistence of existences.'[16] In no sense does he wish to deny the reality of the enduring subject – to deny the reality of the subject is akin to denying the reality of the piece of music – but he wishes to eschew wholly the metaphor inherent in the term 'sub-ject' or 'thrown under': *There are changes but not, under the change, things that change: change has no need of a support. There are movements, but there is not an inert, invariable, object that moves: movement does not imply a mobile.*[17] Hume correctly failed to discover an underlying subject but incorrectly failed to attend to and understand the enduring subject. Bergson's fundamental claim is that the consciousness that takes itself as object, that is, the enquirer who attends to his or her own process of enquiry, may, through and by attending, understand himself or herself as a subject who endures, a subject whose unity is the taking up of the past and the anticipation of the future. It is well known that Bergson distinguished a superficial and a deep subject.[18] The deep subject is not a construct. It is not a transcendental ego, not a 'metaphysical' self, not an invented abstraction to solve an *aporia*; it is simply oneself as enduring. One comes to know oneself as enduring by attention and understanding. The superficial subject is the construct. It is, first, a practical construct more or less inherent in an everyday language that serves us well enough for practical purposes but that philosophically 'leads us astray' – and, second, a philosophical construct emergent from that language. When someone says 'I did A' and 'I did B' there exists the nearly unavoidable, and certainly not always avoided, temptation to suppose the 'I' to be some underlying (*substans*, 'standing under') subsisting core. If the sentence 'I am an enduring subject' is the first approach to an expression of the basic insight, the negative complement of that sentence is 'There is no unchanging, underlying, "I".' Both assertions emerge from the same attentiveness and are complementary expressions and clarifications of the single understanding.

What is true of the subject, of the 'I', is true of the mind. The mind (*esprit*) is not imagined – and that the mind is commonly imagined is hardly deniable with once again 'a picture leading us astray' – as a static, complete, ghostly, invisible body. 'Mind' is the name for a developing, creative, historical set of interrelated activities. Each increment of knowledge moves from experience through enquiry to hypothesis, to critical reflection and judgement. Later increments emerge from earlier and coalesce to form open backgrounds or contexts. Mind, with memory, expectation and anticipation, is process, open and never-to-be-completed virtuality.[19] The question 'Do humans have minds?', with its almost unavoidable metaphorical weight, is reformulated to become 'Do humans think?' or, better, 'Do I think?' and, better still, 'Do I think durationally?' Dualism and materialist monism may be overcome by discerning their common hidden metaphor, and the question becomes 'Are there in the one durational being distinguishable activities – for example, physical, chemical, biochemical, psychological, intellectual – and how are these related?'

Bergson distinguishes 'possibility' and 'virtuality'.[20] These become terms of art: to say that some state of affairs is a possibility is to say that its actuality can be derived, given certain conditions, from an already present state of which it is a possibility; to say that a being is virtual is to say that its future cannot be derived from its present. His suggestion is that in our attentiveness to our consciousness we discover its creativity, that is, we discover that its future is more than its present: future understanding is not simply the discovery of what is already implied in present knowledge but the invention of the radically new. We discover ourselves to be virtualities whose realisations cannot be discerned in advance because they are more than implications of the present.[21]

The understanding that our future is more than our present, that is, the discovery of ourselves as virtualities, allows one to break out of the confined circle variously described by Collingwood, Foucault and Rorty, among others. Radical relativism includes this logical impasse: our knowing is confined within contexts, horizons, sets of presuppositions; basic axioms allow some developments and prevent others; these basic axioms are unchangeable; accordingly, two people with incompatible sets of axioms will eventually come to incompatible conclusions about which there can be, between them, no further argument. In other words, radical relativism involves a static conception or image of mind in which the mind is conceived as a closed system, the future states of which are contained in its present and consequently calculable in principle.[22] It is Bergson's contention that attention to one's conscious activities may elicit the insight that one's durational subjectivity is virtuality (which is another way of saying that the mind is not a closed system).

Method is a recurrent practice to yield a result. Basic intellectual method is a movement from enquiry, through insight and hypothesis to tentative judgement. There are less basic methods that take basic method – often without adverting to it – for granted. Thus, for example, if a John Austin suggests that the appropriate philosophic method is the enquiry into the way words are used, he presupposes basic method. Bergson's intention, however, is to illuminate basic method. A consciousness that takes itself as the object of enquiry is an enquiring activity that takes enquiring activity as its object. Accordingly, the discovery that conscious-ness endures, that I am an enduring subject, is a discovery about the process of enquiry itself. 'To think intuitively is to think durationally'[23] is, therefore, not an injunction, not a suggestion that we might consider thinking in this way; it is much more the discovery that this is the way in which we actually do think but that the way has been impeded – and cer-tainly understanding has been impeded – partially by everyday concerns and partially by a mistaken theory of knowing and a consequent mistaken theory of substance.

Things change slowly, often imperceptibly. For convenience of analysis one may favour a synchronic perspective that acts *as if* the object under investigation were essentially static – and so Saussure could study the state of the French language at an assigned period, but, as he knew, that state (that 'stasis', 'stand', 'stillness') was a fiction. But the fictional charac-ter of the model state – whether in the development of a language or in the growth of a frog – may be forgotten, eliminated by the dominance of the sense of sight that, perhaps more than the other senses, more even than touch, provides a world of unchanging objects. When knowing is imagined as seeing, the route is clear to the static beings and to the static Being of Parmenides and Zeno. The ideal of knowledge becomes contemplation by the static onlooker of static Being: the Theorist faced with the One.

Against this danger Bergson sets the experience of hearing music. Still, hearing is only a less misleading metaphor. The crucial experiment is to attend to and to discover the moving subject that one already is. In one's effort to know anything at all one consciously is, and, by attention and understanding, may discover oneself to be, a developing subject. Further, in any instance of knowing something, in any instance of passing from ignorance to conclusion, one is consciously engaged in what is only one instance of knowledge among many, and through attention and under-standing one may grasp oneself as a subject developing, through the iter-ation of many such instances, a context of habitual knowledge from which to develop further. 'The business of the human mind in this life seems to be, not contemplation of what we know, but relentless devotion to the task of adding to a merely habitual knowledge.'[24] The subject is not an achieved thing that does these things but a to-be-achieved thing through the doing of them. Already, in his *Discourse on Metaphysics*,[25] Leibniz noted that the notion of Alexander cannot be grasped until Alexander's death, because what Alexander is, his essence, his notion, is only then, if then, completely explicit. Leibniz, however, unlike Bergson, is deterministic, so that what is revealed in a life is what is already implicit in the notion, much as Goldbach's conjecture is, if true, already implicit in the notion of prime number.[26] For Leibniz, time is the unfolding of 'possibility'; but for Bergson it is the vehicle of creation and choice, that is, 'virtuality': 'there is neither an immutable substratum nor are there distinct states that appear and pass like actors on a stage. There is simply the continuous melody of our interior life, a melody that runs and will run, indivisible, from the beginning to the end of our conscious existence.'[27]

Notes

1 See B. J. F. Lonergan, *Insight* (London, Longmans, 1957), *passim*; B. J. F. Lonergan, 'Cognitional Structure', in *Collection* (London, Darton, Longman and Todd, 1971); B. J. F. Lonergan, *Method in Theology* (London, Darton, Longman and Todd, 1972), esp. ch. 1.

2 See James Buchanan, 'What should Economists do?', *The Southern Economic Journal*, 30 (3) (1964), pp. 213–22.

3 Jean-Louis Vieillard-Baron makes this distinction in his *Bergson* (Paris, Presses Universitaires de France, 1991), p. 100.

4 CM, p. 13/12; OE, p. 1255. Translations from the French are my own, though corresponding pages from the published English translations will be cited.

5 See Lonergan, *Insight*, ch. 5, especially section 5, and R. B. Lindsay and H. Margenau, *Foundations of Physics* (New York, Dover, 1957), ch. 1. Because physics studies the interaction of particles and because the same events can be described differently, spatial and temporal reference frames must be introduced to correlate different accounts. In the discussion between them Einstein remarks (M, p. 1346) that 'there is no such thing as philosophers' time; there is only a psychological time different from physicists' time'. But time and space in physics are understood abstractly; there is also the concrete understanding of space and time as the condition of the possibility of change, development and creation. It is to this understanding that Bergson's work contributes greatly and Einstein's not at all.

6 CM, p. 13/12; OE, p. 1255. But here, as Peter Schäublin has remarked to me, one must beware of metaphor, because the 'attention that focuses itself' remains durational. Durational consciousness becomes the object of enquiry and is 'fixed', 'focused', but the enquiring consciousness – the enquiring subject – remains durational.

7 Jean Lacroix, 'L'Intuition, méthode de purification', in Albert Béguin and Pierre Thévanez (eds), *Henri Bergson* (Editions de la Baconnière, Neuchâtel, 1943), p. 196. In my translation 'mind' translates 'esprit'.

8 See on this St Thomas Aquinas, *Summa Theologiae*, 1.87.1, where he distinguishes between the knowledge of oneself that is identical with intellectual activity and the knowledge of oneself that is the tentative and fallible result of reflection on intellectual activity.

9 Lacroix, 'L'Intuition', p. 197.

10 CM, p. 165/195; OE, p. 1399.

11 ME, p. 206; OE, p. 943.

12 See CM, pp. 81–3/95–8; OE, 1322–3.

13 *Inter alia*, TFW, pp. 105–6, 111, 125, 127–8; L, pp. 150–1/158; CM, pp. 19/19, 71/83, 127/150–1, 147/174, 149/176; OE, pp. 71, 74, 83, 84–5, 459, 1261, 1312, 1364, 1382, 1384. The experience upon which the metaphor is based is of listening to, not of composing, a piece of music.

14 See CM, pp. 71/83–4, 127/150–1; OE, pp. 1312, 1364.

15 How difficult it is to grasp Bergson's idea of subject and subjectivity if one has not yet adequately performed the experiment and repeated the insight or intuition for oneself is illustrated by Georges Poulet's essay on Bergson in his *Histoire de la pensée indéterminée* (Paris, Presses Universitaires de France, 1990), vol. 3, pp. 5–10, in which he finds great difficulty in getting over the image of duration as necessarily associated with a 'thing' (body) that endures: 'in Bergsonian thought, nothing, strictly speaking, endures, that is, nothing conserves itself identical with itself [rien ne se conserve identique à soi-même]'. This way of expounding Bergson tends, I think, to obscure what he himself thought was essentially simple once understood: 'To reply to those who have seen in this "real" duration something ineffable and mysterious, I shall say simply that it is the clearest thing in the world: real duration is what has always been called time, but time perceived as indivisible' (CM, p. 149/176; OE, p. 1384). He does not at all deny the identity of the subject over a lifetime. His effort is to work out a clearer way of understanding this identity. He denies that there is an 'underlying thing' because he grasps the essential incoherence of that idea or image.

16 CM, p. 305, n. 23; OE, p. 1420, n. 1.

17 CM, p. 147/173; OE, pp. 1381–2, italics original. The text of the lecture reproduced in M, pp. 904–5, reads 'There are movements but not necessarily invariable objects that move.' The elimination of the adverb 'necessarily' from the later recension in *Œuvres* indicates an important clarification: no longer does change require an underlying object (body) that does not change; change cannot be understood unless such an underlying, inert, invariable, unchanging substratum is excised. The attached footnote (CM, p. 305, n. 19; OE, p. 1382) is illuminating: 'From the fact that a being is action, may one conclude that its existence is evanescent? … Does an existence so conceived ever cease to be present to itself, since real duration implies the persistence of the past in the present and the indivisible continuity of an unfolding?' The term 'unfolding' here translates 'déroulement'. Both are metaphors and both mislead, since both carry, however faintly, the imprint of the original image of something already present becoming visible. Compare St Thomas Aquinas's idea of God as 'pure act' (see note 19 below).

18 Already and centrally in TFW, chs 2 and 3, but recurrently thereafter.

19 'being [être] as copula is static, inserted in a static world of the projection of objectified representations. The same goes for beings. Contrariwise, Being [Etre] … is dynamic activity; as the great philosophers from Aristotle to Saint Thomas (Gilson) – and perhaps even Leibniz, Bergson, Hegel, Heidegger – have seen' (Michel Villey, *Les Carnets*, ed. Marie-Anne Frison-Roche and Christophe Jamin (Paris, Presses Universitaires de France, 1995), XVI, p. 39).

20 CM, pp. 91–106/107–25, especially pp. 99 ff./117 ff.; OE, pp. 1331–45, especially pp. 1339 ff. See also his résumé of the conference of the same title given at Oxford on 24 September 1920, in M, pp. 1322–6. See also Deleuze's discussion of the distinction in his *Le Bergsonisme* (Paris, Presses Universitaires de France, 1966), ch. 3.

21 Bergson, here close enough to Popper and Hayek, rejects the determinist account of possibility according to which time exists for no other reason than to allow what must happen actually to happen so that the present, as for Laplace, is no more than the actualised implication of the past. The present is in the past as the conclusion is implied in its premises. For Bergson, on the contrary, time is 'the vehicle of creation and choice' (CM, p. 93/110; OE, p. 1333).

22 Collingwood was unhappy with the radical relativism towards which his conclusions seemed to lead. He was convinced that it was possible to break through radical confinement, but was unable to provide an entirely satisfactory account of how this was to be done. See the endnote to chapter 5 of his *An Essay on Metaphysics* (Oxford, Oxford University Press, 1940). On the whole issue, see Barden, *After Principles* (Notre Dame, Ind. and London, University of Notre Dame Press, 1990). On the closed system and calculability, see CM, pp. 103–4/121–3; OE, pp. 1342–3.

23 CM, p. 34/38; OE, p. 1275.

24 Lonergan, *Insight*, p. 278

25 G. Leibniz, *Discourse on Metaphysics* (Manchester, Manchester University Press, 1953), ch. 3. The manuscript of this work dates from 1685–6; it was first published in 1846.

26 In a letter to Euler, Goldbach conjectured that every even number is the sum of two prime numbers. Neither an example to refute, nor a proof to demonstrate, the conjecture has yet been found.

27 CM, p. 149/175–6; OE, p. 1384.

II

ONTOLOGY

3

gilles deleuze

translated by melissa mcmahon

BERGSON'S CONCEPTION OF DIFFERENCE

The notion of difference must throw a certain light on Bergson's philosophy, but inversely, Bergsonism must bring the greatest contribution to a philosophy of difference. Such a philosophy always plays on two levels, methodological and ontological. On the one hand, it is a matter of determining the differences of nature between things: it is only in this way that we will be able to 'return' to things themselves, to account for them without reducing them to something other than themselves, to grasp them in their being. But on the other hand, if the being of things is, in a certain way, in their differences of nature, we can hope that difference itself is something, that it has a nature, finally that it will deliver Being to us. These two problems, methodological and ontological, perpetually refer to each other: the one of differences of nature, the other of the nature of difference. In Bergson, we encounter them in their bond, we discover the passage from the one to the other.

What Bergson essentially reproaches in his predecessors is not having seen the true differences of nature. The constancy of such a critique signals to us at the same time the importance of the theme in Bergson. Where there were differences of nature, we have retained only differences of degree. No doubt the opposite reproach sometimes appears: where there were only differences of degree, we have introduced differences of nature, for example between the so-called perceptive faculty of the brain and the reflex functions of the marrow, between the perception of matter and matter itself.[1] But this second aspect of the same critique has neither the frequency nor the importance of the first. In order to judge what is most important, we must ask ourselves about the aim of philosophy. If philosophy is to have a positive and direct relation with things, it is only to the extent that it claims to grasp the thing itself in what it is, in its difference from all that it is not, which is to say in its *internal difference*. The objection will be made that internal difference makes no sense, that such a notion is absurd; but then one must deny at the same time that there are differences of nature between things of the same kind. If there are differences of nature between individuals of the same kind, we must effectively recognise that difference itself is not simply spatio-temporal, that it is not generic or specific either, in short that it is not exterior or superior to the thing. This is why it is important, according to Bergson, to show that general ideas, at least most of the time, present to us extremely different givens in merely utilitarian groupings: 'Suppose that in examining the states grouped under the name of pleasure we find nothing in common between them except that they are states which man is seeking: humanity will have classified these very different things in one genus because it found them of the same practical interest and reacted towards all of them in the same way.'[2] It is in this sense that differences of nature are already the key to everything: we must start from them, we must in the first place find them again. Without prejudicing what the nature of difference as internal difference is, we already know that it exists, *if we suppose that there are differences of nature between things of the same kind*. Thus, either philosophy proposes *this* way and *this* aim for itself (differences of nature in order to arrive at internal difference), or else it will only have a negative and generic relation with things, it will end up as criticism or generality, in any case in a merely external state of reflection. Placing himself within the first point of view, Bergson proposes the ideal of philosophy: to tailor 'for the object a concept appropriate to the object alone, a concept one can barely say is still a concept, since it applies only to that one thing'.[3] This unity of the thing and the concept is internal difference, which is reached via differences of nature.

Intuition is the *jouissance* of difference. But it is not only the pleasure of the result of the method, it is the method itself. As such, it is not a unique act, it proposes to us a plurality of acts, a plurality of efforts and directions.[4] Intuition in its first impulse [*effort*] is the determination of differences of nature. And since these differences are between things, it is a matter of a veritable distribution, of a problem of distribution. Reality must be divided according to its articulations,[5] and Bergson cites Plato's famous text on carving and the good cook. But the difference of nature between two things is not yet the internal difference of the thing itself. We must distinguish *articulations of the real* from *lines of facts* which define another impulse of intuition.[6] And if, in relation to the articulations of the real, Bergsonian philosophy presents itself as a veritable 'empiricism', in relation to the lines of facts it will present itself rather as a 'positivism' or even a probabilism. The articulations of the real distribute things according to their differences of nature, they constitute a differentiation. The lines of facts are directions, each of which are followed to the end, directions which converge on one and the same thing; they define an integration, each one constitutes a line of probability. In *Mind–Energy*, Bergson shows us the nature of consciousness at the point of convergence of three lines of facts.[7] In *The Two Sources of Morality and Religion*, the immortality of the soul is at the convergence of two lines of facts.[8] In this sense intuition is not opposed to the hypothesis, but envelops it as hypothesis. In short, the articulations of the real correspond to a cutting-out [*découpage*], and the lines of facts to a 'recutting' [*recoupement*].[9] Certainly they are not the same paths in each case, but the important thing is the sense or direction in which they are taken, following the divergence or towards a convergence. We always sense the two aspects of difference: the articulations of the real give us the differences of nature between things; the lines of fact show us the thing itself identical to its difference, the internal difference identical to a thing.

To neglect differences of nature in favour of genres is thus to belie philosophy. We have lost these differences of nature. We find ourselves before a science which has substituted in their place simple *differences of degree*, and before a metaphysics which has more specially substituted *differences of intensity*. The first question concerns science: how is it that we only see differences of degree? 'We make the qualitative differences melt into the homogeneity of the space which subtends them.'[10] Bergson invokes, as is known, the conjugated operations of need, of social life and language, of intelligence and space, space being what intelligence makes from a susceptible matter. In short we substitute purely utilitarian modes of grouping for the articulations of the real. But this is not the most important thing, utility cannot ground what makes it possible. We must thus insist on two points. In the first place degrees have an effective reality and, *in a form that is not spatial*, are already comprehended in a certain way in differences of nature: 'behind our qualitative distinctions' there are often numbers.[11] We will see that one of Bergson's most curious ideas is that difference itself has a number, a virtual number, a sort of numbering number. Utility thus only liberates and spreads out the degrees comprehended in difference until this difference is only one of degree. But on the other hand, if degrees can be liberated to form differences themselves, we must seek the reason for this in the state of experience. What space presents to the understanding, and what the understanding finds in space, are things, products, results and nothing else. However, between things (in the sense of results), there are never and can never be anything but differences of proportion.[12] It is not things nor states of things which differ in nature, it is not characters, but *tendencies*. This is why the conception of specific difference is not satisfactory: it is not to the presence of characters that we must pay attention, but to their tendency to develop themselves. 'The group must not be defined by the possession of certain characters, but by its tendency to emphasise them.'[13] Thus Bergson will show throughout his works that the tendency is not only primary in relation to its product, but in relation to the causes of these products in time, causes always being obtained retroactively starting from the product itself: a thing in itself and in its true nature is the expression of a tendency before being the effect of a cause. In a word, simple difference of degree would be the correct status of things separated from the tendency and grasped in their elemental causes. Causes effectively belong to the domain of quantity. According to whether it is considered in its product or in its tendency, the human brain, for example, will show, in relation to the animal brain, a simple difference of degree or a whole difference of nature.[14] Thus Bergson tells us that, *from a certain point of view*, differences of nature disappear, or rather, cannot appear. By placing oneself within this point of view, he writes in relation to static and dynamic religion, we would perceive 'transitions and differences, ostensibly of degree, between two things which are as a matter of fact radically different in nature'.[15] Things, products, results are always *mixtures*. Space will never show, intelligence will never find, anything but mixtures, a mixture of the closed and the open, of the geometrical order and the vital order, of perception and affection, of perception and memory … And what must be understood is that no doubt the mixture is a blend of tendencies which differ in nature, but, as such, it is a state of things in which it is impossible to establish any difference of nature. The mixture is what we see from the point of view where nothing differs in nature from anything else. The homogeneous is the mixture by definition, because the simple is always something which differs in nature: only tendencies are simple, pure. In this way, we can only find what really differs by finding the tendency again, beyond its product. We must use what the mixture presents to us, differences of degree or proportion, since nothing else is available to us, but we use them only as a measure of the tendency, in order to arrive at the tendency as the sufficient reason of the proportion. 'This very difference in proportion will suffice to define the group, if we can establish that it is not accidental, and that the group, as it evolves, tends more and more to emphasise these particular characters.'[16]

For its part, metaphysics retains hardly anything but differences in intensity. Bergson shows us this vision of intensity that traverses Greek metaphysics: because this metaphysics defines space and time as a simple relaxation [*détente*], a diminishing of being, it finds only differences of intensity between beings themselves, situating them between the two limits of perfection and nothingness.[17] We will see how this illusion is born, and what in turn grounds it in differences of nature themselves. We can notice already that it is based less on mixed ideas than on pseudo-ideas, disorder, nothingness. But these latter are still kinds of mixed ideas,[18] and the illusion of intensity is based in the final instance on that of space. In the end there is only one sort of false problem: problems whose expression does not respect differences of nature. One of the roles of intuition is to denounce their arbitrary quality.

In order to reach true differences, we must rejoin the point of view where the mixture divides itself. It is tendencies that are dually opposed to each other [s'opposent deux à deux], that differ in nature. It is the tendency that is the subject. A being [être] is not the subject, but the expression of the tendency, and furthermore, a being is only the expression of a tendency in so far as this is contrasted with another tendency. It is in this way that intuition presents itself as a method of difference or division: that of dividing the mixture into two tendencies. This method is something other than a spatial analysis, more than a description of experience and less (in appearance) than a transcendental analysis. It certainly raises itself to the conditions of the given, but these conditions are tendency-subjects, they are themselves given in a certain way, they are lived. Moreover, they are at the same time the pure and the lived, the living and the lived, the absolute and the lived. The essential thing is that the foundation be a foundation, but that it is nevertheless *experienced* [constaté], and we know how much Bergson insists on the empirical character of the *élan vital*. We must not raise ourselves to the level of conditions as conditions of all possible experience, but as conditions of real experience: Schelling already gave himself this aim and defined his philosophy as a superior empiricism. The formula suits Bergson just as well. If these conditions can and must be grasped in an intuition, it is precisely because they are the conditions of real experience, because they are no broader than the conditioned, because the concept they form is identical to its object. We should thus not be surprised to find in Bergson a kind of principle of sufficient reason and of indiscernibles. What he refuses is a distribution which places reason in the genre or in the category, and which leaves the individual in the realm of the contingent, which is to say in space. Reason must go right up to the individual, the true concept right up to the thing, comprehension to 'this'. Why this rather than that? Bergson always poses this question of difference. Why does a perception evoke such and such a memory rather than another?[19] Why does perception 'gather' certain frequencies, why those rather than others?[20] Why such and such a tension of duration?[21] In fact reason must be the reason of what Bergson calls the *nuance*. In psychical life there are no accidents: the nuance is the essence.[22] As long as the concept which suits the object itself has not been found, 'the unique concept', we are satisfied with explaining the object by several concepts, general ideas 'in which it is deemed to "participate"':[23] what then escapes is that the object is this one rather than another of the same genre, and that in this genre it has these proportions rather than others. Only the tendency is the unity of the concept and its object, such that the object is no longer contingent nor the concept general. But none of these details concerning method seems to avoid the impasse to which it appears to lead. For the mixture must be divided into two tendencies: the differences of proportion in the mixture itself do not tell us how we will find these tendencies, what the rule of division is. Moreover, given two tendencies, which is the right one? The two are not equivalent, they differ in value, there is always a dominant tendency. And it is only this dominant tendency which defines the true nature of the mixture, it alone is the unique concept and the one which is pure, since it is the purity of the corresponding thing: the other tendency is the impurity which comes to compromise and contrast with it. The behaviour of animals presents instinct to us as the dominant tendency, that of humans, intelligence. In the mixture of perception and affection, affection plays the role of the impurity which mixes itself with pure perception.[24] In other words, the division has a right and a left side. What rule do we use to determine them? We rediscover in this way a difficulty that Plato has already encountered. How can he respond to Aristotle's remark that the Platonic method of difference was only a weak syllogism, incapable of deciding in which half of the divided genre the sought idea could be found, since it lacked a middle term? Moreover, Plato seems better armed than Bergson, because the idea of a transcendent Good can effectively guide the choice of the right half. But Bergson generally refuses the aid of finality, as if he wanted the method of difference to suffice in itself.

The difficulty is perhaps illusory. We know that the articulations of the real do not define the essence and the aim of the method. No doubt the difference of nature between the two tendencies marks a progress in relation to differences of degree between things: it nevertheless remains an exterior difference, a difference that is still external. At this point, Bergsonian intuition, in order to be complete, does not so much lack an exterior term that it could use as a rule, on the contrary, it still presents too much exteriority. Let us take an example: Bergson shows that abstract time is a mixture of space and duration, and that, more profoundly, space itself is a mixture of matter and duration, of matter and memory. Thus there is the mixture which divides itself into two tendencies: matter is in effect a tendency, because it is defined as a relaxation [*relâchement*]; duration is a tendency, being a contraction. But if we consider all the definitions, descriptions and characters of duration in Bergson's work, we realise that difference of nature, in the end, is not *between* these two tendencies.

47

Finally, difference of nature is itself *one* of these tendencies, and is opposed to the other. What in effect is duration? Everything that Bergson says about duration always comes back to this: duration *is what differs from itself*. Matter, on the contrary, is what does not differ from itself, what repeats. In *Time and Free Will* Bergson shows not only that intensity is a mixture which divides itself into two tendencies, pure quality and extensive quantity, but above all that intensity is not a property of sensation, that sensation is pure quality, and that pure quality or sensation differs in nature from itself. Sensation is what changes in nature and not in magnitude.[25] Psychical life is thus difference of nature itself: in the psychical life there is always *otherness* without there ever being *number* or *several*.[26] Bergson distinguishes three sorts of movements, qualitative, extensive and evolutionary,[27] but the essence of all these movements, even that of pure transference like Achilles' race, is alteration. Movement is qualitative change and qualitative change is movement.[28] In short, duration is what differs, and what differs is no longer what differs from something else, but what differs from itself. What differs has become itself a thing, a *substance*. Bergson's thesis could be expressed in this way: real time is alteration, and alteration is substance. Difference of nature is thus no longer between two things or rather two tendencies, difference of nature is itself a thing, one tendency opposing itself to the other. The decomposition of the mixture does not simply give us two tendencies which differ in nature, it gives us difference of nature as one of the two tendencies. And in the same way that difference has thus become substance, movement is no longer the character of something, but has itself taken on a substantial character, it presupposes nothing else, no moving object.[29] Duration, tendency is the difference of self from self; and what differs from itself is *immediately* the unity of substance and subject.

At once we know how to divide the mixture and choose the right tendency, since on the right there is always what differs with itself, that is to say duration, which in each case is revealed to us in one of its aspects, in one of its 'nuances'. We can nevertheless note that, according to the mixture, a same term will be sometimes on the right, at other times on the left. The division of animal behaviour places intelligence on the left side, since duration, the *élan vital*, expresses itself through them as instinct, while it is on the right in the analysis of human behaviour. But intelligence cannot change sides without revealing itself in turn as an expression of duration, this time in humanity: if intelligence has the form of matter, its sense is duration, because it is the organ of the domination of matter, a sense uniquely manifested in man.[30] We should not be surprised that duration has several aspects in the form of its nuances, as it is that which differs from itself; and we must go further, right to the end, to the point of finally seeing matter as a last nuance of duration. But in order to understand this last point, which is the most important one, we must first of all recall what difference has become. It is no longer between two tendencies, it is itself one of the tendencies and is always on the right. External difference has become internal difference. *Difference of nature has itself become a nature.* Moreover, it was so from the beginning. It is in this sense that the articulations of the real and the lines of fact referred to each other: the articulations of the real also sketched lines of fact, which at least showed us internal difference as the limit of their convergence, and conversely the lines of fact also gave us the articulations of the real, as for example with the convergence of three diverse lines which lead us in *Matter and Memory* to the true distribution of subjectivity and objectivity.[31] Difference of nature was only external in appearance. Even in this appearance it already distinguished itself from difference of degree, from difference in intensity, and from specific difference. But in the state of internal difference we have now to make other distinctions. In effect, if duration can be presented as substance itself, it is to the extent that it is simple, indivisible. Alteration must maintain itself and find its status without letting itself be reduced to plurality, or even to contradiction, or to alterity even. Internal difference will have to be distinguished from *contradiction, alterity, negation.* This is where the Bergsonian theory and method of difference is opposed to that other method, to that other theory of difference that is called the dialectic, as much Plato's dialectic of alterity as Hegel's dialectic of contradiction, both implying the power and presence of the negative. The originality of the Bergsonian conception is in showing that internal difference does not go and must not go to the point of contradiction, to alterity, to the negative, because these three notions are in fact less profound than it or are merely external views of this internal difference. To think internal difference as such, as pure internal difference, to reach the pure concept of difference, to raise difference to the absolute, such is the direction of Bergson's effort.

Duration is only one of the two tendencies, one of the two halves; but if it is true that in all its being it differs from itself, does it not contain the secret of the other half? How would it still leave outside of itself *that from which* it differs, the other tendency? If duration differs from itself, that from which it differs is still duration, in a certain way. It is not a matter of dividing duration in the way the mixture was divided: duration is simple, indivisible, pure. It is a matter of something else: the simple does not divide itself, *it differentiates itself.* Self-differentiation is the very essence of the simple or the movement of difference. Thus the mixture decomposes itself into two tendencies, one of which is the indivisible, but the indivisible differentiates itself into two tendencies, the other of which is the principle of the divisible. Space is decomposed into matter and duration, but duration differentiates itself into contraction and relaxation, relaxation being the principle of matter. Organic form is decomposed into matter and the *élan vital*, but the *élan vital* differentiates itself into instinct and intelligence, intelligence being the principle for the transformation of matter into space. It is evidently not in the same way that the mixture is decomposed and the simple is differentiated: the method of difference is these two movements taken together. But now we must ask questions regarding this power of differentiation. This is what will lead us to the pure concept of internal difference. The final determination of this concept will be in showing *in what way* what differs from duration can still be duration.

In *Duration and Simultaneity*, Bergson ascribes to duration a curious power of enveloping itself, a power both to separate itself out into different fluxes and to concentrate itself in a single current, according to the nature of attention.[32] In *Time and Free Will* the fundamental idea of *virtuality* appears, which will be taken up again and developed in *Matter and Memory*: duration, the indivisible, is not exactly what cannot be divided, but what changes in nature in dividing itself, and what changes in nature in this way defines the virtual or the subjective. But it is above all in *Creative Evolution* that we will find the necessary information. Biology shows us the process of differentiation at work. We are seeking the concept of difference in so far as it cannot be reduced to degree or to intensity, to alterity or to contradiction: such a difference *is* vital, even if its concept is not itself biological. Life is the process of difference. Here Bergson is thinking less of embryological differentiation than of the differentiation of species, which is to say, evolution. With Darwin the problems of difference and life come to be identified in this idea of evolution, even though Darwin himself had a false conception of vital difference. Against a certain mechanism, Bergson shows that vital difference is an *internal* difference. But also that internal difference cannot be conceived as a simple *determination*: a determination can be accidental, or at least its being can only be attached to a cause, end or chance, it thus implies a subsisting exteriority; moreover, the relation of several determinations is only ever one of association or addition.[33] Not only will vital difference not be a determination, it will rather be its opposite, it will lean towards indetermination itself. Bergson always insists on the unpredictable character of living forms: 'indeterminate, *i.e.* unforeseeable'.[34] And with Bergson, the unpredictable and the indeterminate is not the accidental, but on the contrary the essential, the negation of accident. In making of difference a simple determination, we either give it over to chance, or we can make it necessary as a function of something only by at the same time making it still accidental in relation to life. But the tendency to change is not accidental in relation to life; moreover, the changes themselves are not accidental,[35] the *élan vital* 'is the fundamental cause of variations'.[36] Which is to say that difference is not a determination, but, in this essential relation with life, a differentiation. No doubt differentiation comes from the resistance life encounters in matter, but it comes first and above all from the internal explosive force that life carries in itself. 'The essence of a vital tendency is to develop itself fan-wise, creating, by the mere fact of its growth, the divergent directions, each of which will receive a certain portion of the impetus [élan]':[37] virtuality exists in such a way that it realises itself in dissociating itself, in such a way that it is forced to dissociate itself in order to realise itself. Self-differentiation is the movement of a virtuality which actualises itself. Life differs from itself, so much so that we find ourselves before divergent lines of evolution and, on each line, before original procedures; but it is still only with itself that it differs, such that, on each line we will also find certain apparati, certain identical organ structures obtained by different means.[38] Divergence in series and identity of certain apparati: such is the double movement of life as a whole. The notion of differentiation posits at once the *simplicity* of virtuality, the *divergence* of the series in which it realises itself and the *resemblance* of certain fundamental results that it produces in these series. Bergson explains to what extent resemblance is an important biological category:[39] it is the identity of what differs from itself, it proves that a same virtuality realises itself in the divergence of series, it shows the *essence* subsisting in change just as divergence showed change itself operating in the essence. 'What likelihood is there that, by two entirely different series of accidents being added together, two entirely different evolutions will arrive at similar results?'[40]

In *The Two Sources of Morality and Religion* Bergson comes back to this process of differentiation: dichotomy is the law of life.[41] But something new appears: beside biological differentiation a properly historical differentiation appears. No doubt biological differentiation finds its principle in life itself, but it is no less linked to matter, so much so that its products remain separated, exterior to one another. 'The material form they (the species) have assumed prevents them from reuniting to bring back again, stronger than it was, more complex, more fully evolved, the original tendency.' On the level of history, in contrast, it is in the same individual and in the same society that the tendencies which have constituted themselves by dissociation evolve. From that point on, they evolve successively, but in the same being: man will go as far as possible in one direction, then turn back towards the other.[42] This text is all the more important in that it is one of the rare ones where Bergson recognises a specificity of the historical in relation to the vital. What does this mean? It means that with man and man alone difference becomes conscious, raises itself to self-consciousness. If difference itself is biological, consciousness of difference is historical. It is

true that we must not exaggerate the function of this historical consciousness of difference. According to Bergson, it liberates the old even more
than it brings on the new. Consciousness already existed, with and in
difference itself. Duration by itself is consciousness, life by itself is consciousness, but it is so *by right*.[43] If history is what reanimates consciousness, or rather is the place in which it reanimates itself and posits itself in
fact, it is only because this consciousness identical to life was asleep,
numbed in matter, annulled consciousness, not no consciousness at all.[44]
Consciousness in Bergson is not at all historical, history is just the only
point where consciousness re-emerges, having traversed matter. So much
so that there is an identity in principle [*de droit*] between difference itself
and consciousness of difference: history is only ever a matter of fact. This
identity in principle of difference and the consciousness of difference is
memory; memory must finally give us the nature of the pure concept.

But again, before reaching this point, we must see how the process of
differentiation suffices to distinguish the Bergsonian method from the
dialectical method. The great resemblance between Plato and Bergson is
that they both made a philosophy of difference where difference is thought
as such and is not reduced to contradiction, *it does not go* to the point of
contradiction.[45] But the point of separation, not the only one but the most
important, seems to be in the necessary presence in Plato of a principle of
finality: only the Good accounts for the difference of the thing and lets us
understand it in itself, as in the famous example of Socrates seated in his
prison. Thus Plato needs the Good in his dichotomy as the rule of the
choice. There is no intuition in Plato, but an inspiration by the Good. At
least one of Bergson's texts is, in this sense, very Platonic: in *The Two
Sources of Morality and Religion* he shows that in order to rediscover the
true articulations of the real, we must ask ourselves questions about function. What use is each faculty, what is, for example, the function of the faculty of 'myth-making' [*fabulation*]?[46] Here the difference of the thing
comes from its use, its end, its destination, the Good. But we know that the
cutting-out or the articulations of the real are only an initial expression of
the method. What presides over the distribution [*découpage*] of things is
evidently their function, their end, so much so that at this level they seem
to receive their difference in itself from the outside. But it is precisely for
this reason that Bergson both criticises the notion of finality and does not
stop with the articulations of the real: the thing itself and the corresponding end are in fact one and the same thing, envisaged on the one hand as
the mixture it forms in space, and on the other hand as the difference and
simplicity of its pure duration.[47] There is no more need to speak of an end:
when difference has become the thing itself, there is no more need to say
that the thing receives its difference from its end. Thus Bergson's concep-

tion of difference allows him to avoid, in contrast to Plato, any real recourse to finality. We can in the same way predict, using certain of Bergson's texts, the objections he would make to a Hegelian-style dialectic, which he is actually much further away from than that of Plato. In Bergson, and thanks to the notion of the virtual, the thing differs from itself *in the first place, immediately.* According to Hegel, the thing differs from itself because it differs in the first place from all that it is not, such that difference goes to the point of contradiction. The distinction between contrast and contradiction matters little to us here, contradiction being only the presentation of the whole as the contrary. In any case, in both instances the game of determination has been substituted for difference. 'There is scarcely any concrete reality upon which one cannot take two opposing views at the same time and which is consequently not subsumed under the two antagonistic concepts.'[48] It can then be claimed that with these two views the thing has been recomposed, it will be said for example that duration is a synthesis of unity and multiplicity. But if the objection that Bergson made against Platonism was that it stopped at a *still external conception of difference*, the objection that he makes to a dialectic of contradiction is that it remains with a *merely abstract conception of difference*. 'This combination [of two contradictory concepts] can present neither a diversity of degrees nor a variety of forms: it is or it is not.'[49] What comprises neither degrees nor nuances is an abstraction. Thus the dialectic of contradiction lacks difference itself, which is the logic [*raison*] of nuance. And contradiction, finally, is only one of the many retrospective illusions that Bergson denounces. What differentiates itself into two divergent tendencies is a virtuality, and as such is something absolutely simple that realises itself. We treat it as something real by composing it using the characteristic elements of the two tendencies, which have nevertheless only been created by its own development. We believe that duration differs from itself because it is in the first place the product of two contrary determinations, we forget that it differentiated itself because it was in the first place what differs from itself. Everything comes back to the critique that Bergson makes of the negative: to reach a conception of difference without negation, which does not contain the negative – such is Bergson's greatest effort. In his critique of disorder as much as in those of nothingness or contradiction, he tries to show that the negation of a real term by the other is only the positive realisation of a virtuality which contained both terms at once. 'Struggle is here only the superficial aspect of an advance.'[50] It is thus by virtue of an ignorance of the virtual that we believe in contradiction, in negation. The opposition of two terms is only the realisation of the virtuality which contained them both: which is to say that difference is more profound than negation, than contradiction.

However important differentiation is, it is not what is most profound. If it were, there would be no reason to speak of a concept of difference: differentiation is an action, a realisation. What differentiates itself is *first* what differs with itself, which is to say, the virtual. Differentiation is not the concept, but the production of objects which find their reason in the concept. But if it is true that what differs from itself must be such a concept, the virtual must have a consistency, an objective consistency which enables it to differentiate itself and to produce such objects. In some essential pages dedicated to Ravaisson, Bergson explains that there are two ways of determining what colours have in common.[51] *Either* one extracts the abstract and general idea of colour, extracted 'by taking away from red what makes it red, from blue what makes it blue, from green what makes it green': one then ends up with a concept which is a genre, with several objects which have the same concept. There is a duality of concept and object, and the relation of the object to the concept is one of subsumption. One thus stops at spatial distinctions, at a state of difference exterior to the thing. *Or*, one passes the colours through a converging lens which directs them on to a single point: what we obtain, in this case, is 'pure white light', which 'brought out the differences between tints'. In this case the different colours are no longer *under* a concept, but the nuances or degrees of the concept itself, degrees of difference itself and not differences of degree. The relation is no longer one of subsumption, but participation. White light is still a universal, but a concrete universal, which enables us to understand the particular because it is itself at the extreme of the particular. Just as things have become the nuances or degrees of the concept, the concept itself has become the thing. It is a universal thing, we could say, since the objects are sketched therein as so many degrees, but a concrete thing, not a kind or a generality. Strictly speaking there are no longer several objects with the same concept, as the concept is identical to the thing itself, it is the difference between the objects related to it, not their resemblance. Such is internal difference: the concept become concept of difference. What did this superior philosophical aim require? We had to renounce thinking in space: the spatial distinction 'comprises no degrees' in effect.[52] We had to substitute temporal differences for spatial ones. The specificity of temporal difference is to make the concept into a concrete thing, because things there are so many nuances or degrees which present themselves at the heart of the concept. It is in this sense that Bergson has placed difference, and with it the concept, in time. 'If, in fact, the humblest function of spirit is to bind together the successive moments of the duration of things, if it is by this that it comes into contact with matter and by this also that it is first of all distinguished from matter, we can conceive an infinite number of degrees between matter and fully-developed spirit.'[53]

The distinctions between the subject and object, body and spirit, are temporal, and in this sense are a matter of degree, but they are not simple differences of degree.[54] Thus we can see how the virtual becomes the pure concept of difference, and what such a concept can be: such a concept is *the possible coexistence of degrees or nuances*. If, despite the apparent paradox, we call *memory* this possible *coexistence*, as Bergson does, we must say that the *élan vital* is less profound than memory, and memory less profound than duration. *Duration, memory, élan vital form three clearly distinct aspects of the concept.* Duration is difference with itself; memory is the coexistence of degrees of difference; the *élan vital* is the differentiation of difference. These three stages define a schematism in Bergson's philosophy. The meaning of memory is to give the virtuality of duration itself an objective consistency which makes it a concrete universal, which enables it to realise itself. When virtuality realises itself, which is to say differentiates itself, it is through life and in a vital form; in this sense it is true that difference *is* vital. But virtuality could only differentiate itself using the degrees which coexist in it. Differentiation is only the separation of what coexists in duration. The differentiations of the *élan vital* are, more profoundly, the degrees of difference itself. And the products of differentiation are objects which conform absolutely to the concept, at least in their purity, because in truth they are nothing other than the complementary position of different degrees of the concept itself. It is in this sense again that the theory of differentiation is less profound than the theory of nuances or degrees.

The virtual now defines an absolutely positive mode of existence. Duration is the virtual; such or such a degree of duration is real to the extent that this degree differentiates itself. For example, duration is not psychological in itself, but the psychological represents a certain degree of duration which realises itself between and among others.[55] No doubt the virtual is, in itself, the mode of the non-active, since it only acts in differentiating itself, in ceasing to be itself, all the while keeping something of its origin. But it is in this very respect that it is the mode of *what is*. This is a particularly famous thesis of Bergson's: the virtual is pure recollection [*le pur souvenir*], and pure recollection is difference. Pure recollection is virtual because it would be absurd to seek the mark of the past in something actual and already realised,[56] a memory is not a representation of something, it represents nothing, it *is*, or if we must still speak of representation, 'it does not present [*représente*] to us something which has been, but simply something which is … it is a *memory of the present*';[57] in effect, it does not have to be made, to be formed, it does not have to wait for perception to disappear, it is not subsequent to perception. *The coexistence of the past with the present that it was is an essential theme in Bergsonism.* But according to these characteristics, when we say that recollection, defined in this way, is difference itself, we are saying two things at once. On the one hand the pure recollection is difference because no one memory resembles another, because each memory is immediately perfect, because it is at once what it will always be: difference is the object of recollection as resemblance is the object of perception.[58] It is enough to dream in order to approach this world where nothing resembles anything else; a pure dreamer would never leave the particular, he would only grasp differences. But recollection is difference in yet another sense, it *carries* difference; for if it is true that the requirements of the present introduce some resemblance between our memories, recollection, conversely, introduces difference in the present, in the sense that it constitutes each subsequent moment as something new. By virtue of the very fact that the past conserves itself 'the following moment always contains, over and above the preceding one, the memory that the latter has left it',[59] 'inner duration is the continuous life of a memory which prolongs the past into the present, whether the present distinctly contains the ever-growing image of the past, or whether, by its continual changing of quality, it attests rather the increasingly heavy burden dragged along behind one the older one grows'.[60] In a different way from Freud, but just as profoundly, Bergson saw that memory was a function of the future, that memory and will were but one and the same function, that only a being capable of memory could turn away from its past, detach itself, not repeat it, do something new. In this way the word 'difference' designates both *the particular that is* and *the new which is made*. Recollection is defined both in relation to the perception with which it is contemporaneous and the following moment in which it prolongs itself. Reuniting the two senses produces a bizarre impression: that of acting and being 'acted' at the same time.[61] But how can these two senses not be reunited, since my perception is already the following moment?

Let us begin with the second sense. We know what importance this idea of *novelty* will take on for Bergson, in his theory of the future and freedom. But we must study this notion on the most precise level, at the moment it is formed, in the second chapter of *Time and Free Will*, it seems. To say that the past is conserved in itself and that it is prolonged into the present is to say that the next moment appears without the previous one having disappeared. This supposes a *contraction*, and it is contraction that defines duration.[62] Opposed to contraction is pure repetition or matter: repetition is the mode of a present which only appears when the other has disappeared, the instant itself or exteriority, vibration, relaxation. Contraction, by contrast, designates difference, because in its essence it makes repetition impossible, because it has destroyed the very condition of any possible repetition. In this sense difference is the new, novelty itself. But how can we define the appearance of something new *in general*? In the second chapter of *Time and Free Will* we will find this problem to which Hume's name is attached taken up again. Hume posed the problem of causality by asking how a pure repetition, a repetition of similar cases which produces nothing new in the object, can nevertheless produce something new in the spirit which contemplates it. This 'something new', expectation to the nth degree, this is *difference*. The reply was that, if repetition produced a difference in the spirit which observed it, it was in virtue of the principles of human nature, and notably of the principle of habit. When Bergson analyses the example of the tolls of a bell or the blows of a hammer, he poses the problem in the same way, and resolves it in an analogous way: the new that is produced is nothing in the objects but a 'fusion', an 'interpenetration', an 'organisation' in the spirit which contemplates them, a conservation of what precedes which has not disappeared when the next thing appears, in short, a contraction which occurs in the spirit. There is even a further resemblance between Hume and Bergson: in the same way that, in Hume, similar cases melted together in the imagination but remained at the same time distinct in the understanding, in Bergson states merge in duration but at the same time keep something of the exteriority from which they come; it is thanks to this last point that Bergson accounts for the construction of space. Thus contraction begins by happening in a sense *within* the spirit, it is like the origin of the spirit, it gives birth to difference. Afterwards, but only afterwards, spirit takes difference up again on its own account, it contracts, and contracts itself, as can be seen in the Bergsonian theory of freedom.[63] But it is enough to have grasped the notion in its origin.

Not only do duration and matter differ in nature, but what so differs is difference itself and repetition. We thus rediscover a former difficulty: difference of nature was at the same time between two tendencies and, more profoundly, one of the two tendencies. And these were not the only two states of difference, there were also two others: the privileged tendency, the right-hand tendency differentiated itself into two, and it could differentiate itself because, at a more profound level, difference contained degrees. It is these four states that we must now gather together: *difference of nature*, *internal difference*, *differentiation* and *degrees of difference*. Our guiding thread is the idea that (internal) difference differs (in nature) from repetition. But we can see only too well that such a statement does not balance out: difference is said to be both internal and yet differing from the outside. If we can nevertheless perceive the outlines of a solution, it is because Bergson makes an effort to show us that difference is still a repetition, and repetition already a difference. In effect, repetition, matter, is indeed a difference; the oscillations are quite distinct in so far as 'one has faded away when the other appears'. Bergson does not deny that science attempts to capture difference itself, and almost succeeds; he sees in infinitesimal analysis an effort of this kind, a true science of difference.[64] Moreover, when Bergson shows us the dreamer living in the particular to the point of only grasping pure differences, he tells us that this region of the spirit rejoins matter,[65] and that to dream is to become disinterested, indifferent. It would thus be wrong to confuse repetition with generality, generality on the contrary supposes the contraction of the spirit. Repetition creates nothing in the object, it lets it be, it even maintains it in its particularity. Repetition does indeed form objective kinds, but these kinds are not in themselves general ideas, because they do not envelop a plurality of objects which resemble each other, but only present us the particularity of an object which repeats itself in an identical way.[66] Repetition is thus a sort of difference; only it is a difference that is always exterior to itself, a difference that is indifferent to itself. Inversely, *difference is in turn a repetition*. We have seen in effect that difference was, in its very origin and in the act of this origin, a contraction. But what is the effect of this contraction? It raises to coexistence what otherwise was repeated. In its origin the spirit is only the contraction of identical elements, and it is in virtue of this that it is memory. When Bergson speaks to us of memory, he always presents it in its two aspects, the second aspect more profound than the first: memory-recollection and memory-contraction.[67] In contraction, the repeated element coexists with itself, multiplies itself, we might say, retains itself. It is in this way that the degrees of contraction are defined, each one presenting to us on its own level the self-coexistence of the element itself, which is to say the whole. There is thus no paradox in memory being defined as coexistence in itself. For all the possible degrees of coexistence themselves in turn coexist and form memory. The identical elements of material repetition merge in a contraction; this contraction shows us at the same time something new – difference – and the degrees which are the degrees of this difference itself. It is in this sense that difference is still a repetition; Bergson returns constantly to this theme: 'The same psychical life, therefore, must be supposed to be repeated an endless number of times on the different stories of memory, and the same act of the mind may be performed at varying heights';[68] the sections of the cone are 'so many repetitions of the whole of our past life';[69] 'everything happens, then, as though our recollections were repeated an infinite number of times in these many possible reductions of our past life'.[70] We can see the distinction that remains to be made between this psychical repetition and material repetition: it is at the same moment that all of our past life is infinitely repeated and that repetition is virtual. Moreover, virtuality has no other consistency than that which it receives from this original repetition. 'These planes … are not given as ready-made things superposed the one on the other. Rather they exist virtually, with that existence which is proper to things of the spirit.'[71] At this point we could almost say that for Bergson it is matter which is succession and duration, coexistence: 'An attention to life, sufficiently powerful and sufficiently separated from all practical interest, would thus include in an undivided present the entire past history of the conscious person.'[72] But duration is a virtual coexistence; space is a coexistence of a wholly other kind, a real coexistence, a simultaneity. This is why the virtual coexistence that defines duration is at the same time a real succession, while ultimately matter gives us less a succession than the simple matter of a simultaneity, a real coexistence, a juxtaposition. In short, the degrees of the psyche are so many virtual planes of contraction or levels of tension. Bergson's philosophy triumphs in a cosmology where everything is a change in tension and nothing else.[73] Duration, as it is given to intuition, presents itself as capable of a thousand possible tensions, of an infinite diversity of relaxations and contractions. Bergson reproached the mere combination of antagonistic concepts for only being able to present a thing *en bloc*, without degrees or nuances. Intuition on the contrary gives us 'a choice between an infinity of possible durations',[74] 'a whole continuity of durations which we should try to follow either upward or downward'.[75]

Do the two senses of difference join up: difference as the particularity which is and difference as personality, indetermination, novelty which creates itself? The two senses can only be united through and in the coexisting degrees of contraction. Particularity effectively presents itself as the greatest relaxation, a spreading out, an expansion; in the sections of the cone, it is the base which carries memories in their individual form. 'They take on a more common form when memory shrinks more, more personal when it widens out.'[76] The more the contraction relaxes, the more individual the memories are, distinct from each other, and localised.[77] The particular is found at the limit of relaxation or expansion, and its movement will be prolonged by the matter itself which it prepares. Matter and duration are two extreme levels of relaxation and contraction, as are the pure past and the pure present in duration itself, recollection and perception. We can thus see that the present will be defined as resemblance or even universality. A being that lived in the pure present would evolve in the universal, 'habit being to action what generality is to thought'.[78] But the two terms opposed in this way are only the two extreme degrees which coexist. Opposition is only ever the virtual coexistence of two extreme degrees: a memory coexists with what it is a memory of, with the corresponding perception; the present is only the most contracted degree of memory, it is an *immediate past*.[79] Between the two we will thus find all the intermediate degrees, which are those of generality, or rather which themselves form the general idea. We can see to what extent matter was not generality: true generality supposes a perception of similarities, a contraction. The general idea is a dynamic whole, an oscillation: 'the essence of the general idea, in fact, is to be unceasingly going backwards and forwards between the plane of action and that of pure memory', 'it consists in the double current which goes from the one to the other'.[80] But we know that the intermediate degrees between two extremes are apt to reconstruct these extremes as themselves the products of a differentiation. We know that the theory of degrees founds a theory of differentiation: it is enough that two degrees be opposed to each other in memory for them to be at the same time the differentiation of the intermediary into two tendencies or movements which are distinguished in nature. Because the past and the present are two opposed degrees, they are distinguished in nature, they are the differentiation, the splitting of the whole. At each instant duration splits itself into two symmetrical spurts, 'one of which falls back towards the past, while the other springs forwards towards the future'.[81] To say that the present is the most contracted degree of the past is also to say that it is opposed by nature to the past, that it is an *imminent future*. We enter into the second sense of difference: something new. But what exactly is this new? The general idea is this whole which differentiates itself into particular images and a corporeal attitude, but this differentiation itself is still the sum of the degrees which go from one extreme to the other, and which put one into the other.[82] The general idea is what places the memory into action, what organises memories with acts, what transforms a memory into a perception, more precisely what makes the images which come from the past itself 'more and more capable of inserting themselves into the motor diagram'.[83] The particular put into the universal – such is the function of the general idea. Novelty, something new, lies precisely in the particular being in the universal. The new is obviously not the pure present: the pure present, just as much as the particular memory, tends towards the state of matter, not by virtue of its spreading-out, but by virtue of its instantaneity. But when the particular descends into the universal or the memory into movement, the automatic act gives way to the voluntary and free act. Novelty is the specificity of a being which, at the same time, comes and goes between the universal and the particular, opposes them to each other and places the latter in the former. Such a being at the same time thinks, wills and remembers. In short, what unites and reunites the two senses of difference are all the degrees of generality.

It can happen that for many readers Bergson gives a certain impression of vagueness and incoherence. Vague, because what he finally teaches us is that difference is unpredictable, indetermination itself. Incoherent, because he seems to take back for himself, one by one, each of the notions that he has criticised. His critique concerned degrees, but here they are returning to the forefront in duration itself, to the point where Bergsonism is a philosophy of degrees: '*We pass by imperceptible stages [degrés], from recollection strung out along the course of time to the movements which indicate their nascent or possible action in space*',[84] 'the memory thus gradually transforms itself into perception';[85] in the same way there are degrees of freedom.[86] The Bergsonian critique touched especially on intensity, but then relaxation and contraction are invoked as the fundamental explanatory principles: 'between brute matter and the mind most capable of reflection there are all possible intensities of memory or, what comes to the same thing, all the degrees of freedom'.[87] Finally his critique concerned the negative and opposition, but here they are reintroduced with the notion of inversion: the geometric order is negative, it is born of 'the introversion of the true positivity', of an 'interruption';[88] if we compare science and philosophy, we see that science is not relative, but 'bears on a reality of inverse order'.[89] And yet we do not believe that this impression of incoherence is justified. In the first place it is true that Bergson comes back to degrees, but not to differences of degree. His whole idea is this: that there are no differences of degree in being, *but degrees of difference itself*. The theories which proceed by differences of degree have precisely confused everything, because they have not seen the differences of nature, they have lost themselves in space and in the mixtures that it presents us with. It remains that what differs in nature is ultimately what differs in nature *from itself*, so much so that what it differs from is only its lowest *degree*; such is duration, defined as difference of nature in itself. When the difference of nature between two things becomes one of the two things, the other is only its *last* degree. It is in this way that difference of nature, when it appears in itself, is precisely the virtual coexistence of two *extreme* degrees. As they are extremes, the double current which goes from one to the other forms the intermediate degrees. These constitute the principle of mixtures, and make us believe in differences of degree, but only if we consider them for themselves, forgetting that the extremities that they reunite are two things which differ in nature, being in truth the degrees of difference itself. Thus what differs is relaxation and contraction, matter and duration as the degrees or intensities of difference. And if Bergson does not in this way fall back on differences of degree in general, nor does he, in particular, come back to the vision of differences of intensity. Relaxation and contraction are only the degrees of difference itself because they are opposed and in so far as they are opposed. As extremes, they are the *inversion* of each other. What Bergson reproaches in metaphysics is that, not having seen that relaxation and contraction are inverse to each other, it believed that they were only two more or less intense degrees in the degradation of a same immobile, stable and eternal Being.[90] In fact, in the same way that degrees are explained by difference rather than the other way around, intensities are explained by inversion and presuppose it. A stable and immobile being is not the first principle; *what we must start from* is contraction itself, the duration whose inversion is relaxation. We always encounter in Bergson this concern to find the true beginning, the true starting-point: thus for perception and affection, 'instead of starting from *affection*, of which we can say nothing, since there is no reason why it should be what it is rather than anything else, we start from *action*'.[91] Why is it that relaxation is the inversion of contraction, and not contraction the inversion of relaxation? Because to do philosophy *is precisely to start with difference*, and difference of nature is duration, of which matter is only its lowest degree. Difference is the true beginning; it is in this respect that Bergson diverges most from Schelling, at least in appearance; by beginning from something else, from a stable and immobile being, something indifferent is posited as the first principle, a less is taken for a more, we fall into a simple vision of intensities. But when he founds intensity on inversion, Bergson only seems to escape this vision by coming back to the negative, to opposition. There again such a reproach would not be correct. In the final instance the opposition of two terms which differ in nature is only the positive realisation of a virtuality which contained them both. The role of intermediary degrees is precisely in this realisation: they place one in the other, the memory in movement. We thus do not think that there is any incoherence in Bergson's philosophy, but on the contrary a great deepening of the concept of difference. Nor do we think, finally, that indetermination is a vague concept. Indetermination, unpredictability, contingency, liberty always signify an independence in relation to causes: it is in this sense that Bergson credits the *élan vital* with many contingencies.[92] What he means is that the thing comes in a sense *before* its causes, that we must indeed start with the thing itself because causes come afterwards. But indetermination never signifies that the thing or the action could have been otherwise. 'Could the act have been otherwise?' is a question devoid of sense. The Bergsonian demand is to understand why the thing is this rather than something else. It is difference which explicates the thing itself and not its causes. 'Freedom must be sought in a certain shade [*nuance*] or quality of the action itself and not in a relation of this act to what it is not or to what it might have been.'[93] Bergsonism is a philosophy of difference, and of difference's realisation: there we find difference in itself, and it realises itself as novelty.

Notes

1 MM, pp. 10–11/23–4, 78–9/71; OE, pp. 175, 218.
2 CM, pp. 52/59–60; OE, pp. 1293–4.
3 CM, p. 175/207; OE, p. 1408.
4 CM, p. 184/217; OE, p. 1416.
5 CM, pp. 29/31–2; OE, p. 1270.
6 ME, p. 7; OE, p. 817.
7 ME, chapter one, pp. 3–36; OE, pp. 815–36.
8 MR, p. 264; OE, p. 1200.
9 MR, p. 294; OE, p. 1225 (I am assuming Deleuze is referring to Bergson's example of an 'orange' world which only 'will have' been made of yellow and red once these have been distinguished. The real is what at the same time carves and recarves itself [*se découpe et se recoupe*] – Trans.).
10 CE, p. 228/216; OE, p. 679.
11 CM, p. 59/68; OE, p. 1300.
12 CE, pp. 111–12/106; OE, p. 585.
13 CE, p. 112/106; OE, p. 585.
14 CE, pp. 192–4/182–5, 277–8/263–4; OE, pp. 650–1, 718.
15 MR, p. 214; OE, p. 1157.
16 CE, p. 112/106; OE, p. 585.
17 CE, pp. 340–2/322–4; OE, pp. 768–9.
18 CE, pp. 235–6/222–3; OE, p. 684.
19 MM, p. 213/164; OE, p. 303.
20 CM, p. 59/68; OE, p. 1300.
21 CM, p. 185/218; OE, p. 1417.
22 CM, pp. 159–60/188; OE, p. 1394.
23 CM, pp. 177–8/209; OE, p. 1410.
24 MM, p. 60/58; OE, p. 207.
25 TFW, chapter one, pp. 1–74; OE, pp. 5–51.
26 TFW, p. 104; OE, p. 70.
27 CE, pp. 320–1/304; OE, p. 752.
28 MM, p. 258/196; OE, p. 331.
29 CM, pp. 147/173, 150/177; OE, pp. 1382, 1385.
30 CE, pp. 280–1/266, 284–5/270; OE, pp. 721, 724.
31 CM, p. 77/90–1; OE, p. 1318.
32 DS, p. 52; M, pp. 105–6.
33 CE, chapter one, pp. 1–102/1–97; OE, pp. 494–578.
34 CE, pp. 132–3/126; OE, p. 602.
35 CE, p. 90/85; OE, p. 568.
36 CE, p. 92/87; OE, p. 570.
37 MR, pp. 293–4; OE, p. 1225.
38 CE, pp. 56–8/53–5; OE, pp. 540–1.
39 CM, pp. 56–7/65–6; OE, p. 1298.
40 CE, p. 57/54; OE, p. 541.
41 MR, pp. 294–5; OE, p. 1226.
42 MR, p. 295; OE, p. 1226.
43 ME, p. 17; OE, p. 824.
44 ME, pp. 14–15; OE, p. 822.
45 We nevertheless do not think that on this point Bergson was influenced by Plato.

Closer to him was Gabriel Tarde, who characterised his own philosophy as a philosophy of difference and distinguished it from philosophies of opposition. But the conception that Bergson has of the essence and process of difference is quite different from Tarde's.

46 MR, p. 108; OE, p. 1066.
47 CE, pp. 93–4/88–9; OE, pp. 570–1.
48 CM, p. 176/208; OE, p. 1409.
49 CM, p. 184/218; OE, p. 1416.
50 MR, p. 297; OE, p. 1228.
51 CM, pp. 225–6/267–8; OE, pp. 1455–6.
52 MM, p. 295/221; OE, p. 355.
53 MM, pp. 295–6/221; OE, p. 355.
54 MM, p. 78/71; OE, p. 218.
55 CM, pp. 186–7/220; OE, p. 1418.
56 MM, p. 173/135; OE, p. 278.
57 ME, p. 167; OE, pp. 918–19 (emphasis in Bergson's original text, though not in Deleuze – Trans.).
58 MM, pp. 206–7/159; OE, p. 299.
59 CM, p. 164/193; OE, p. 1398.
60 CM, p. 179/211; OE, p. 1411.
61 ME, p. 170; OE, p. 920.
62 CE, pp. 210–11/199–200; OE, pp. 664–5.
63 TFW, chapter three, pp. 140–221; OE, pp. 93–145.
64 CM, pp. 190–1/225; OE, p. 1422.
65 CE, pp. 220–1/209; OE, p. 672.
66 CM, pp. 58–9/68–9; OE, p. 1300.
67 MM, pp. 25/34; OE, p. 184.
68 MM, pp. 128–9/105; OE, pp. 250–1.
69 MM, p. 220/168; OE, p. 307.
70 MM, p. 220/169; OE, p. 308.
71 MM, p. 322/242; OE, p. 371.
72 CM, pp. 152/179–80; OE, p. 1387.
73 MM, p. 266/201; OE, p. 337.
74 CM, p. 185/218; OE, p. 1417.
75 CM, p. 187/221; OE, p. 1419.
76 MM, p. 220/169; OE, p. 308.
77 MM, p. 224/171; OE, p. 310.
78 MM, p. 201/155; OE, p. 296.
79 MM, pp. 193–4/150; OE, p. 291.
80 MM, pp. 210/161, 211/162; OE, pp. 301, 302.
81 ME (Deleuze gives no page reference, but ME, p. 165; OE, pp. 917–18 comes close to Deleuze's wording – Ed.).
82 MM, p. 209/161; OE, p. 301.
83 MM, pp. 160–9/125–31; OE, pp. 270–5.
84 MM, p. 88/79; OE, p. 225 (emphasis in Bergson though not in Deleuze – Trans.).
85 The page reference Deleuze provides does not contain this line, but MM, p. 162/127; OE, p. 271 comes close to Deleuze's wording – Ed.
86 TFW, p. 166; OE, p. 109.
87 MM, p. 296/222; OE, p. 355.
88 CE, p. 231/219; OE, p. 681.

89 CE, p. 243/230; OE, p. 690.
90 CE, pp. 342–7/324–9; OE, pp. 769–73.
91 MM, p. 67/63; OE, p. 211 (emphasis in the original, though not in Deleuze – Trans.).
92 CE, pp. 268–9/255; OE, p. 711.
93 TFW, pp. 182–3; OE, p. 120.

4

timothy s. murphy

BENEATH RELATIVITY: BERGSON AND BOHM ON ABSOLUTE TIME

Perhaps there are times of inherent excellence,

As when the cock crows on the left and all
Is well, incalculable balances,
At which a kind of Swiss perfection comes

And a familiar music of the machine
Sets up its Schwärmerei, not balances
That we achieve but balances that happen …
       Wallace Stevens, *Notes Toward a Supreme Fiction* (part 1, section 7)

I

No scientific theory since Darwin's model of evolution by natural selection has had the broad cultural impact of former Berne patent clerk Albert Einstein's theory of relativity. As the crowning achievement of pre-war German technocracy, it spelled the symbolic end of the nineteenth-century European cultures that produced it and provided ideological legitimation for the varieties of modernism in the arts and human sciences that arose alongside and after it. It did this by dismantling the classical assumption of a single absolute frame of spatio-temporal reference for the measurement of motion, and from there it was only a short metaphorical step to the cultural relativism that underlay the rise of scientific ethnology and the subjective relativism that underlay the widespread adoption of stream-of-consciousness techniques, among others, in literature. The speed of this transformation was no doubt a function of the extraordinary power of legitimation that was conferred upon 'science' during the late nineteenth and early twentieth centuries, a power that also included ascendancy over the previous intellectual claimant to legitimating judgement, philosophy. The victory of Einstein's model of time not only over classical notions but also over the alternative modernism of Henri Bergson's philosophy of duration is evidence of this.

The triumph of relativity has never been complete, however. Neils Bohr's original 'Copenhagen Interpretation' of quantum physics is at odds with relativity, and Einstein himself noted that 'in the Schrödinger [wave] equation, absolute time ... play[s] a decisive role', though the concept had been 'recognised by the theory of relativity as inadmissible in principle'.[1] David Bohm and Basil J. Hiley point out that 'the basic orders implied in relativity theory and in quantum theory are qualitatively in complete contradiction. Thus relativity requires strict continuity, strict causality and strict locality in the order of the movement of particles and fields. And ... in essence quantum mechanics implies the opposite.'[2] The quantum phenomenon of non-locality in particular has implications that call into question the 'Swiss perfection' of relativity. Furthermore, J. S. Bell's theorem on the necessary structure of quantum-mechanical formalism insists that a comprehensive theory taking into account all of the experimentally determined facts of quantum behaviour can remain realistic, in other words can insist on the existence of its objects independent of human observation, only if it includes the possibility of non-local interactions.[3] With this proof, the stage has been set for a direct confrontation between quantum theory, whose indeterministic implications Einstein always refused to accept, and his own deterministic relativity theory.[4] This confrontation constitutes a restaging of the post-World War I debate between Einstein and Bergson over the nature of time as it appeared within the theory of relativity.

Relativity is based largely on the principle that nothing can move faster than the speed of light in a vacuum. On this basis, Einstein dismantles the intuitive notion of the simultaneity of events and demonstrates that the only practical simultaneity is constructed or conventional, based on signs (clocks) that are themselves subject to distortion due to relative movement. He does so by showing that two events which would be considered simultaneous by an observer who is stationary with respect to those events would be considered sequential by an observer who was moving simultaneously towards one event and away from the other; this is because of the finitude of the velocity of light, which must catch up to an observer who is receding from one event and who is rushing to meet the light coming from the event towards which she moves.[5] There are actually two theories of relativity, the special and the general. The special theory is limited to the claim and proof that the equations of physics, which are the mathematical representations of natural laws, hold good only for systems in constant, uniform motion, that is, unaccelerated systems. In the special theory, any such system can be taken as a frame of reference and simply substituted for another. If, for example, a train passes by a tree, that motion can be treated as movement of the train in one direction at a particular speed, or movement of the tree and landscape in the opposite direction at the same speed; the two perspectives are mathematically equivalent. The general theory demonstrates how the laws may be transformed for accelerated systems, that is, those in inconstant motion and those involving gravitational fields that are mathematically equivalent to inconstant motion. In the general theory, substitution is more difficult, because an accelerated frame will have features that are not directly equivalent, like the jerks caused by turns, acceleration or braking of the moving object. General relativity is the source of the famous 'paradox' of the twins who age asymmetrically, first proposed by Paul Langevin in 1911, to which we will return in a moment.[6]

The Lorentz equations allow us to convert measurements taken by the stationary observer into measurements valid for the moving observer and vice versa.[7] This principle of convertibility or 'covariance' (also called in some circumstances 'invariance') reduces time to a dependent variable rather than an independent one, as it had been assumed to be in classical mechanics from Newton to the end of the nineteenth century, by enabling the physicist to choose frames of reference in which apparent temporal sequences could be inverted or suspended in order to simplify the process of calculation. 'By this procedure time lost its absolute character, and was adjoined to the 'spatial' co-ordinates as of algebraically (nearly) similar character. The absolute character of time and particularly of simultaneity was destroyed, and the four-dimensional description was introduced as the only adequate one.'[8]

The qualification 'nearly' in the first sentence above refers to the fact that in the equations that define space–time as a four-dimensional continuum (for example $c^2 t^2 - x^2 - y^2 - z^2 = 1$), the three spatial co-ordinates x, y and z are subtractive when the temporal co-ordinate t is additive and vice versa.[9] On the basis of this reduction, Einstein generalises the possibility that an appropriate choice of reference-frame allows the physicist to transform any experimental situation into the one with which the equations of physics can most easily deal.

In *Duration and Simultaneity*, Bergson chastised relativity theorists for what he felt was their failure to recognise the purely instrumental nature of their use of the Lorentz transformation equations. Early relativity theorists (a group not immediately including Einstein) claimed, following Langevin, that if one member of a set of twins was sent on a round-trip journey to a star a hundred light-years away and accelerated to nearly the speed of light on the way, he would age only 2 years while the other twin, who remained on earth, would age 200 years. Bergson insisted that this was a false claim that was based on the fact that the travelling twin was imagined from the point of view of the earthbound twin, and that in fact they would age at the same rate, according to the direct substitutability of frames of reference. The travelling twin was merely an *image*,[10] or a *puppet*,[11] what Gilles Deleuze calls an empty 'symbol' or sign whose experience could not be lived as the earthbound twin's could. For Bergson, this critique demonstrated the irreducibly singular nature of duration, the irreversible time of the movements and perceptual processes of the subject and other, non-human observers.[12] Because of his insistence on this independence of time with respect to space, many physicists assumed that Bergson was attempting to refute the theory of relativity and recuperate the classical notion of a single absolute time. Nothing could be further from the truth.

Bergson actually asserts the unity and singularity of an irreversible virtual time, duration, out of which all the other specific, conventionally measurable times of the various possible reference-frames can be derived through spatialisation. This process of abstract spatialisation, of subordinating movement or change in time to the spatial co-ordinate system that measures that movement, is the basis of all mathematico-scientific cognition, and as such is practically useful but conceptually reductive. On the other hand, 'a single duration will pick up along its route the events of the totality of the material world; and we will then be able to eliminate the human consciousness that we had initially had available, every now and then, as so many relays for the movement of our thought; there will now only be impersonal time in which all things will flow'.[13] Deleuze interprets this to mean that the separate fluxes of the different reference-frames 'communicat[e] in a single and identical Time, which is, as it were, their condition … There is only one time (monism), although there is an infinity of actual fluxes (generalised pluralism) that necessarily participate in the same virtual whole (limited pluralism).' In this model, 'our duration (the duration of the spectator) [is] necessary both as flux and as representative of Time in which all fluxes are engulfed'.[14] This Bergsonian claim, Deleuze insists, was intended to 'give the theory of Relativity the metaphysics it lacked',[15] to cut the last bonds that tied relativity to the classical model of time reduced to space.

There can be little doubt that Bergson misunderstood the theory of relativity, or rather understood only the special theory of the relativity of systems in uniform motion, according to which his critique would have been correct. But since the twin's journey required at least two moments of acceleration, one at the beginning of each half of the trip, the problem must be treated under general relativity, and under general relativity the time asymmetry cannot be cancelled out. The twin accelerated to a substantial fraction of the speed of light would manifest time dilation, or slowing of proper time, that the unaccelerated twin would not; this phenomenon has been experimentally verified by accelerating a sensitive atomic clock, previously synchronised with another such clock that remains immobile, in a jet.[16] Bergson almost realises this irreducibility of acceleration: in a footnote, he notes that the twins paradox 'raises certain difficulties, because we are here really no longer in special relativity. As soon as speed changes direction, there is acceleration and we are dealing with a problem in general relativity. But, in any case, the solution given above completely removes the paradox and does away with the problem.'[17] Deleuze admits that 'Bergson's reasoning involves a misunderstanding of Einstein. But Bergson's reasoning itself has also often been misunderstood.'[18] According to Deleuze, despite Bergson's misattribution of the twins paradox to special relativity instead of general relativity, he has arrived at a concise and correct basic criticism of relativity theory in general: in constructing a model for the transformation or substitution of different time-flows between different frames of reference, Einstein has actually tried to prove, as he himself often admitted, that time is a phenomenological illusion without physical reality.

'For us convinced physicists,' Einstein wrote, 'the distinction between past, present and future is an illusion, although a persistent one.'[19] From the point of view of physics, time and the events it measures are always reversible in principle, which means that time has no substance or reality. Time's avatars in relativity, in the form of reference-frames, are multiple, but its quality is not even singular but merely illusory; for Einstein time can be reduced to an additional dimension of space, 'adjoined to the "spatial" co-ordinates' in a 'four-dimensional description', as Bergson claimed it had always already been in the history of Western philosophy. From Bergson's point of view, it is Einstein's relativity, then, that remains within the classical model of time. Thus Einstein flatly rejected Bergson's suggestion of a 'philosopher's time' that remains unaffected by relativity as 'only a psychological time' without objective reality,[20] and he may have been partially and indirectly responsible for the decline in influence of the Bergsonian philosophy in general after the 1920s. But Bergson's critique of Einstein anticipates Bohm and Hiley's 'ontological' interpretation of quantum mechanics, as we will see, which renews the confrontation with absolute or independent time that Einstein successfully parried in 1922.

II

Einstein himself threw down the gauntlet that led to the renewed confrontation between relativity and quantum theory in an article published in 1935, long after the Bergson polemics had effectively ended.[21] Along with his collaborators Boris Podolsky and Nathan Rosen, Einstein attacked what he called the apparent 'incompleteness' of quantum theory as it was then structured in Bohr and Heisenberg's interpretation. By this they meant that Bohr's 'Copenhagen Interpretation' of quantum theory, centred around the notion of the complementary indeterminacy of linked variables like position and velocity, presented itself as a complete description of reality even though it actually gave no account of many physically evident aspects of that reality. Their proof of this 'incompleteness' took the form of a thought-experiment, as disagreements often do in physics. The proof depends upon several points: the Heisenberg Principle of the complementary indeterminacy of position and velocity; the principle of the conservation of energy, in this case the conservation of angular momentum; and the constancy of the speed of light. We begin with two-particle molecules, which have zero total angular momentum, and then split the molecules into their component particles, which will have equal and opposite angular momenta according to the conservation law. Einstein, Podolsky and Rosen, or EPR as they came to be known, postulated an apparatus for measuring the angular momenta of the component particles of those molecules after they had been separated from each other. The momenta of the components would be indeterminate, according to Heisenberg's Principle, until they were so measured.

The interest of the thought-experiment lies in the arrangement of the apparatus (see diagram). EPR suggested that the molecule be split into two component particles before measurement; according to the law of the conservation of momentum, the two particles' angular momenta must add up to the momentum of the original molecule. Then, the two particles would be allowed to move far apart before a device determined the momentum of each part. During this separation period, the Schrödinger Wave Function for the two-particle system would develop as many virtual resultant states as there are actual momentum states for the two particles to occupy upon measurement. According to the Heisenberg Principle, the interaction of one particle with the measuring device would precipitate that particle into one of these virtual states of momentum, and would require the other particle to precipitate into a complementary state in order to conserve the momentum of the entire system. If the measuring devices were sufficiently far apart, however, the two particles' momenta could both be determined before any signal could

Simplified EPR thought-experiment

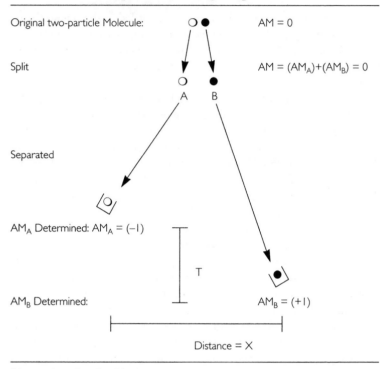

Original two-particle Molecule: $AM = 0$

Split $AM = (AM_A) + (AM_B) = 0$

A   B

Separated

AM_A Determined: $AM_A = (-1)$

T

AM_B Determined: $AM_B = (+1)$

Distance $= X$

Distance from A to B = X
Time between determination A and determination B = T
X/T = velocity necessary for A–B communication > c = speed of light

pass, at the speed of light, between them. Quantum mechanics predicts that, in such an arrangement, the correlation of complementary momenta will still be observed, which means that the angular momentum of the system will be conserved. But how could this happen if no signal could possibly 'inform' particle B of the state into which particle A had been precipitated? For EPR, this meant that rather than being indeterminate until determined by interaction with a measuring device, as Heisenberg and Bohr would have it, the momenta of the particles are actually determined at separation and remain fixed until they are measured. This fixity or determination cannot be described in the mathematical formalism of quantum mechanics and in fact runs completely counter to the conceptual edifice constructed by Bohr, Heisenberg and others; therefore EPR claimed that quantum mechanics was incomplete as a description of reality and should be augmented or replaced by a more deterministic model.

Bohr immediately refuted the deterministic results of the EPR thought-experiment from the point of view of the Copenhagen Interpretation. He pointed out that the EPR critique assumed that all of the terms of quantum mechanical mathematics corresponded to separate, distinct, precisely defined elements of reality, when in fact the significance of the Heisenberg Principle and the Schrödinger Wave Equation is to deny just this correspondence on the quantum level. Bohr insisted that quantum events had to be comprehended as indissociable wholes that were only roughly and statistically definable as 'separate parts'; assuming as we must that the apparatus used to measure the quantum event is itself composed of particles acting according to quantum principles, how can we rigorously distinguish the quantum behaviour of the particle being studied from the quantum behaviour of the particles that make up the experimental apparatus?[22] In this, Bohr's refutation of determinism in the quantum realm repeats key aspects of Bergson's defence of free will as the impossibility of breaking up a process of movement or change in duration: 'Freedom is the relation of the concrete self to the act which it performs. This relation is indefinable, just because we *are* free. For we can analyse a thing, but not a process; we can break up extensity, but not duration.'[23] As Deleuze points out, duration, like a quantum ensemble, is a virtual multiplicity that changes in quality or kind when its dimensions or quantity changes; it is one of Wallace Stevens's 'incalculable balances'. Einstein accepted Bohr's refutation with good grace (though he did not recognise its similarity to Bergson's philosophical attempt of a dozen years earlier), but refused to accept once and for all the premise that 'we shall never get any insight into these important changes in the single systems, in their structure and their causal connections'.[24] Even so, Bohr's refutation of EPR was also a crucial moment in the polemic against 'hidden variable' theories like Louis de Broglie's and the first (1952) version of Bohm's, because such 'hidden variables' would have to meet the same indeterminacy criteria that EPR had failed to meet.[25]

There is another way to understand the situation, however. If we wish to maintain the objective indeterminacy implied by quantum theory and the results of the EPR thought-experiment, we can posit that the two component particles remain in the undetermined states of momentum required by the wave equation until one is determined, and then they correlate their momenta with one another instantaneously (or apparently so).[26] In other words, the two component particles will 'communicate' *faster than the speed of light* in order to avoid violating the conservation law. Einstein recognised that such supraluminal communication violated his cherished belief that all physical interaction must be local, that is, that all interaction takes place through spatial contiguity (physical contact) or through continuous fields of force (like electromagnetism or gravity).[27] The experimental data do not warrant such a belief, however. In fact, Bell based his theorem of quantum non-locality and realism on the EPR model taken as a *support* for quantum theory rather than as a criticism. Such apparently non-local correlations have been observed in experiments conducted by Alain Aspect and others in 1982, experiments which also confirmed the statistical predictions of Bohr's and Heisenberg's indeterminate quantum theory against the determinism of EPR's implicit model of reality.[28]

The phenomenon of non-locality implies that faster-than-light connections exist not only between separated sub-atomic particles, but also between widely separated parts of the larger universe; indeed, if the Big Bang Theory of the origin of the universe is correct in any one of its variant forms, then the universe as a whole can be treated as a single immense quantum system bound together by conservation laws and thus by a multiplicity of non-local effects. Many recent interpretations of quantum theory include non-locality, but they do not place it at the conceptual centre of the interpretation as David Bohm's work does, and therefore they can temporarily avoid the confrontation with relativity. On the macroscopic scale of the universe, however, we cannot avoid confronting quantum non-locality with the theory of relativity, which can be and often is ignored on the sub-atomic scale. Bohm and Hiley insist that their 'ontological interpretation helps bring out a fundamental inconsistency between relativity and quantum theory, centred on the question of nonlocality'.[29]

As we have seen, relativity in its most compact and simple form states that *'the general laws of nature are to be expressed by equations which hold good for all systems of coordinates, that is, are co-variant with respect to any substitutions whatever (generally co-variant)'*.[30] This means, essentially, that physical laws remain the same for all frames of reference and so all frames of reference may be transformed into one another, using the Lorentz equations, without loss of relevant information.[31] In other words, there is no naturally and necessarily privileged frame of reference for the implementation of experiments, no absolute frame or ether that must ground a test of physical laws. Any frame of reference can be designated as ground, because all physical laws will be transformable into equations that can account equally well for events in any frame.

Clearly quantum non-locality violates the theory of relativity, because it posits apparently instantaneous (or at least extremely rapid) communication, real simultaneous determination, between widely separated objects. Non-locality returns strict simultaneity to physics and also breaks the limit of the speed of light in a vacuum. This means that, to use Einstein's terminology, the quantum theory will no longer be fully covariant or invariant, no longer fully transformable from any frame of reference to any other frame on the basis of the Lorentz equations, which depended on the absolute value of the speed of light. Bohm and Hiley admit that 'The concept of a particle guided in a nonlocal way will, in general, not be Lorentz invariant ... one therefore has to assume some definite frame in which the connections are to be described as instantaneous, while in other frames they are described as working either backwards or forwards in time ... Briefly, what this means is that there is always a unique frame in which the nonlocal connections operate instantaneously.'[32] In the most fundamental way possible, non-locality undoes the reduction of time to space performed by relativity theory and establishes an irreducibly privileged frame of temporal reference for physical experiments.

This does not mean that the ontological interpretation will immediately give different experimental results than the Copenhagen Interpretation does: 'the ontological interpretation gives the same *statistical* results for all measurement-manifestation processes as does the usual interpretation. This means that our interpretation will have a co-variant content for all statistical consequences of the measurement-manifestation process. But the only quantum experiments that can be performed thus far are of this statistical nature',[33] rather than the nature of an individual particle, therefore we must await an advance in our ability to construct experiments in order to test this concept directly. This also means that relativity is spared for the present, because this statistical covariance cancels out the effects of non-locality at the macroscopic, Newtonian level of human experience; in other words, relativity still holds in the large-scale world because 'the statistical distribution of manifestations of [quantum/non-local] processes in the ordinary large-scale world of experience will be the same in [the ontological] interpretation as in the usual interpretation [which is covariant]'.[34] But *beneath* relativity, in the ubiquitous quantum underworld, the potential paradoxes of non-locality hold sway.

Bohm and Hiley go so far as to describe the privileged reference-frame of non-locality as a 'universal order of succession',[35] which is a 'hyperplane of constant time ... obtained by considering at each point in space–time, the line connecting it to the presumed origin of the universe'[36] and founded on Bohm's 'pilot wave' or 'quantum potential' field.[37] Such a 'universal order of succession' bears a striking resemblance to Bergson's concept of duration, to what Deleuze called the 'representative of time'. In practice, though, this privileged frame or 'time of inherent excellence' would have to coincide with or be transformable to the laboratory frame of reference in order to avoid temporal paradoxes,[38] and indeed in order to be observable at all. Thus the 'universal' or 'unique' time of non-local interactions would be multiple in principle, or 'virtual' as Bergson and Deleuze would say, since it would be determined in each singular case by the experimental arrangements of the particular laboratories involved in investigating it. In a very real sense, then, the observer or spectator defines the universal order by interfering in it, but this does not necessarily privilege the human subject. Recall that, for Bohm and Hiley as for Deleuze, 'In a certain sense we could say that the overall quantum world measures and observes *itself*. For the classical 'sub-world' that contains the apparatus [the laboratory, for example] is inseparably contained within the quantum world, especially through those nonlocal interactions that bring about the classical [or Newtonian] behaviour.'[39] Bergson called this aspect of duration the 'impersonal time in which all things will flow'. As Stevens suggests, such impersonality means that these are 'not balances / That we achieve but balances that happen'.

This Bergsonian 'representative of Time' also describes Deleuze's own early formulation of the pure and empty form of time that he later, in *The Logic of Sense*, calls 'Aion', the transcendental virtual generator of multiple actual times ('Chronos') that plays such an important role in his own ontology.[40] In *Difference and Repetition* he describes this form of time as follows: 'every structure has a purely logical, ideal or dialectical time. However, this virtual time itself determines a time of differenCiation, or rather rhythms or different times of actualisation which correspond to the relations and singularities of the structure and, for their part, measure the passage from virtual to actual.'[41] The capital C in temporal 'differenCiation' serves to mark its differential relation to the 'differenTiation' of space; together the two terms constitute the double concept of 'differenT/Ciation',[42] which is comparable to Jacques Derrida's double (spatio-temporal) term 'différance'. Deleuze's further elaboration defines virtual time in terms of acceleration and deceleration, which make its debt to and difference from Einstein's relativity evident:

> if, from the point of view of actualisation, the dynamism of spatial directions determines a [temporal] differenciation of types, then the more or less rapid times immanent to these dynamisms ground the passage from one to the other, from one differenciated type to another, either by deceleration or by acceleration. With contracted or extended times and according to the reasons for acceleration or delay, other spaces are created … In principle, the temporal factor allows the transformation of dynamisms, even though these may be asymmetrical, spatially irreducible and completely differenciated – or rather, differenciating.[43]

In this way Deleuze has adopted the Bergsonian concept of duration in order to clarify and extend it within the discipline of philosophy, just as Bohm and Hiley did within physics.[44] Like duration itself, which Bergson claimed was a virtual multiplicity capable of generating many different actual time-flows, his concept of it has proven to be a virtual multiplicity as well, generating creative thought and activity in these distinct domains.

Bergson's concept of virtual time, so long ignored both by scientists and by philosophers, is now being reassessed not only by Deleuze, Bohm and Hiley, but also by theorists like Ilya Prigogine and Isabelle Stengers, who have written that although 'Bergson was certainly "wrong" on some technical points [of relativity theory] … his task as a philosopher was to attempt to make explicit inside physics the aspects of time he thought science was neglecting.'[45] This he did do, though it has taken physicists more than half a century to comprehend this explication and make it productive, and then only once his attempt to 'give the theory of Relativity the metaphysics it lacked' had been reconstructed within the formalism of quantum mechanics by Bohm. The rapidly expanding field of complex dynamics, which includes chaos theory and fractal geometry, is another, more direct heir of Bergson's studies in duration, as several recent critical works have pointed out.[46] Complex dynamics studies the behaviour of highly unstable systems far from equilibrium, and finds that they obey a temporal law as iron-bound as the spatial laws of relativistic motion and the statistical laws of quantum mechanics: the second law of thermodynamics, which allows order to be created only at the expense of the production and accumulation of greater disorder elsewhere. The measure of this disorder, entropy, defines the irreversibility of time. *Contra* Einstein, then, we can say that time is real, and it is also irreducible to space. In this sense, and this sense alone, time is absolute. The reality of this absolute time, however, is virtual, in the sense Deleuze gives that term: generative of many different times of actualisation, many different laboratory frames of non-local reference, many different rates of entropy.[47] Duration as Bergson conceived it, then, is a virtual multiplicity,[48] a *singular* reservoir of potential times, but this does not mean that time is not also, in actualisation, irreducibly *multiple*.

Notes

1 Albert Einstein, 'Physics and Reality', in his *Ideas and Opinions*, trans. Sonja Bargmann (New York, Crown, [1936] 1954), pp. 290–323: p. 318.

2 David Bohm and Basil J. Hiley, *The Undivided Universe: an Ontological Interpretation of Quantum Theory* (New York, Routledge, 1993), p. 351.

3 J. S. Bell, 'On the Einstein–Podolsky–Rosen Paradox', in his *Speakable and Unspeakable in Quantum Mechanics* (Cambridge, Cambridge University Press, 1987), pp. 14–21: p. 20.

4 For the purposes of this essay, the term 'deterministic' is understood to mean 'precisely predictable in each individual case', while 'indeterministic' on the contrary is taken to mean 'only statistically predictable, on the basis of a large sample of similar cases'. Relativity is deterministic because it makes precise predictions of the outcomes to be expected in individual experiments, for example in the rate of time dilation for a given acceleration (Gary Zukav, *The Dancing Wu Li Masters: an Overview of the New Physics* (New York, Bantam, 1979), pp. 139–40) or the number of degrees of arc of the precession of Mercury's perihelion (*ibid.*, p. 180). The Lorentz transformation equations reflect this, as we will see. Quantum theory is indeterministic because it cannot precisely predict the results of any single-particle measurement, but can only predict what the statistical range of possible results of that measurement will be (*ibid.*, pp. 34–5). Both Heisenberg's Indeterminacy Principle and Schrödinger's Wave Equation reflect this, as we will also see.

5 Albert Einstein, *Relativity: the Special and General Theory*, trans. Robert W. Lawson (New York, Crown, [1916] 1961), pp. 25–7. Though presented by Einstein himself, this demonstration can be misleading in that it may be taken to show that, when the observer moves towards the light coming from an event, the speed of the light and the speed of the observer towards the light add together to produce a resultant speed of their approach to each other that exceeds the speed of light. This is not the case because, as Einstein also demonstrates, speeds are not simply additive as we imagine in classical mechanics, but can only be combined by dividing them by their ratio to the square of the speed of light. The upshot of this is that, if one were to travel towards a star at half the speed of light, the light coming from the star would still approach one only at the speed of light, not at one-and-a-half times the speed of light. This is part of the demonstration of the absolute value of the speed of light in relativity theory (Einstein, *Relativity*, pp. 38–41).

6 See Paul Langevin, 'L'Evolution de l'espace et du temps', *Revue de la Métaphysique et de Morale*, 19 (1911), pp. 455–66: pp. 465–6, where it is not actually specified that the traveller and the person who remains on earth must be twins. This case requires general relativity to explain it, despite the fact that Einstein did not formulate the general theory until 1915–16.

7 H. A. Lorentz, 'Michelson's Interference Experiment' and 'Electromagnetic Phenomena in a System Moving with Any Velocity Less than that of Light', in A. Einstein, H. A. Lorentz, H. Weyl and H. Minkowski, *The Principle of Relativity*, trans. W. Perrett and G. B. Jeffery (New York, Dover, 1952), pp. 3–34 (originally published in German in 1895 and 1904); A. Einstein, 'On the Electrodynamics of Moving Bodies', in Einstein, Lorentz, Weyland and Minkowski, *The Principle of Relativity*, pp. 35–65: pp. 37–51 (originally published in German in 1905); Einstein, *Relativity*, pp. 30–4, 115–20.

8 Einstein, 'Physics and Reality', p. 308.

9 See Hermann Minkowski, 'Space and Time', in Einstein, Lorentz, Weyland and Minkowski, *The Principle of Relativity*, pp. 73–91: p. 77 (originally published in German in 1908), and Albert Einstein, 'The Foundation of the General Theory of Relativity', *ibid.*, pp. 109–64: pp. 118–19 (originally published in German in 1916) for a description of some of the variants of this equation. I would like to thank Laurence S. Hordon for clarifying this point for me.

10 DS, p. 74; M, p. 127.

11 DS, p. 80; M, p. 133.

12 The critique of the 'paradox of the twins' is in DS, pp. 72–9, 163–72; M, pp. 124–32, 216–25; his defence of duration is contained in chapter three of DS as a whole.

13 DS, p. 47; M, p. 100, translation modified.

14 Gilles Deleuze, *Bergsonism*, trans. Hugh Tomlinson and Barbara Habberjam (New York, Zone Books, [1966] 1991), p. 82. Milič Čapek comes to a conclusion concerning Bergson's 'simultaneity of flows' that is remarkably similar to Deleuze's in 'What is Living and What is Dead in the Bergsonian Critique of Relativity', in Milič Čapek, *The New Aspects of Time: its Continuity and Novelties* (Dordrecht, Kluwer, 1991), especially pp. 311–19.

15 Deleuze, *Bergsonism*, p. 116.

16 Zukav, *The Dancing Wu Li Masters*, pp. 141–2.

17 DS, p. 78, n. 3; M, p. 131, n. 1.

18 Deleuze, *Bergsonism*, p. 130, n. 20. Bergson was not exclusively misunderstood, however: Louis de Broglie, who developed the first 'hidden variable' interpretation of quantum mechanics in the 1920s and later inspired Bohm in his fuller version of it, notes the many similarities between quantum theory and Bergson's work as a whole in his *Physics and Microphysics*, trans. Martin Davidson (New York, Harper, 1955), chapter nine (unfortunately this chapter is only summarised in the English translation; the complete text is translated in P. A. Y. Gunter (ed.), *Bergson and the Evolution of Physics* (Knoxville, University of Tennessee Press, 1969), pp. 46–62).

19 Einstein cited in Ilya Prigogine and Isabelle Stengers, *Order Out of Chaos: Man's New Dialogue with Nature* (New York, Bantam, 1984), p. 294.

20 Einstein cited in M, p. 1346; translated in Gunter, *Bergson*, p. 133.

21 The next two paragraphs constitute a rather loose paraphrase of Einstein, Podolsky and Rosen (Can Quantum-Mechanical Description of Physical Reality be Considered Complete?) in *Physical Review*, 47 (1935), pp. 777–80, a paraphrase which also draws on David Bohm's discussion in David Bohm, *Quantum Theory* (New York, Prentice-Hall, 1951), pp. 611–23 and Zukav, *The Dancing Wu Li Masters*, pp. 283–93.

22 Niels Bohr, 'Can Quantum-Mechanical Description of Physical Reality be Considered Complete?', in *Physical Review*, 48 (1935), pp. 696–702: pp. 697, 701.

23 TFW, p. 219; OE, pp. 143–4.

24 Einstein, 'Physics and Reality', pp. 317–18.

25 Bohm in fact accepted Bohr's refutation of 'hidden variables' at first and defended it in his *Quantum Theory* textbook on pp. 619–23. Bohm's public statement of apostasy followed the publication of this text by less than a year.

26 We should clarify here that no one has yet determined whether non-local interactions are truly instantaneous or merely much faster than light. Bohm and Hiley propose some experiments that would allow us to distinguish the two forms, but these are unrealisable at present; see Bohm and Hiley, *The Undivided Universe*, pp. 293–5.

27 Albert Einstein, 'Autobiographical Notes', in Paul Schilpp (ed.), *Albert Einstein, Philosopher-Scientist* (New York, Harper & Row, 1949), p. 85; Einstein, *Relativity*, p. 48.

28 Alain Aspect, interview in P. C. W. Davies and J. R. Brown (eds), *The Ghost in the Atom* (Cambridge, Cambridge University Press, 1986), pp. 40–4: pp. 41–3; Zukav, *The Dancing Wu Li Masters*, pp. 294–5.

29 Bohm and Hiley, *The Undivided Universe*, p. 289.

30 Einstein, 'The Foundation of the General Theory of Relativity', p. 117. See also Einstein, *Relativity*, for a more discursive account of relativity.

31 Lorentz, 'Michelson's Interference Experiment' and 'Electromagnetic Phenomena'; Einstein, 'On the Electrodynamics of Moving Bodies', pp. 37–51; Einstein, *Relativity*, pp. 30–4, 115–20.

32 Bohm and Hiley, *The Undivided Universe*, p. 285.

33 *Ibid.*, p. 282, emphasis added.

34 *Ibid.*, p. 288.

35 *Ibid.*, p. 290.

36 *Ibid.*, p. 292.

37 *Ibid.*, pp. 31–8. The pilot wave model, which is the foundation of Bohm's theory of the 'implicate order', has been explicated in many places, most notably in Bohm's own *Wholeness and the Implicate Order* (New York, Routledge, 1980). Briefly, it contends that sub-atomic particles are influenced by an as-yet-undetectable 'pilot wave' that 'informs' them of the state of the entire universe instantaneously, a wave which in effect guides them in all their motions. This wave, which would operate in the orders of magnitude between what we can currently observe (down to about 10^{-16} cm) and the lowest level of physical activity consistent with current physical theory (about 10^{-33} cm), accounts for the paradoxical determinations of non-locality in Bohm's model.

38 Bohm and Hiley, *The Undivided Universe*, p. 285.

39 *Ibid.*, p. 179. On non-subjective observers see Gilles Deleuze and Félix Guattari, *What is Philosophy?* trans. Hugh Tomlinson and Graham Burchell (New York, Columbia University Press, [1991] 1994), pp. 128–32.

40 Gilles Deleuze, *The Logic of Sense*, trans. Mark Lester with Charles Stivale (New York, Columbia University Press, [1969] 1990), pp. 60–5, 162–8. Though Deleuze's linkage of Aion and Chronos derives in large part from Bergson (but also from Hume, Hölderlin and Nietzsche), it manages in large measure to evade one of the most problematic elements in Bergson's own formulation of the problem of time: 'heterogeneous continuity', changing sameness, which is the paradoxical phrase Bergson uses to synthesise the indeterminable creation of novelty that constitutes freedom in *Time and Free Will* with the perpetual but virtual presence of the pure past that constitutes memory in *Matter and Memory* (see TFW, pp. 234–40; OE, pp. 153–6 and MM, pp. 319–23/239–42; OE, pp. 369–72). Though Bergson apparently did not perceive a problem in their relation, some critics of Bergson do: how can genuine novelty continue to emerge when the past is virtually omnipresent? This question of Bergson's consistency goes beyond the scope of my essay, though it is indirectly related both to Bergson's argument with Einstein and to Bohm and Hiley's reformulation of that argument in physical terms. In brief, I would suggest that the difficulty can be overcome by way of a detour, like the one Deleuze takes, through Nietzsche's eternal return understood as repetition into the future rather than continuity with the past. The key element of duration for Deleuze is not its constant relation to memory but its function as a reservoir of other time-flows, which act as alternate historical trajectories on to which the present can be switched (like a train at a junction) at any time – in principle. See Gilles Deleuze, *Nietzsche and Philosophy*, trans. Hugh Tomlinson (New York, Columbia University Press, [1962] 1983), particularly chapter two. I would like to thank John Mullarkey for bringing this issue to my attention.

41 Gilles Deleuze, *Difference and Repetition*, trans. Paul Patton (New York, Columbia University Press, 1994), pp. 210–11 (originally published in French in 1968).

42 *Ibid.*, p. 209.

43 *Ibid.*, p. 216.

44 This is not to suggest that Bohm and Hiley drew directly on Bergson's arguments; indeed, they do not cite Bergson at all, nor does Bohm do so in any of his solo texts that I have examined. The conceptual parallelism is all the more striking for its lack

of direct causality.

45 Prigogine and Stengers, *Order Out of Chaos*, pp. 301–2.
46 In addition to Prigogine and Stengers, see also the essays collected in David Ray Griffin (ed.), *Physics and the Ultimate Significance of Time: Bohm, Prigogine and Process Philosophy* (Albany, NY, SUNY Press, 1986); other relevant essays are included in David Ray Griffin, *The Re-enchantment of Science* (Albany, NY, SUNY Press, 1988) and N. Katherine Hayles (ed.), *Chaos and Order: Complex Dynamics in Literature and Science* (Chicago, University of Chicago Press, 1991).
47 Brian Massumi has suggested that Deleuze's conception of virtuality has a number of significant resemblances to the attractors of chaos theory; see Brian Massumi, *A User's Guide to Capitalism and Schizophrenia: Deviations from Deleuze and Guattari* (Cambridge, Mass., MIT Press, 1992), pp. 58–68.
48 Deleuze, *Bergsonism*, p. 85.

III

MIND

introduction by ryu jiseok[1]
translated by john mullarkey

A LETTER FROM BERGSON TO JOHN DEWEY

It is highly likely that Bergson met Dewey for the first time during his visit to Columbia University in 1913, a prospect Bergson was looking forward to, as his letter indicates. But Bergson already knew Dewey's writings, as can be seen from his 1902 essay 'Intellectual Effort', even if this is the only reference to the American philosopher in his work.[2] As for Dewey, the article Bergson's letter refers to is probably the first text Dewey devoted to the French philosopher, for none of his writings before 1912 makes any mention of Bergson. Thereafter, Dewey's references to Bergson are numerous, and he dedicates a number of studies to him.[3]

The following letter is a moderate reply to a detailed critical study by Dewey of the first chapter of *Matter and Memory*.[4] Dewey's article begins by remarking on the 'twofold strain' implicit in Bergson's theory: on the one hand, there are the features of perception, common-sense knowledge and science explained via the influence of action, and, on the other hand, Bergson's critique of the errors stemming from applying to metaphysics practical conclusions and methods formed through the influence of a particular action. In short, he highlights two interpretative possibilities in Bergsonism – *pragmatic* and *mystical* – and then denounces Bergson's oscillation between these two contradictory tendencies. It is not surprising that Dewey, an instrumentalist who was hostile to dualism, would not hide his preference for the first approach while resolutely turning his back on the second. In his article, Dewey therefore rejects some elements of Bergson's analysis at the same time as selecting and revising those parts which are compatible with his own philosophical tendency.

In his letter, Bergson contents himself with drawing attention to certain essential points of his work in order to indicate his disagreement with Dewey's interpretation. Their difference in opinion, in our view, originates in an interpretation limited to analysing the first chapter of *Matter and Memory*, often derided as difficult and obscure.[5] To grasp fully the meaning of the text in question it would be necessary to understand the preparatory and hypothetical character of the notion of 'pure perception' – diametrically opposed to pure memory – as well as the very specific use of the term 'image'[6] around which the plan of the book is structured, as the title of each chapter indicates.

From the start of the first chapter, Bergson invites his readers to engage with this problematic term in defining the material world as an ensemble of images.[7] The author's intention is to bypass the traditional dichotomy of subject and object by establishing common ground between the privileged image of our body and the other images which surround it. Bergsonian epistemology adopts a realist perspective as it situates at the origin of our perception the given world. This is a world of images overflowing perception, in that perception, always oriented towards action, limits itself only to certain, utilisable images. Images therefore exist independently of us. But Bergson at the same time makes a concession to idealism by adopting the word 'image', which is analogous to representation, and by admitting that every reality has a connection or relationship with consciousness through which we grasp things, that is, images.[8] This is why Bergson writes to William James saying that he uses the term 'image' to designate a reality which is neither subjective nor objective,[9] and attempts thereby to resolve the dichotomy of realism and idealism.

Villa Montmorency
18 Avenue des Tilleuls
Auteuil, Paris
3 January 1913

Dear Mr Dewey

As I had failed to put my hands on the issue of *Journal of Philosophy* where your article 'Perception and Organic Action' appeared, it would probably have escaped me had you not been so kind as to send it to me. I have all the more reason now to thank you for sending it and especially for writing it, as it is a very deep, very sharp critique of the first chapter of *Matter and Memory*. Unfortunately, I cannot reply right now to the objections that you raise: I am sending you this hasty letter as I am snowed under with work and various duties, and I would need a good deal of time and space to tackle one by one such subtle and penetrating criticisms as those you make. In general, I believe that the explanation for all these criticisms, and the point of departure for all my replies, is your implicit refusal to accept the *partial realism* of the doctrine I set out. As I say in the introduction to *Matter and Memory*, I place myself in a position mid-way between realism and idealism,[10] but in a certain measure I am realist; and, as regards matter, I reckon that the geometry which it contains, and which it mani-fests all the more in the measure in which we delve more deeply into it, pertains to what is real *in itself*. That is why, here as elsewhere, it would be impossible for me to define *all* reality in terms of action, unless one greatly stretches the meaning of this word. I believe that this is the essential point which separates us.

According to my position, the action of things on us, be it real or virtual, is a part of their reality, but only a part. Besides, I do not see any difficulty in confusing our virtual action on things with the virtual action of things on us. The action by which we utilise things is essentially a contact, and in that contact it is irrelevant whether one says that we act on the thing or that the thing acts on us.[11]

But, once again, it would be necessary to go through all the points of your argument one by one. I would like to be able to do this later, in a work where I would develop anew some of the points in *Matter and Memory*.[12] By then, I will have had the great pleasure of making your acquaintance in America.[13]

Best wishes

H. Bergson

Notes

1 I must thank Annie Neuburger for kindly authorising the publication of this letter, as well as Pierre Trotignon, Pete Gunter, Frédéric Worms and John Mullarkey for their help.

2 The reference to Dewey's 'The Psychology of Effort' can be found in ME, p. 215; OE, p. 949.

3 'Bergson on Instinct', *New Republic*, 83 (1073) (1935), pp. 200–1; 'Time and Individuality', in D. W. Hering (ed.), *Time and Its Mysteries: Four Lectures Given in the James Arthur Foundation* (New York, New York University Press, 1940), pp. 85–109; 'Spencer and Bergson', *Revue de Métaphysique et de Morale*, 70 (3) (1965), pp. 325–33.

4 'Perception and Organic Action', *The Journal of Philosophy, Psychology and Scientific Methods*, 9 (24) (1912), pp. 645–68.

5 The meaning of Bergson's argument in the first chapter will only emerge fully in the light of the rest of the book, each part of which, though distinct with its own character, none the less collectively comprise a unifying coherence. The complexity of the philosophical argument deployed across multiple levels is without doubt one of the major obstacles to understanding the profound significance of *Matter and Memory*. See the excellent commentary by Frédéric Worms, *Introduction à* Matière et mémoire *de Bergson* (Paris, Presses Universitaires de France, 1997).

6 CM, pp. 77/90–1; OE, p. 1318; 'Lettre à G. Lechalas', in M, pp. 410–13.

7 MM, pp. 2–3/18; OE, p. 170. The introduction to the original French edition of *Matter and Memory* does not give any preliminary analysis of the 'image'. It is from the seventh edition onwards that Bergson replaced the old introduction with a new one which spends a good deal of time clarifying the notion of the image, regarded by many readers as obscure. We note, besides, that this new version was initially written in 1910 as an introduction to the English translation of this work (MM, pp. xi–xxi/9–16; OE, pp. 161–8.

8 It seems that, overall, Dewey retains this idealist aspect of Bergson and criticises it as a form of pan-psychical idealism; see Dewey, 'Perception and Organic Action', p. 658.

9 M, p. 660.

10 MM, pp. xi–xii/9–10, 12–16/24–8, 281–91/211–18; OE, pp. 161, 176–9, 346–53.

11 MM, pp. 57–8/56–7; OE, p. 205.

12 Some months later, Bergson would give a lecture on themes relating to *Matter and Memory*, '"Phantoms of the Living" and "Psychical Research"' (ME, pp. 75–103; OE, pp. 860–78). Yet it seems hard to consider this as a response to the American philosopher's critique. He would develop these themes again in the Gifford Lectures on personality (1914) which rely on the conclusions of *Creative Evolution* (M, pp. 1051–86). But it is impossible for us to verify whether Bergson is thinking here of this series of lectures.

13 Bergson is alluding to his trip to the USA. Among others, he would deliver two lecture courses at Columbia University, where Dewey was teaching. For the occasion Columbia University Press published a Bergson bibliography – the first bibliography systematically prepared – for which Dewey wrote the introduction: *A Contribution to a Bibliography of Henri Bergson* (New York, Columbia University Press, 1913), pp. ix–xii.

frédéric worms
translated by pelagia goulimari

MATTER AND MEMORY ON MIND AND BODY: FINAL STATEMENTS AND NEW PERSPECTIVES

The following essay is taken from the concluding part of a book called *Intro-duction à* Matière et Mémoire de Bergson.¹ Its purpose is to establish Bergson's final statement on the mind–body problem, and to show how relevant it may still be for contemporary theory. It relies first on Bergson's own 'Summary and Conclusion' which ends *Matter and Memory* and so allows for a review of the whole book. It then develops the book's main results on the three different levels of theory of knowledge, psychology and metaphysics, thus covering the whole range of the philosophy of mind and mapping out the main meeting-points with contemporary issues. Bergson's pragmatic theory of knowledge, hierarchical, top-down theory of mind, and metaphysical dualism (grounded in degrees of duration) thus combine in a quite coherent and original per-spective.²

I

The idea that we have disengaged from the facts and confirmed by reason-ing is that our body is an instrument of action, and of action only.³

So reads the opening sentence of the 'Summary and Conclusion' of *Matter and Memory*.

Why, at the point of concluding, does Bergson re-emphasise an aspect of the book which is certainly important, but partial, a hypothesis con-cerning the body and that alone?⁴ How, starting from this point, can the entire content of the book come together again, including its initial hypothesis on memory, where the action of the body seemed to be but one element among others?

The paradox and the essential lesson of *Matter and Memory* are never-theless exactly where Bergson wants them to be: that is, in defining the body by its action, and its action *only*. The problem covered by this 'only' is in fact the following: how to deduce from the action of our body (that is to say from its movements, as they transform the configuration of material objects) what appears to be opposed to it, that is our knowledge or our *representation?* More precisely still, we must reconstitute Bergson's implicit reasoning here: if the body can do nothing but act, *and if nevertheless we represent things to ourselves*, we must be able to account for this representation by recourse to something *other than* the body. One thus seems to be condemned, by this initial hypothesis, to a dualism that would be clear-cut, radical or, to use Bergson's term, 'vulgar'.

At this point there intervenes what appears to us to be Bergson's *tour de force* in this book: it consists in explaining representation not only in one but in *two* ways other than by recourse to the body, by bringing in *not one, but two principles other than the body!* The consequence of this will itself be double, and doubly fundamental:

- not only will the real metaphysical contradiction no longer be between the action of the body and the representation of our mind, but *between two forms of representation*;
- but furthermore, in an astonishing reversal, the action of the body will be able to play the role of a *mediation* between these two forms of representation or of reality!

We could then summarise the movement of this conclusion, and at the same time of the entire book, in the following manner: *from the action of the body as opposed to our representation, to the action of the body as mediation between our representation and that of things, between our mind and matter*.

But such a conclusion at once necessitates recalling the main stages of the book and its structure. That is to say the following moments:

a) To begin with, if the role of the body is limited to its action, a first consequence follows concerning the representation of external objects or, said otherwise, *perception*: this initial hypothesis obliges us to situate perception outside the body, obliges us to suppose that the external world as such is made of *images*. The purpose of the first chapter of the book was certainly to prove this hypothesis and even to derive from it a complete theory of knowledge.[5]

b) But if the role of the body is limited to its action, a second explanation, completely different from the first one, will be necessary in order to account for, not this time the pure representation of external objects, but the representation of absent objects and the preservation of the departed moments of time, that is, *memory*. Now it has become necessary to assume, not that the external universe is a set of images, but that individual consciousness is a set of memories and an act of recollection, and that it is radically opposed to perception itself. Hence the psychological dualism of the two central chapters,[6] already overcome at the centre of the book (in the figure of the 'cone')[7] through the double meaning given to the body, and to its action. Here reappeared the initial hypothesis set forth in the original introduction,[8] concerning the 'planes of consciousness'.

c) Thus the action of the body took place between two kinds of representation, exactly because it could not explain either of them by itself! But if the dualism is displaced by a notch, being between two forms of representation, is it now easier to overcome? Only in the last chapter of his book did Bergson establish that matter,[9] to which we are introduced by perception, and mind, which is revealed to us by memory, are connected through a profound metaphysical analogy, which leads to conceiving them as two degrees of the same activity: *tension* in time and *extension* in the extended, or in other words, duration in general. From then on the action of the body took its full metaphysical significance, as mediation between two degrees of the same act and two different kinds of reality, matter where it inscribes itself on the one hand, mind which appropriates it on the other.

Thus the genuine opposition is not between body and soul, but between *the external world* and *individual consciousness* or – the title of the book finally becoming totally explicit – between *'matter'* and *'memory'*. If henceforth the 'and' of the title can take its double meaning of duality and unity, the subtitle of the book has itself become explicit, by making apparent the mediating role of the body: the theoretical and general analogy culminates in a practical and individual participation, the 'relation of body towards mind'.[10] Such, then, is the overall conclusion of *Matter and Memory*: one escapes neither dualism nor union, but the choice of *the correct point of departure* profoundly transforms the meaning of both.

But this conclusion presupposes the overall movement of the book, in its three profoundly distinct stages: that is why this conclusion cannot be set forth without a 'summary'[11] which repeats this movement in accelerated form.

Furthermore, it is only by setting forth the philosophical theses which would result from each one of its stages, and which would present us with as many still open theoretical options, that we would ourselves be led back to re-examine the overall unity of the work, and then to return to the meaning that *the very problem of dualism* could retain for us today.

II

Certainly, through the three stages of his demonstration,[12] Bergson has first achieved the unique aim of the book, which was to affirm and to go beyond the thesis of dualism, starting from the principle of the action of the body: the action of the body can and must be thought as *a mediation between two different orders of representation and of reality*.

But one can and must go further.

In fact, this unique conclusion not only comes to light at the end of a continuous and linear course. It can also be found at the point of convergence of three distinct critical points, points which each stage of the book has allowed to be established independently, and which it is important to formulate concisely *for themselves*, so as to give the book its full import.

Moreover, not only does each thesis that Bergson was led to defend in each part of the book open in each domain a philosophical debate that would ask to be reopened, even today, but especially, each one of these theses reopens and displaces *the problem of dualism itself*, starting from the initial principle of the action of the body. The comprehensive re-opening of this problem, which gives *Matter and Memory* its unity, depends on three results which give it its intrinsic diversity. Briefly considering this triple displacement will allow us to have a triple glance at the unity of the book.

In short, it seems that starting from the action of the body Bergson reaches in succession:

1) a thesis relevant to the *theory of knowledge*: the action of the body would suffice to understand the distance and the agreement between 'image' and 'reality'; what we would thus have gone beyond is the epistemological dualism between realism and idealism; we would understand at the same time why the entire book is organised around the notion of *image*, and how important this dimension of the problem remains today;

2) a *psychological* thesis: the action of the body would suffice to make a profound distinction between two types of representation, 'perception' and 'memory'; the psychological theory of Bergson would thus be opposed to all theories of 'association' between homogeneous representations: we would finally understand why the entire book is centred on the hypothesis of 'planes of consciousness', which allows it to go beyond its own dualism, and the great significance which this theory ought to retain in the debates of 'cognitive psychology';

3) finally, a *metaphysical* thesis: the action of the body would suffice to bring together and connect two types of reality, 'matter' and 'mind' ['esprit'];[13] Bergson's theory would thus be opposed equally to 'materialism' and to any simple 'spiritualism': it is indeed the notion of *duration* –

because it simultaneously provides the criterion for all reality and allows us to establish differences between realities – which plays, so to speak, the key role in the denouement of the book; its significance cannot be over-estimated, even today.

We must briefly go back over each of the above decisive points:

1) The first thesis or the first philosophical option adopted by Bergson could be stated as follows: *we must replace sensation or sensibility with the action of the body as the first principle of the theory of knowledge.*

In this way, by pushing a notch further than traditional empiricism what could be called the 'naturalisation' of knowledge – that is, by not being content with replacing all 'innate ideas' with sensations coming from things, but instead replacing sensations themselves with the real actions of a living body in an external milieu – we would find a better foundation, or rather the authentic foundation for this knowledge.

In fact, as Kant has shown, all theories of knowledge which start with sensation, that is from a subjective given, are forced to show how this given agrees with the thing which has produced it, that is with its object: put differently, if the *matter* of knowledge is in us or relative to us, it must pass through universal *forms* in order, as it were, to reconquer its objectivity, without any guarantee that it has caught up with *the thing* in itself that way.

The strength of Bergson's chosen point of departure lies in the rigorous inversion of the above outcome: in starting from the action of the body, one is led to presuppose a real matter, exterior to us, on which this action imposes a relative aspect or form, relative, that is, to its practical needs.

Such is indeed the meaning of the Bergsonian notion of the image, with which we can now conclude: it designates the external object itself, or rather *that part of external matter which has been carved out as an object for the purpose of our action.*

In this way, if the *matter* of the image is real and exterior to us, its *form*, that is to say, primarily its spatial contour, is imaginary and relative to us. Thus we have indeed a real foundation for the object of knowledge, or rather knowledge does not have to agree with its object since the object is assumed to be part of external reality; but we also have the first data of subjective knowledge, with 'images' being relative not to the structure of our sensibility, but to the requirements of our action.

We understand then why the whole book is organised around 'images': if the first chapter shows how they carve themselves out against the background of matter, as soon as a body acts on it, the following two parts of the book will return them to two *totalities* which are themselves no longer constituted by images, even if images can each time be obtained from them by a psychological effort which involves primarily this privileged 'form of action' that we call *space*:

- the two central chapters of the book return images to the indistinct totality of *pure memory*, from where an effort of consciousness can draw them out in order to respatialise them as distinct objects;
- the last chapter of the book will finally return images to the totality out of which they had been drawn in the first chapter: this totality *is matter* or the material universe.

Above all, it is two completely general and fundamental theses that Bergson reaches and defends with his notion of the image.

- Unlike the 'sensation' of the empiricists or 'representation' in general, the image, the 'datum' or the first 'mental' content is part of *exteriority* itself. Bergson defends, in an apparently extreme form, the thesis of an 'exteriority of the mind'. This thesis gives straight away an objective foundation to all our knowledge, to all *human* knowledge and science.
- On the other hand, what explains the relativity or subjectivity of our knowledge is no longer the fact of sensation but *the obligation to act*, which 'detaches' strictly speaking the image from its content, without for all that absorbing it into a psychological interiority. Here as well Bergson seems to be pushing to its extreme the thesis of a pragmatism or of a biological naturalisation of our knowledge, which would take seriously the strict materiality of a body that is incapable of distinguishing itself in nature from other parts of the universe!

Each one of these two theses would rightfully enter into the most important debates of our contemporary 'philosophy of mind'.

Above all, they allow Bergson, starting from the action of the body, to pose and at the same time to go beyond a first dualism which would serve as a foundation for all the others. In fact, if there is a distance between image and reality, this is not a distance between the world and its representation in a consciousness, or its double in a brain: it is *at the interior of matter itself* that appears a *duality* or an epistemological dualism which is certainly irreducible as such, but which, to put it this way, has already been overcome even before it has been initiated!

2) Yet what is particular to Bergson in *Matter and Memory* is that he does not stop there.

If the action of the body allows us to found our knowledge by obliging us to assume images, the psychologist nevertheless notes, although confining himself to this same initial principle, that our practical knowledge does not consist *only* in these images, or in some combinatorial action, so to speak, that our mind would just carry out on them.

Bergson is therefore led to his second fundamental thesis: *we must replace the hypothesis of a single level of representations which are con-*

nected to each other through a horizontal work of association with that of a plurality of levels of representations, connected to each other through a vertical work of interpretation or comprehension.

In fact no theory of knowledge can content itself with answering the question of the *origin* or the foundation of our representations, whether they be sensations or images. We must also understand how these originary – or elementary, if you wish – representations are preserved and made use of in the autonomous deployment of our *knowledge* and of our psychological life.

In this respect, does it suffice to give oneself sensations, preserved in the form of memories, and combined or associated with each other, as Hume believed? Or rather, must we add to them, as did Kant, an active power to synthesise them in concepts which would characterise our understanding, itself irreducible to sensibility?

Bergson's thesis fits with neither of these fundamental positions: he notes an irreducible heterogeneity between our representations, which forbids us to reduce them all to images; but this difference must be situated not between sensations and concepts but between sensations, or rather perceptions, and *memories*! Put differently, the mere preservation of our perceptions in an individual memory would change their nature profoundly, and this difference of nature would manifest itself in each and every complex operation of our 'mental life'. It is thus not the universal and objective concept which would be opposed to subjective sensation, it is on the contrary the objective and external perception which would find itself caught up and even supplanted by internal and individual memories.

We understand then the place, at the centre of the book, of the theory of *planes of consciousness* and the metaphor or the figure of the cone: it took the first chapter to establish the initial 'plane' of perception, a surface carved out against the background of the matter of the universe; it took the chapters on memory to establish the specific status of recollections, and their meeting-point with the action of a body that would not know how to produce them or contain them; finally it took the fourth chapter to give to this dualism, which is for the time being functional and psychological, a meaning which could well be considered substantial and metaphysical.

On the psychological level itself, it is again two completely general and fundamental theses which Bergson reaches and defends in *Matter and Memory*, and which ought to find their place at the heart of most contemporary debates of the 'philosophy of mind':

– The difference of nature between perceptions and memories, which stops us from reducing all our 'mental contents' to a single genre of 'representations', is certainly not yet the metaphysical distinction between matter and mind: and yet it already covers the fundamental distinction between the diversity of the representations of *objects* and the unity of the consciousness of a *subject*, or rather of an individual person. The indistinct and unconscious unity of memories refers to the unity of an individual history in time. More generally, we can ask ourselves whether all theories postulating an irreducible diversity of levels of representations are not led to ascribe a dynamic unity to the subject of knowledge, whether it be in the brain (as is the case with so-called 'connectionist' theories today) or in the unconscious (as is the case with psychoanalysis). In any case, such would be – and it is very far from being dated or outdated – the broadest sense of Bergson's fundamental debate with 'associationism' in this book!

– Furthermore, Bergson's analysis of the 'convergence' between memories and perceptions leads to a second thesis of general significance: not only would memories indeed collaborate with perceptions in every complex and complete knowledge, they would precede them and *anticipate* them through a vertical movement which is not 'bottom–up' but 'top–down', inverting the apparently simpler order that we would have wanted to establish between our representations! It is the general theory of *interpretation* or of comprehension which is at stake here. Once again, this theory brings into play two radically opposed theoretical models between which Bergson obliges us to choose – a choice which, still today, engages our full philosophical responsibility.

However the case might be with these two debates – which are undoubtedly more open than ever with the development of the 'cognitive sciences', and whose properly philosophical significance appears clearly here – a new step in the general movement of the book has indeed just been accomplished. If a psychological dualism must be radically affirmed, according to Bergson, the unity of psychological experience, founded on the very action of the body, must be equally affirmed. Its only precariousness – and how painful it is – rests on the affections or the lesions of the body itself. At least it does not run the purely theoretical risk of being cut in half by a theoretical abstraction, incapable of giving an account of the unity of our thought or of our life.

3) In order to establish the third fundamental thesis of *Matter and Memory*, 'the action of the body' can no longer suffice.

Now it is no longer a question of founding knowledge or psychological experience, which are henceforth completely described. It is a question on the contrary of overcoming the carving-out that this action and this knowledge impose on perception and memory, in order to see if the latter, in their primitive totality, would not refer back to autonomous and different realities.

But even if this were the case, would not the action of the body remain the mediating point between the two realities?

We must be more precise: the action of the body will in fact be able retrospectively to reveal, *this side of it*, an originary point of contact between two realities whose pure difference it also reveals: this is pure perception. It will also be able to show, *beyond itself* this time, an ultimate reason for being or acting which unites these two realities, no matter how different they are: this is liberty.

In any case this is how the third fundamental thesis of *Matter and Memory* could be formulated, as emerges from its last chapter: *we must replace the difference of substance between mind and matter with a difference of degree within a single scale of reality, allowing us to understand their respective and irreducible independence from each other, as well as their analogy or even their mutual participation.*

This time it is about asking oneself the question of the difference of *nature* between the subject of knowledge and its object, between the sensing and the sensed, so to speak, in the sensation itself: so must we assume that this difference is irreducible, while attempting to give an account of the union and also the contact that characterise them, as is the case with Descartes's metaphysical dualism? Or, must we, on the contrary, fold sensations back on to matter, abolishing all difference of nature, as is the case, for example, with Taine's materialism; or inversely must we fold matter back on to sensation, abolishing there as well all difference of nature, as is the case with Berkeley's 'immaterialism'?

It is in order to answer this question that Bergson brings in the notion of *duration*: not only in order to define through it, rather than through sensation, the inmost nature of our mind, but mainly in order to have it, rather than space, define the inmost nature of matter itself. In this way matter and mind would come under the 'same' irreducible reality, or rather the 'same' *act* of preservation of time, which does not contradict time's succession, and beyond which there is nothing to search for.

However, though coming under the same act, matter and mind remain entirely different and independent, because of a difference of degree founded exactly on the fact that duration denotes *an act and not a thing. Only acts have degrees or intensities*: if duration 'was' the flux of time as such, how could we look inside it for differences? But inversely, if duration [*la durée*] denotes not a thing, such as time, but the always individual act by which time is retained and prolonged in a consciousness, then we understand not only that there can be differences of degree or of rhythm, but above all that every difference of degree can correspond to a pure difference, to a difference of nature, to a type of reality.

Thus, well beyond all 'monism' of duration, well beyond also any undifferentiated plurality of durations, Bergson's philosophy is a philosophy of a *determined* plurality of durations or of a plurality of durations which are always determined and *individual*, starting with the duality which opposes *our* duration to that *of matter*, and which makes his doctrine that of a *dualism* which is irreducible to all others. As Gilles Deleuze has shown, 'Bergsonism' is indeed a *philosophy of difference*.

But we must add straight away that the plurality of durations, precisely because it remains a plurality *of durations*, makes their interaction or their mutual participation not only thinkable but directly and immediately sensible. This certainly has nothing to do with the fusion or confusion of individual realities. On the contrary, each time, a specific effort of thought is required in order to determine *the exact point of contact* between the temporal and individual realities which alone exist. This 'point' had initially been defined by Bergson, in *Time and Free Will*, within ourselves, *between us and ourselves*, at the heart of the relation to the self. The point of departure and the point of destination of *Matter and Memory* have consisted in searching for this point, this time, between us and matter, in the originary act of pure perception and in the ultimate destination of the free act. Thus Bergson's philosophy is *not only* a philosophy of difference: it is also, as shown this time by Maurice Merleau-Ponty, *a philosophy of immanence*, that is to say of contact, no matter how limited and partial, between realities which are part of, which take part in, the same reality.

Such is – in any case, between duality and unity, between difference and immanence – the summit of Bergson's work in *Matter and Memory*. It took him the entire book to get there. Perhaps, also, the perspectives which we touched on in the preceding remarks would suggest that we have not yet exhausted all its effects.

Notes

1 *Introduction à* Matière et Mémoire *de Bergson* (Les Grands Livres de la philosophie) (Paris, Presses Universitaires de France, 1997).
2 My warmest thanks go to John Mullarkey for inviting this contribution and discussing it with me, and to the Presses Universitaires de France for granting permission for this translation. These endnotes are new additions.
3 MM, p. 299/225; OE, p. 356.
4 The hypothesis can be found in what was the original introduction to *Matter and Memory* (see OE, pp. 1490–1, and below, note 8), where the body plays only a limited role.
5 The first chapter of *Matter and Memory* is entitled 'The Selection of Images for Representation. The Role of the Body'. [The English translation of *Matter and Memory* renders the French title as 'Of the Selection of Images for Conscious Presentation. What Our Body Means and Does'. – Ed.] It supposes that the world is made of images, as virtual representations, which it takes a work of selection to make actual.

It thus allows for a partial 'idealism', the world being made of possible 'ideas' (as Berkeley would have put it).

6 Chapters two and three of *Matter and Memory* deal with *memory* and lead to a distinction between images stemming from the perceptions of objects and images stemming from the pure memories of a subject.

7 The psychological dualism mentioned in the preceding note is completed by the junction of both kinds of representation in the perception itself, to which memories descend as though down the slope of a cone.

8 The original introduction (see note 4 above) was replaced by Bergson with a new one in the English translation (1911) of *Matter and Memory* and from then on in the French editions also. Both introductions are crucial to the book.

9 The fourth and last chapter is entitled 'The Delimiting and Fixing of Images. Perception and Matter. Soul and Body', showing that, beyond images, there should be something *limitless*, and in *movement*, something analogous to a mind, a soul, though different from it.

10 There is a subtitle to *Matter and Memory*, 'Essay on the Relation of Body Towards Mind', which should always be kept in mind. One can only wonder why this subtitle was omitted from the English translation of *Matter and Memory*, and whether such an important omission was intentional on Bergson's part (he gave great attention to the translation).

11 *Matter and Memory* is one of the very few philosophical books which ends not only with a 'conclusion' but with a 'summary and conclusion', showing the importance of reading it as a whole and of considering it as a complete picture.

12 They have been thus summarised analytically by Bergson in his 'Summary, and Conclusion' – we proceed on our part to a synthetic study.

13 'Esprit' is normally rendered as 'mind', although this French word could also refer to the metaphysical 'soul' or cognitive 'knowledge'. This is also the central ambiguity of any 'philosophy of mind' *in any language*.

marie cariou
translated by melissa mcmahon

BERGSON: THE KEYBOARDS
OF FORGETTING

Even while stating from the outset that his book is 'frankly dualistic', Bergson indeed intends, in *Matter and Memory* (1896), to correct the errors of a vulgar dualism and, in so doing, to reconcile materialism and idealism. In order to do this he analyses a specific example borrowed from experience: that of recollection [*souvenir*].

It is in fact common in Bergson's method to rediscover the point where contrasting terms meet up with each other by showing how two theories which seem relentlessly to clash and oppose one another in fact commit the same error and should be placed side by side: neither the one nor the other are able to resolve a badly posed problem. And both pose it badly. For 'badly stated' questions, 'lame' answers.[1] In this case materialism and idealism thus limp along together for the same reason: attributing a speculative role to perception instead of situating it in relation to a field of possible action, a homogeneous spatial field, which must be defined as a 'network which we stretch beneath material continuity in order to render ourselves masters of it'.[2]

In order to think 'the relationship of the body to mind' in a new way, we must then in the first place forget 'philosophers' discussions' and try to place ourselves within the perspective of a mind which is in a sense 'naive', which would assimilate matter to an image. The first chapter of the book studies this gaze turned towards matter, the fourth will draw out its conclusions. Between the two comes the analysis of memory, in its dual relationship to the mind and the brain, which provides 'precise indications' indispensable to anyone wishing to pose a problem in the light of 'facts'.[3]

It is important to note the central character of the notion of the image from start to finish of the book:

It is in fact due to the originality of his thesis on *the extensity of the sensible*, it seems, that Bergson has been able to subvert the whole theory of knowledge. We are wrong, according to him, to have concluded that our sensations are unextended under the pretext that they are only 'vaguely localised'. From purely subjective, purely interior sensations we should thus pass via a complicated process of objectification to the reconstruction of external images in space. This scheme rests on a reversal of the experimental situation. Instead of starting from the entire set [*l'ensemble*] of images, it starts from a singular subject, and in so doing entails a series of 'false problems': how can unextended sensations allow us to form the idea of extension? How can we explain their definite order in space? How can we account for an agreement between consciousnesses in these conditions?

Whereas by starting from an initially indefinite field of images, the singularity of the subject will be experienced in a body which will itself appear as an image, a particular image which is reflecting, operative, central: a *reflecting* image, a sort of mirror which captures the images of matter and which is in a sense modelled by the action which objects exercise upon it; an *operative* image, since the body carries out a selection with a view to action. Without this operation, consciousness could not emerge. We would in a sense be an object among objects, as the material universe is itself a kind of consciousness, but a neutralised consciousness in which all the images appear to each other, are in constant interaction, without the possibility of choice, of limitation, in other words without the possibility of *distinction*.

It is the function of 'discernment' which characterises the image of the body and which is the first sign of a consciousness which will be defined as reflexivity, intuition, spirit. 'To perceive all the influences from all the points of all bodies would be to descend to the condition of a material object. Conscious perception signifies choice, and consciousness mainly consists in this practical discernment.'[4] The body is thus essentially a *central* image to which all the others are referred. It is obtained by the successive limitations of perception which, starting from multiple images, stops at this particular image possessing a sensori-motor power, this 'privileged', 'favoured' image, my body. 'It is this particular image which I adopt as the center of my universe and as the physical basis of my personality.'[5] Sartre and Merleau-Ponty will remember this masterly lesson whose train of argument we must now clarify.

Bergson's statements can seem peremptory: the body is only an instru-ment of action, 'to no extent, in no sense, in no way does it serve to pre-pare and even less to explain a representation'. It retains only the imprint of motor habits which play out the past but store no memories. It cannot be attributed a decisive role even at the level of sense-impressions. The mechanisms that it sets in motion illuminate sketches of action, not, strictly speaking, perceptions. Bergson will thus maintain a paradox: the union of soul and body will be shown by pushing dualism to its extreme.

The difficulties with 'vulgar' dualism come from the fact that it consid-ers the physical and the psychological as duplicates of each other. On this point idealism fares just as badly as epiphenomenal materialism. Seeking within the body the equivalent of the images which are organised around the body is to confuse 'the order which appears to us in perception' with 'the order which works for us in science'. Whether one considers cerebral movements as 'the cause' of our representations, as in materialism, or whether they are considered 'the occasion', as in idealism, in both cases the relationship of consciousness to action is neglected, and we believe we can treat perceptions and memories as operations of pure knowledge.

In order to reverse this perspective, we must thus begin by totally reversing its postulate and, at least for methodological reasons, begin res-olutely with action, even if it is only a matter of a 'possible' action. We can then estimate to what extent perception is not pre-eminently inventive. It is only selective. Its role is in the first place negative: to eliminate, to leave aside everything that does not concern the needs of action. By construct-ing the notion of a 'pure perception' in this way, isolated from any inter-vention of memory, Bergson in fact intends to create an operative concept which allows us to put perception back into things and the brain back into the universe, and, in so doing, to eliminate the false problems of these twin enemies, which are idealism and materialism in his eyes. It is obviously not a matter of describing a concrete psychological situation. He himself will specify that this theory of 'pure perception' must be subsequently completed and qualified by the introduction of affectivity and recollection. We must first think this fiction of a perception which would be only 'a mathematical instant in time', in the same way that in *Time and Free Will* we had first to think this fiction of a pure duration unmixed with space in order to rediscover the fundamental self and rescue freedom, which remains, moreover, the chief preoccupation of *Matter and Memory*.[6]

The consequences of this method of radical distinction in order subse-quently to clarify the conditions of an original union are multiple. In the first place it allows perception to be restored to things and thus renders useless the intervention of a parallelist hypothesis, the relationship of per-ception to reality not being a relationship of cause and effect but simply of the part to the whole. Second, it avoids the false problems of an imbalance between interiority and exteriority and the need to fabricate intermediaries in order to ensure the passage from one to the other. Finally it favours the return to scientific demands and consecrates the end of 'bad metaphysics'. This rests on two Bergsonian leitmotifs:

1 In images there is only a difference of degree and not of nature between being and being perceived. But there is, on the other hand, a difference of nature between perception and recollection.
2 Extension is no more reducible to some 'amorphous space' than duration is reducible to some 'bastard time'.

Perception is not a photographic view nor a scaled-down trace of an object, but the result of a phenomenon of reflection or, as Bergson says, 'an effect of mirage'.[7] Simple to the end, this operation only retains of the luxuriant totality of matter what interests our 'possible action' on it. But this poverty is in fact a richness, since it is the precursory sign of mind: the function of discerning. The mind is nevertheless only 'announced' in this way. In order to celebrate its coming, we must leave a material universe which can be defined as a consciousness where images compensate and neutralise each other and which in so doing become an unconsciousness; we must enter into the thickness of a duration where our memories are forged.

The theory of memory in Bergson is by his own admission like a theoretical consequence and an experimental verification of his theory of pure perception. In effect, to the extent that we imagine that in perception it is the states of the body which engender a representation, it becomes in a way logical to deduce from this that a memory is only a weakening and fading of perception and thus itself the distant echo of cerebral phenomena. In these conditions 'memory is only a function of the brain', and it is indeed in this case that the difference between perception and memory can only be one of degree. Instead of being richer and more complex than what is perceived, what is remembered is on the contrary less intense. But if this creative function of the cerebral state is denied and we only attribute to it the role of a continuous support of psychical activity, we are then in a position to distinguish the originality of recollection, which is that it bears on an absence whereas perception bears on a present object. But the present cannot be a simple idea. It is always 'ideo-motor'.[8] The recourse to experience should allow perception to be torn away from the contemplative and speculative halo in which we tend to plunge it.

The reference to diseases of memory is fundamental here to the extent that, however conditioned by the psychophysiology of the time they are, and whatever corrections we must today make to the information that was available to Bergson, they constitute an experimental basis from which he constructs his major principles. And it is not certain that the evolution of scientific knowledge and especially the introduction of neuroscience in contemporary reflection allow us to refute Bergson's intuitions. It is indeed by 'intuition' that the problems 'should be solved'.[9]

They can be grouped under two essential observations:

First observation: Nobody loses his or her memory. But the faculty of recall can be more or less inhibited, diminished, atrophied in its vitality. It is the mechanisms of contact between the past and the present which no longer function. The brain should ensure their functioning. It is not, however, a reservoir of sleeping images which would awaken spontaneously and effortlessly. The recognition which Bergson calls 'passive' characterises habits, mechanisms whose destruction can explain lesions. But true recognition, which we must call 'active', requires a tension of consciousness. Memory becomes concrete by encountering the sensible, in such a way that we could say that the past–present contact is also the mind–matter contact. We can observe that it is in the name of the same principle and by evoking the *élan* of a consciousness made to endure without anything being able to assign an end to its indefinite prolongation that Bergson also explains the illusions of *déjà vu*.[10]

The second part of the introduction to *Creative Mind* will signal the kinship of these views with those of Freud, especially concerning the complete conservation of the past. Bergson had moreover cited the Freudian theory of aphasia while broaching the question of the location of memories in chapter two of *Matter and Memory*. Freud is rather quickly evoked at the same time as Wysman and Moéli,[11] to whom hardly anything is attributed apart from the merit of having produced an evolution in the history of the schemata of sensory aphasia. Instead of accepting the hypothesis of an 'ideational centre' linked to the diverse language centres, as did Charcot, for example, they multiplied the number of centres according to the nature of the representations (visual, tactile, auditory and so on). Bergson's preoccupation goes further: he wants to destroy centres outright, the images of 'strings', 'conduits' [*fils conducteurs*] or 'interior keyboards' seeming to him more adequate to the psychical reality whose mode of activity he wants to suggest.[12]

Second observation: True memory is creative imagination. If the past never ceases to exist, it can nevertheless cease to be useful, or at least cease to appear such to clear consciousness, for many established habits and acquired mechanisms intervene unconsciously in all our everyday acts, saving us from going through each time the effort that our first learning experiences required. This second and subordinate form of memory that we must rather call habit thus constantly serves as a base for the operations of the one true memory which is creative imagination. But it can only play this role by provoking a phenomenon of inhibition with regard to movements which would call up inopportune reminiscences. Dream allows memories which the waking state shuts out to 'smuggle past'. But action does not admit any 'contraband', nor even any polyphony. We must choose, or else resolve ourselves to inefficacy. And it is because the delirious man deserts efficacy that he is indeed 'maladjusted' for Bergson.[13] There is thus a sort of hygiene of forgetting, a spontaneous asceticism in the memory which, between the two extremes of reverie, too rich, and the impoverished instant which is in any case foreign to any experience, constitutes conscious adaptation, what *Matter and Memory* calls 'mental equilibrium'.[14]

One can certainly object that this train of argument hardly clarifies anything except profitable and salutary cases of memory. We nevertheless find that on many occasions we cannot find the memories that the present action would in fact judge to be useful. Consciousness in no way selects in a way that is so adequate and rational that it always puts aside untimely reminiscences from our best interests and provides the opportune ones advisedly. Bergson is thus defining here more a sort of ideal functioning of memory than proposing an exhaustive description of the phenomena of forgetting. In any case, his explication could clarify a type of forgetting, but not diverse and more complex cases of an at least apparent or momentary disappearance of memory. Simplifying the explication to the extreme by giving considerable importance to the concept of 'utility' sometimes leads to the obscuring of many motives which could account for difficulties in evocation, or even harmful or corrupt evocations. Freudian psychoanalysis thus not only confirms Bergson's views, it should allow them to be enriched and completed by a more rigorous conception of the negativity of forgetting: it is not in effect the simple absence or the simple diminution of a positive act. It is a phenomenon of intense psychical complexity in which a whole work of elaboration, condensation, figuration is accomplished which is also found in dreams and which translates the war of desires. It is a struggle of which Bergson seems little aware, as his analysis sees hardly anything in the unconscious but a sort of psychical constant from which the selection of the present draws what it needs, whereas for Freud the unconscious is made; consciousness is not its residue but its expression.

It remains that the rightly famous distinction between the two memories constitutes an irrefutable strong point in Bergson's demonstration, and we can observe that it is a constant in his *œuvre*: the two selves of *Time and*

Free Will, the two intelligences of *Creative Evolution* and the two religions of *The Two Sources of Morality and Religion* are in each case the figures of a dialectic of the closed and the open which carry contradiction in the heart of a single notion and in a way symbolise the resolution of problems by a change in vocabulary: the true self is personality, the true intelligence is intuition, the true religion is mysticism, and in the present case the true memory is imagination.

The evocation of closure is, moreover, explicit. In the commentary of the famous example of the lesson learnt by heart, habit is defined as a '*closed system* of automatic movements which succeed each other in the same order and, together, take the same length of time'.[15] Its progress is carried out by successive reorganisations, repeated compositions and recompositions which concern action, and are thus opposed to the opening of the event, the unique 'irreducible moment of my history' which does not bear repetition and which alone can be the object of an authentic remembering. We only remember our past, and perhaps we could go so far as to say that we only remember ourselves. To the distinction between two memories corresponds the distinction between two forms of recognition: an 'intellectual' recognition which implies the recording of an event in its spatial and temporal singularity and a 'lived' recognition which guarantees the efficacy of action but which limits itself to 'playing out' the past without truly recognising it. Intellectual recognition is thus indeed the only one which deserves its name, in the same way that only those eminently personal memories which are not merely the fruit of learning but are authentic creations deserve to be called memories. In the end the others are only 'forms of knowledge'. And it is the confusion between these two planes which engenders a 'crude' psychology, 'duped by language', as was already evoked by *Time and Free Will* in order to refute the associationist interpretation of conscious phenomena. Certainly habit is necessary to adaptation, and Bergson no more thinks of challenging its utility than he would deny the inevitable projection of the self into space and with it all the mirror-games which offer us their traps.

He aims only to rescue the understanding of spiritual phenomena from a type of representation which cannot agree with them. It is as easy to establish a system of adequate representations for matter, which is homogeneous with intelligence and created by it, as it is impossible to find systems of representation which are absolutely adequate to spiritual life or indeed to life altogether.

Everything which participates in the cosmic movement of the *élan vital* and is characterised by that 'process of mutual organisation or penetration' which constitutes duration escapes by nature from the divisions and fixity of symbolic representations. We can only seek to convey it through the suggestion of mediating images and the creation of concepts which are as 'fluid' as possible and espouse the mobility of intuition, as the 'Introduction to Metaphysics' would specify in 1903, which also assimilates duration, that fluid concept *par excellence*, to 'the continuous life of a *memory* which prolongs the past into the present'.[16]

It is important here to emphasise that it is in *Matter and Memory* that Bergson establishes the same type of relationship between space and extension as between time and duration.[17] The importance that the commentaries have accorded to the intuition of duration has sometimes ended up making us forget this. And we can moreover lament the fact that Bergson himself did not sufficiently exploit this parallel between these two dialectical structures, notably when he would pose questions on the theory of relativity in *Duration and Simultaneity*.

It remains that this was strongly evoked in *Matter and Memory*, in the first place because the confusion between pure perception and memory corresponds to a confusion between (divisible) space and (indivisible) extension. Extension 'precedes space' just as 'concrete, continuous, diversified, organised' duration precedes time and cannot thus be considered to be assimilable or even necessarily attached to a space which is qualified as 'amorphous', 'inert'. Similarly, extension is 'lived', is 'perceived', while space and time are 'schemata' which may be conceived but never experienced. It thus cannot be reduced to pure spatiality, since it designates only a virtual process, a tendency of bodies towards extension, a tendency which is never completely realised, or, if one prefers, whose absolute realisation constitutes a limit-concept, the extreme point of an eminently theoretical field, which amounts to saying that extension is an 'immediate given of consciousness' and that we get out of it no more than we can get out of duration. In the same way that we can have, through memory, 'a single intuition [of] multiple moments of duration', we can have, through perception, a single intuition of multiple points of extension.[18]

But the condition is that we admit that real extension is neither truly divided nor even divisible, and that it is for the needs of action that we construct a homogeneous space which is 'infinitely divided' and divisible to infinity. But this is a 'bastard' concept obtained by a sort of introduction of time into extension, just as the concept of time is the result of an introduction of space into duration. By requiring a rigorous separation of the immediate realities [*réalités en présence*] in order to rediscover their purity (pure duration; pure perception; pure recollection), we seem to leave the terrain of psychical experience where everything is in fact intermingled. But it is, on the contrary, a very efficient method for distinguishing the specific character of each singular experience and for escaping the interpretations of idealism and realism: from idealism, because if perception is defined by its practical and not speculative role there is no more occasion to state that our knowledge of matter is only subjective (compare English idealism) or only relative (compare Kantian idealism); and from realism because, space being posterior to the existence of material things, there is no more occasion to make it into a milieu in which everything would be suspended (compare 'vulgar' realism) or an ideal form in which the co-ordination of the sensible could be carried out. Neither idealism nor realism can explain the relationship of matter and spirit, since in both perspectives no communication, no true contact is possible between them, space and time constituting a screen or, as the conclusion of *Matter and Memory* puts it, an unbreakable 'barrier'.

We must thus now see how this relationship becomes possible within the Bergsonian perspective of a 'pure' duration and a 'pure' extension. Let us remind ourselves that *Creative Evolution* will take up this thesis again and enrich it, the thesis itself moreover confirming that of *Time and Free Will* by giving it the amplitude of a cosmic dynamic in which space and time are reconciled by the ascent towards their common source: extension and duration. 'Neither is space so foreign to our nature as we imagine, nor is matter as completely extended in space as our senses and intellect represent it.'[19] Rediscovered in their common genesis, time and space are grasped this time in their profound and reciprocal implication. Intelligence is no longer considered as 'ready-made', no longer in its results, but in its exercise, in the process of being made, of becoming intelligence; and similarly matter is no longer considered ready-made, static, piecemeal, but itself also in the process of being made, of elaborating itself in its objective alterity. Matter and spirit thus indeed appear as two concepts which are reciprocally constituted by each other, in a common process. As such, the 'I endure' is only the particular manifestation of a universal evolution in which the self discovers itself as part of a whole and constantly referred to the universe which endures. The divisions carried out by intelligence are then justified by the natural structuration of the world, as nature has indeed a tendency to form 'closed' systems and is quite homogeneous with 'the geometrical order'. But this idea of 'tendency' indicates well that we are in the presence of a group of virtualities which never attain their completion and perfection. Similarly the movement which tends towards the absolute contraction of duration which would be pure spirit never attains its plenitude, and Bergson defines consciousness as the movement back and forth between these two extremes. This reminder is indispensable for the comprehension of the particularly transitional situation of *Matter and Memory* within the Bergsonian problematic of the relationship of the soul and the body.

In the first place, we must begin with the fundamental principle which

Bergson designates by the expression 'spiritual auscultation': homing in on the singularity of an experience.[20] In the context of contemporary controversies and the recent (1881) publication of Théodule Ribot's work on *Les Maladies de la mémoire*, the experimental basis is the pathology of recollection and forgetting. Psychical blindness, diverse amnesias and aphasias, or even the simple illusion of *déjà vu* are so many facts whose reality cannot be contested, but whose interpretation can and must be discussed. The tight correspondence between the impossibility of a recollection and the cerebral zones brought into play by spoken or written language acquisition and the awareness of diverse (visual, tactile and so on) perceptions is at the origin of a confusion in favour of which the materialist thesis of a conservation of memories in the brain in the form of revivable engrams takes on a semblance of probability. It is thus this confusion which must be dispelled, and first of all by recalling that certain aphasias are curable in spite of real cerebral lesions, which is enough to establish the plasticity of a motor system to which no creative power can be attributed. The role of the brain, according to Bergson, is in effect limited to receiving and organising movements which are favourable to the evocation of the past, but the brain can in no way store and less still fabricate images. As such, memories are not 'things' that could be conserved in the brain as in a drawer, but 'acts' which can be facilitated or inhibited by the established mechanisms of habit and our level of 'psychical tension' (Bergson uses a vocabulary closer to Janet than to Freud here). Every act of recognition in effect is accompanied by a phenomenon of a motor order, and we can go so far as to define it as the 'consciousness' of an organised movement.[21] But recognition is not necessarily 'thought'. It is possible that it is only 'acted': to recognise an object is to know how to use it, even if, as is seen in the child, it cannot yet be named. This is why it seems possible to state that in everyday life recognition is first of all 'played out'. But the examination of an attentive and reflective recognition reveals the radical difference between a phenomenon of motor adaptation and an intellectual event. From the fact that perception transmits a shock to the cerebral centres we cannot deduce that this transmission suffices for the production of images and that consequently memory is only a 'function of the brain'.[22]

Memories, in fact, do not occupy any place, whether in such or such a zone of the brain, or indeed outside of the brain or even in the unconscious. They are not of a spatial order and are not conserved anywhere. To make the unconscious into a sort of reservoir where we could bury memories or draw on them would be to succumb to that 'illusion of immanence' which is often denounced by Bergson, who brings up on many occasions the opposition between 'progresses' [*les progrès*] and 'things'.[23] There is no doubt that memories fall into the first category. Matter serves only as an instrument for their dynamism. Cerebral lesions only concern our action. They can thus produce difficulties in evocation, the body no longer assuming the necessary postures for recall, or no longer finding the link with reality which would have incited the activation of the process of reminiscence in the present. But one cannot draw from the deficiency of the tool an argument against the creative power of a spirit which can no longer find its usual means of expression. A memory which cannot actualise itself is not by this fact a 'lost' memory. The past is an integral part of the personality. It is always there. And aphasics or amnesiacs can, moreover, be seen to rediscover it through the intermediary of attentive care or an emotional shock.

Here, as in the explication of the illusion of *déjà vu*, we must refer ourselves to the dynamism of a consciousness tending towards the future and which, by right and in itself, should not stop its *élan*. Only testing situations of fatigue, by producing a diminution in psychical tension and blurring the function of synthesis and organisation, bring on apparent 'memory losses', an improper expression if there ever was one, since the past is never lost.

Bergson is less attentive than Freud to the way in which it reappears disguised, metamorphosed, transferred and even sometimes transfigured. But this is because his effort is essentially directed at refuting a materialist interpretation, and the ruses of desire thus interest him much less than understanding the metamorphoses [*avatars*] of the body.

Prisoners of metaphor, we thus speak of 'lost' or 'rediscovered' memories because we 'hypostatise' [*chosifions*] images as soon as we seek to project them into space under the form of expressible representations. But the inner duration from which they are born is inexpressible by definition if not by becoming dialectical through concepts. The impromptu reminder of a 'method to be followed' at the beginning of chapter four is in fact an invitation to rediscover the purity of *intuition*.[24]

What we believe to be the 'fundamental structure of our spirit' is in fact only the result of superficial habits which are acquired and transmitted in order to respond to the most elemental needs and are bound to the schemata of action. To propose an intuitive method which would escape from these contingent finalities must allow an escape from the claimed relativism of knowledge and remake 'contact' with the living reality which is characterised by dynamism and unity. As Bergson himself recalls,[25] this method already proved itself when the question of freedom was broached in *Time and Free Will*. Neither the defenders of determinism who assimilate our acts to the results of more or less consciously combined mechanisms, nor the supporters of free will who believe us capable of 'creation *ex nihilo*' pose the problem correctly. And a badly posed problem cannot be solved. In order to understand the emergence of an action, we must pose the problem differently: we must place ourselves within an acting duration and not the point of view of a consciousness which watches itself act. The position of spectator spoils everything here. Sartre will remember this: one cannot watch oneself in the process of wringing one's hands. The splitting of a consciousness which presents its acts to itself as objects of study and deliberation betrays the real movement of an action in the process of being carried out, a decision in the process of being taken, where the interaction and interpenetration of previous moments in no way prevents, but on the contrary supports, without being able wholly to produce, the creation of unpredictable novelties. 'Time is invention or it is nothing at all', Bergson affirms and, like an echo, 'Invention gives being to what did not exist.'[26] It is thus by placing oneself within the context of a creative movement that one can offer a new theory of memory analogous to this new theory of liberty.

For this we must start with the Bergsonian definition of *movement* and then analyse these three principal consequences: the refutation of the arguments of Zeno of Elea, the critique of associationism and the overcoming of Kantianism.

1) Bergsonian definition of movement. In the first place, it is 'a simple fact'.[27] If we believe it to be complicated, this is because of the artifices of our imagination which reconstitutes mobility using fixed points which are so many stops or, if one prefers, rests, which is to say the very opposite of what one wants to designate.

We must translate without betraying the reality which is effectively felt in experience: that of a 'passage'. Nevertheless, as we tend to confuse the act of traversal itself with the distance traversed, nothing is more difficult than finding adequate formulae for the indivisible character of a movement. In contrast, nothing is easier than its representation by a series of immobile points: it is naturally inspired in us by the divisibility of the line which it seems to follow in space. The distance, however, does not coincide with the trajectory. In order to understand it we must place ourselves within the pure duration which is characterised by the absence of instants and which, far from being reconstituted by the sum of its parts, excludes the very idea of parts. It is a whole which cannot be broken down without being destroyed in the same gesture. In this sense our systems of representation are always negative: they are only constituted on the background of the interruption of an *élan*. Language is perpetually digging graves because it is only constructed through concepts which are so many 'fixed points', foreign to vital reality, or, to use a suggestive image, death sentences [*arrêts de mort*]. Any movement which is interrupted is also an inverted movement. Stopping an *élan* is thus at the same time and in the

same respect producing its downfall. Expressing movement by the recon-
stitution of a series of immobile points is thus introducing rest into movement and offering a contradictory definition of it.

2) First consequence. We can express our surprise here that Bergson
did not understand to what extent the subtle dialectician Zeno of Elea had
developed his analysis using the same observation and would probably
have admitted that one cannot draw from the contradictory character of
the definition of movement any argument which would serve to negate it.

Zeno showed very admirably the absurdities which are reached each
time one seeks to speak of movement in general as a homogeneous reality.
Nothing is more naive in our opinion than to attribute these absurdities to
him and at the same time to seek to refute them. As was frequently the case
in antiquity (in Lucretius in particular), it was a matter of reasoning from
the absurd demand that becoming be understood as the union of opposites
(as is also seen in Heraclitus). It was thus necessary to be able to say, *at the
same time*, movement and rest, since one is made by the other and vice
versa. It is language which introduces the succession or chronology of one
after the other and thus betrays the experiential indissociability of the one
in the other. Zeno was probably more Bergsonian than Bergson thought.
What humour as well! It is because Bergson takes Zeno literally that he
feels himself justified in refuting him. And we must believe that this refutation is heartfelt because we find it in all of his works.[28]

The essence of his argument is that Zeno is being cinematographic [*fait
du cinéma*]! He in effect applies a spontaneously cinematic *analytic*
method to an object which requires an *intuitive* method able to liberate
itself from the 'natural inclination' of an intelligence which manipulates,
and is manipulated by, space. It operates what Bergson will call, in *Creative
Evolution*, 'a kind of cinematograph inside us';[29] in so doing, it gives the
impression of movement using the succession of a series of immobilities,
forgetting that movement, *qua passage* from one point to another, is a mental synthesis which is not situated in space. It was thus necessary to make
a distinction between two elements of a radically different nature: the
space covered by a moving object which can be considered a homogeneous
quantity, and the act by which it is covered, which must be considered to
be fundamentally qualitative. It is by virtue of a sort of endosmosis
between the two that the illusion perpetuated by the Eleatics is created.

It is a totally sterile illusion, because it teaches us absolutely nothing
about the nature of becoming – everything which is effectively transition,
passage, escapes its own analysis; moreover it is foreign to experience: it
uses language to reconstitute the thing, whereas it is this intellectual habit,
a matrix of error and falsehood, which must be inverted in order to invent
concepts starting from things, concepts which are susceptible to being

moulded 'on the fleeting forms of intuition'. The immobilities used here to reconstitute the movement cannot be given as realities, they are only virtualities. Moreover it is indeed *memory* which retrospectively reconstitutes the multiplicity of points of passage in a synthetic grouping which gives these points only as possible stops, rather than effective stops. And we are certainly very interested in these possible stops, because they are the diverse positions which permit our action upon things. But once again, Bergson denounces this transferring of a practical necessity to the speculative domain, since it has contaminated our whole theory of knowledge.

3) Second consequence. An analysis of the same kind leads Bergson to the critique of associationism. It is a perspective which has effectively merged all planes of consciousness and takes the memories which are closest to the necessities of action, and thus the most ordinary, for less complex memories. Are they not, in fact, less complete? In order to refute this error, it is not enough to state that 'the superior operations of the spirit' cannot be explained by simple laws of association: contiguity, resemblance and so on, which is, as Auguste Comte also observed, the essence of a materialist interpretation. We must interrogate the *nature* of association itself. To associate is not to juxtapose or add. It is an act of thought which requires a true movement of consciousness tracing smaller or larger circles and creating, literally, its own temporality in a perpetual back and forth between the plane of action and the plane of dream. 'Extreme planes', 'extreme limits', repeats Bergson on the same page.[30] We are struck by the observation that these are the same expressions and the same description which define intuition in the 'Introduction to Metaphysics'.[31] In fact duration, memory, intuition, consciousness are all presented as phenomena involving tension: they either relax and move towards a dispersion, a dissipation which, at the point of infinity, would give pure matter; or they become tense and move towards a concentration, a unity which, at the point of infinity, would give pure spirit. But neither this instantaneity nor this eternity is ever attained. We can at least think them. Is not this what Bergson precisely calls 'the course of the spirit'? On the one hand it explains both the selections carried out by memories, the formation of general ideas, the rising and falling *élan*, and allows us to clarify Ravaisson's beautiful expression: 'materiality begets oblivion'.[32] On the other hand, it ultimately becomes merged, in *Creative Mind*, with metaphysics in its entirety.

4) Third consequence. On several occasions Bergson states his desire to go beyond Kantianism, precisely because he admits the power of an intellectual intuition that was refused to us by Kant, even though *The Critique of Pure Reason* had very well established that only this intuition would allow the possibility of metaphysics to be founded: it would be the intuition of a God. Bergson claims to give it to men. His refutation of Kan-

tianism, like that of Zeno, returns in each of his works: in *Time and Free Will* where he reproaches Kant for having drawn his strength and his weakness from the confusion between duration and its symbol,[33] in *Creative Evolution* where he denounces the Kantian conception of a ready-made space, appearing from nowhere, like a *'deus ex machina'*,[34] and in *Creative Mind* where science, assimilated to 'frameworks within frameworks' and metaphysics, assimilated to 'phantoms pursuing phantoms', are referred to as relativism and agnosticism respectively, because they cannot accept that analytical intelligence, homogeneous to the matter that it manipulates and by which it is manipulated, is not the whole of consciousness.[35]

In chapter four of *Matter and Memory* Bergson rejects making space and time into 'forms of our sensibility' and, above all, the alignment of time with space, which ends up making both the knowledge of matter and the knowledge of mind impossible. This orientation constitutes an 'impasse' for which Bergson aims to substitute another path which is, it seems, more an overcoming than a repudiation of Kant. Did not Kant in effect himself make use of the intuition that he refuses us? Does not the distinction between the matter of knowledge and its form rest on an intuition of the distinction between the homogeneous and the heterogeneous? By making use of this superior intelligence, one is not strictly speaking introducing a new intellectual faculty, one only rediscovers the creative thought inherent in the unfolding of a train of argument, or, as Bergson also says, the 'hidden force' of analyses. We must thus go further than Kant by admitting that there are not only sensible intuitions, and that, moreover, true intuition does not take us out of consciousness, since it is on the contrary the act of consciousness *par excellence*, that which brings us closest to that 'concentration of duration' which would be eternity. Kantian understanding being in a sense a shrunken consciousness, we must substitute a dilated consciousness, just as Bergson gives a psychological content to the thirst of reason in Kant: if it wants the unconditioned, this is indeed the sign that it has an intuition of the absolute.

We can certainly ask ourselves if Bergson did not draw from this psychological content more than it contains, in particular in *The Two Sources of Morality and Religion*, for the passage from the limit of an intuition of our duration to the affirmation of a God that someone could see, feel and touch remains susceptible to the Kantian critique of the ontological argument and hardly manages to refute it. But it remains that in *Matter and Memory*, the claim for a specific status of memory as an 'interior force' which breaks with the rhythm of the flow of things announces the restoration of a very particular type of metaphysics which should rather be called a 'metabiology'.

We can see by these analyses that there is no rupture in continuity between matter and spirit once, instead of posing the question of their relationship starting from space, we ask it starting from time: there is no occasion to wonder how the communication between body and soul is carried out, since both participate in the same movement, and in a sense go to meet each other. There is a multitude of possible degrees between the extended and the unextended. The more the soul nears action the more it rejoins extension. The more sensation nears the image the more it rejoins inextension. The traditional dualism, taking only the spatial point of view, can only lead to the parallelist hypothesis or a pre-established harmony. The new dualism, by taking the point of view of duration, considers matter as a sort of very rapid succession of moments each deducible from the other, while spirit constitutes a sort of evolutionary synthesis in which memory plays the role of a liberating 'force', a force which, instead of letting itself go mechanically with the 'rhythm of the flow of things', incessantly creates novelty. We can, however, ask ourselves whether this dualism, obvious on the methodological plane, does not come back to a vitalist monism on the plane of Doctrine. Spirit and matter are in the end the rise and fall of the same *élan vital* that *Creative Evolution* would define as 'an impulse ... from germ to germ',[36] and even though we may well see in this only a 'mediating image', it holds such an essential place in the system that it is difficult not to see in it the extension of the theses of *Matter and Memory*. Bergson himself specifies before concluding: 'Each of these successive degrees, *which measures a growing intensity of life*, corresponds to a higher tension of duration and is made manifest externally by a greater development of the sensori-motor system.'[37] There is thus in nature only multiple forms of more or less dilated [*dilatée*] or concentrated duration, and if it is true that duration is 'the stuff of things', we must indeed understand that this is true of all things, of matter as of mind. But only the mind is capable of 'binding together the successive moments of duration' and accomplishing no longer simply indeterminate actions but reasonable and reflective actions. This is to describe a difference in *function* between the soul and the body much more than a difference of *nature*, and since Bergson admits that between 'brute matter and the mind most capable of reflection there are all possible intensities of memory or, what comes to the same thing, all the degrees of freedom',[38] there seems no justification for transporting the dualism to the level of origins and to consider that it is substantial. It only allows us to remove the habitual difficulties of caricatured oppositions between the extended and the unextended, quantity and quality, necessity and freedom

- *between the extended and the unextended*, since their distinction is not an experimental given and is not the object of an immediate intuition. What is given is an intermediary between the two: *extension*;
- *between quantity and quality*, since if we put perception back into things, we discover that there are only differences of *tension* between the sensible qualities of our representations and their equivalents in calculable changes;
- *between necessity and freedom*, since we can assume that the successive moments of duration which characterise nature cannot be deduced from each other in a quasi-mathematical way, but in fact constitute a sort of latent consciousness, and that the most developed form of consciousness which is not only capable of movements in space, but also of a powerful movement in time, can 'all the more easily pass through the mesh of necessity' by virtue of the fact that it is also capable of creation and internal indetermination.

We have retained the famous expression: 'freedom is not in nature an *imperium in imperio*',[39] and freedom is indeed the last word of *Matter and Memory*.[40] But we still have to elucidate the relationship between movement in space and movement in time. The first tends towards the second in such a way that matter is a sort of aspiration towards mind, of evolution towards spirituality, but also a moment of mind: its negative moment, its fall, but a fall which is not a death nor an abolition, for it retains the traces, the vestiges of an initial *élan* in its dispersed state. If it were total dispersion, it would escape our knowledge.

We must thus analyse the movement in both directions, but here as in Heraclitus, is it not the same path which goes up and goes down? Are there indeed two movements? 'The progress of living matter' leads to an increasingly complex nervous system, capable of organisation and concerted actions. But is this progress not also called upon by the spirit as if by its final cause, which amounts to saying that the motor of this double movement is consciousness, and as consciousness is identified with a very elaborate and very individualised form of life, we can conclude without hesitation that Bergsonism is indeed a vitalism? The desire to keep it away from this has only reinforced the *aporiai* of the old spiritualism and the avatars of the new materialism. But what Bergson himself calls a 'metaphysics of the vital' can only have a sense if it refuses both and is constructed on their ruins.

Contemporary science certainly has at its disposal the means for observing the cerebral movements that Bergson could not even suspect, but of which he dreams! 'If, moreover, we cast a glance at the minute structure of the nervous system ...'. The fiction of a man who could observe what happens in the brain during the formation of memories, the elaboration of language or emotional response, is today a reality. But what, Bergson says, will one see?: 'conducting lines', 'threads', 'this is all that is seen'.[41] What more do we see in the era of scanners and magnetometry? More numerous and complex reactions. The information increases in quantity as in quality. But it still does not allow us to affirm that cerebral movements are productive of consciousness, any more than it allows us to deny it. Once one enters into the metaphysical interpretation of observed phenomena, one leaves the domain of scientific explanation, and it is to Kant that we must give the last word: we must substitute faith for knowledge.

Notes

1 MM, p. 45/48; OE, p. 197.
2 MM, p. 308/231; OE, p. 362.
3 MM, p. xvii/13; OE, p. 164.
4 MM, p. 46/49; OE, p. 198.
5 MM, p. 64/61; OE, p. 209.
6 See especially pp. 301–2/227; OE, p. 358 and the conclusion.
7 MM, p. 30/37; OE, p. 187.
8 MM, p. 74/68; OE, p. 215.
9 MM, p. 75/69; OE, p. 216.
10 See 'Memory of the Present and False Recognition' in *Mind–Energy* (ME, pp. 134–85; OE, pp. 897–930).
11 MM, p. 158/124; OE, p. 268 and notes.
12 MM, especially pp. 165–6/128–9; OE, pp. 273–4.
13 MM, p. 225/172; OE, p. 311.
14 MM, p. 228/174; OE, p. 313.
15 MM, p. 90/80; OE, p. 225, emphasis added.
16 See CM, pp. 179/211, 190–1/224–5; OE, pp. 1411, 1422, emphasis added.
17 See especially MM, pp. 32–3/39, 45–6/48, 244–5/186–7, 307–8/231–2; OE, pp. 189, 197, 323, 362.
18 See MM, pp. 303/228, 307–8/231; OE, pp. 359, 362.
19 See CE, p. 214/202; OE, p. 667.
20 CM, p. 175/206; OE, p. 1408.
21 MM, pp. 112–13/94; OE, p. 240.
22 MM, p. 119/99; OE, p. 244.
23 See TFW, pp. 137–8, 181, 198; OE, pp. 91, 119, 130; MM, pp. 162/127, 192–3/149; OE, pp. 271, 290; CM, p. 188/222; OE, p. 1420.
24 MM, pp. 241–2/185; OE, p. 321.
25 MM, pp. 242–3/185; OE, pp. 321–2.
26 See CE, p. 361/342; OE, p. 784; CM, p. 51/59; OE, p. 1293.
27 MM, p. 249/190; OE, p. 326.
28 In TFW, chapter two, p. 112; OE, p. 75; here in chapter four of MM, p. 251/191; OE, p. 326; then in CE, chapter four, p. 325/308; OE, p. 755; and again in 1911 in 'The Perception of Change', a text included in CM, p. 144/170; OE, p. 1379.

29 CE, p. 323/306; OE, p. 753.
30 MM, pp. 323–4/242–3; OE, p. 372.
31 CM, pp. 187/220–1; OE, p. 1419.
32 *La Philosophie en France au XIXe siècle*, cited in MM, p. 232/177; OE, p. 316.
33 TFW, pp. 91–2, 102–3; OE, pp. 62, 69.
34 CE, pp. 215–16/204–5; OE, pp. 668–9.
35 CM, pp. 27–8/29–30, 127–8/150–1, 138–9/163–4, 305, note, 195/231; OE, pp. 1269, 1364, 1374, 1393, note, 1427.
36 CE, p. 90/85; OE, p. 568.
37 MM, p. 296/221; OE, p. 355, emphasis added.
38 MM, p. 296/222; OE, p. 355.
39 MM, p. 331/248; OE, p. 377.
40 MM, p. 332/249; OE, p. 378.
41 MM, p. 227/173; OE, p. 312.

eric matthews

BERGSON'S CONCEPT OF A PERSON

At the beginning of the revised Introduction which Bergson wrote specially for the English translation of his book *Matter and Memory* he says, 'This book affirms the reality of spirit and the reality of matter, and tries to determine the relation of the one to the other by the study of a definite example, that of memory. *It is, then, frankly dualistic.*'[1] It quickly becomes clear, however, that whatever 'frankly dualistic' means here, it does *not* mean what we normally take it to mean in philosophy, namely, a two-substance view of the kind which received its classical expression in Descartes. Bergson himself sometimes describes this Cartesian or substantial dualism as 'ordinary dualism' and plainly distinguishes it from his own position: 'ordinary' dualism leads to one or other of two untenable theories about our position in relation to the external world, namely, either classical realism or idealism. His own view, on the other hand, makes it possible, as he sees it anyway, to retain what is right about realism and idealism, while discarding the unacceptable elements in both theories. What I seek to do in this essay is to expound and, in so doing, to defend the main outlines of Bergson's position, which I consider to have much to contribute to our contemporary discussions in philosophy of mind and metaphysics.

I

In order to see what Bergson considered to be wrong about 'ordinary dualism' and to understand better the view which he himself wanted to propose, we must first examine his account of philosophical method. We could regard Bergson as a variety of phenomenologist, though this is not a label he actually attached to himself. By this term I mean that he saw philosophy, not as the construction of explanatory *theories*, but rather as an attempt to get away from theorising in order to concentrate on the purest possible *description of the way we actually experience the world*. Theorising or generalising, such as occurs not only in the sciences but even in everyday life, is, for Bergson, an inescapable human activity. It takes the form of analysing or distinguishing one thing from another, and then of comparing the things so distinguished in terms of what they have in common with other things. The outcome of this comparison is generalisations, of which the outstanding examples are the laws of science.

Important, indeed essential though this work of analysis and generalisation (the work of *intellect*) may be, however, we should not regard it, in Bergson's view, as giving us real insight into the ultimate nature of things. We engage in it, not in order to gain such insight, but for a specific purpose which is necessary to our shared lives as *social beings*: as such, we need to see our own individual experience of reality as simply one perspective on the world, which can be complemented and corrected by other individual perspectives in order to form a more 'objective' or detached view of how things are. That way of thinking about ourselves and our experience implies a view of ourselves as simply one other object in the world, standing in causal and spatial relations to other objects: we look on ourselves, as it were, from the outside, as not in any sense at the centre of things. (As Thomas Nagel expresses it, it is 'the view from nowhere'.)[2] And this is essential, if we are to be able to communicate factual information about objects to other subjects as we need to do in order to live in society, and in particular to engage in shared practical activity with other human beings.

This detached, impersonal, intellectual view of the world and ourselves, however true it may be within its own limits, cannot be the ultimate truth, if only because it presupposes another view. It is formed for the purpose of sharing experience between individuals, which implies that the individual experiences are logically prior to their sharing. But considered apart from that sharing, of course, what is here called the individual experience is not truly individual at all: it can be called 'individual' only by comparison with those of other individuals, in which case it is *relative* or *perspectival*. Apart from the context of communication, however, it is absolute or ultimate: paradoxically, it is no longer specifically *my* experience or *yours*. Bergson's word for our acquaintance with this absolute or ultimate is 'intuition'. Since metaphysics is supposed to be our knowledge of the absolute or ultimate, it is clear that intuition, our acquaintance with experience as such, rather than intellect or analysis, the basis of the impersonal view, must for him be the basis of metaphysics.

But what exactly does Bergson mean by 'intuition'? Perhaps the fullest attempt at a definition is given in his essay 'Introduction to Metaphysics': 'By intuition is meant the kind of *intellectual sympathy* by which one places oneself within an object in order to coincide with what is unique in it and consequently inexpressible.'[3] But this definition itself requires some interpretation. In my own book *Twentieth-Century French Philosophy*[4] I suggested that a straightforward reading of this definition would make 'intuition' equivalent to 'empathy', the power of thinking oneself into someone's position, of knowing, as Thomas Nagel puts it, 'what it is like to be' someone or something.[5] I also argued there that intuition read in this way would have only limited application. It would be applicable, primarily, to oneself as a conscious being, and then derivatively, by imaginative extension, to other conscious beings, to beings such that there is something it is like to be them. And such a limited scope of application could hardly constitute intuition as the basis for a general method of metaphysics.

Further reflection, however, has convinced me that we need to read the definition taking account of other things which Bergson says about 'intuition'. He contrasts it, as said earlier, with 'intellect', and this contrast is made in several different, though related, ways. In *Matter and Memory*, for instance, he distinguishes intuition in terms of *immediacy, continuity and practical disinterestedness*. 'That which is commonly called a *fact*', he says, 'is not reality as it appears to immediate intuition, but an adaptation of the real to the interests of practice and to the exigencies of social life. Pure intuition, external or internal, is that of an undivided continuity.'[6] The opposition between 'pure intuition' and intellectual analysis or theorising is here presented as that between our awareness of the objects of our experience (whether persons or things), as it is *before* we begin to seek to classify and explain them for the purposes of communication and practical intervention and as it is *after* such classification. Intuitive or immediate awareness is, as Bergson says, 'of an undivided continuity', of a seamless web of reality, in which there is no clear distinction between external and internal, or between one object and another (indeed, the very use of the term 'object' seems scarcely appropriate).

The work of intellect is then seen as (literally) that of 'analysis', of breaking up this undivided continuity into discrete objects, which can then be treated as homogeneous units to the extent that they have properties in common with each other, and so are seen as extended in a homogeneous space. A further important distinction introduced by intellect is that between inner and outer, subject and object, thus generating the idea of an 'objective world', existing in complete independence of the experiencing subject. And intellect breaks up the original continuity, as Bergson says, in order to adapt the real 'to the interests of practice and to the exigencies of social life'. As he puts it elsewhere, we need, as active beings, to have a view of the world which will 'provide our activity with points to which it can be applied'.[7] To be active requires us to distinguish between ourselves as agents and the things we act upon, and to classify those things in general terms in order to have general rules for action.

This can be related to the definition of 'intuition' in 'Introduction to Metaphysics'. If we are not, in intuition, detached from what we experience, then we are 'coinciding with' it; and if we do not regard it as a member of a general class, then we coincide with 'what is unique in it'. Bergson goes on to say that what is unique is 'consequently inexpressible', but it is not entirely clear what this means. What he seems to be saying in this passage is that what we intuit cannot be expressed in language at all, and it is easy to see why someone should say this. Language cannot 'express' what is unique in something by the use of terms which refer only to one instance, because there are not and could not be such terms. Language can identify particulars only by the use of general terms, including terms of spatial and temporal location. It seems a natural conclusion that intuition of the unique as such is inexpressible in language.

But there is a problem here, if intuition is the method of metaphysics. For surely metaphysics must be communicable in some way, and that seems to require the use of language, for which general terms, as just argued, are essential. Bergson does indeed say, a page or two later in 'Introduction to Metaphysics', that metaphysics seizes reality 'without any expression, translation or symbolic representation' and so is 'the science which claims to dispense with symbols'.[8] This seems plain enough: an intuitively based metaphysics dispenses with symbols and so is incommunicable. Towards the end of the 'Introduction', however, Bergson (no doubt through recognition of the difficulties caused by this doctrine) appears to change his tune. Now it is not so much that metaphysics dispenses with all symbolism, but that it has a symbolism of its own: it does not do without concepts altogether, but only without 'pre-existing concepts'.[9] Intuitive knowledge, he says 'installs itself in that which is moving and adopts the very life of things'.[10] Its concepts will be 'fluid concepts, capable of following reality in all its sinuosities and of adopting the very movement of the inward life of things'.[11]

Clearly, it is only if there can be some sort of language of intuition that intuition can be the basis of a metaphysics worthy of the name, if, for example, intuition is not to be simply our ineffable awareness of our own inner states, but a communicable awareness, not only of our selves, but even of the essential reality of all living things, as Bergson insists it is in *Creative Evolution*. But then to say, as Bergson does in his definition, that intuition is 'inexpressible' must be, to say the least, misleading.

But what kind of language can it be that can communicate what is unique? The first thing to be said is that we *do* in fact succeed in communicating our own unique experiences to others. We do it every day, in the context of our close personal relationships, where we talk about our thoughts and feelings, not in the generalising way of scientific psychology, but in expressive ways which, if we are lucky and if the person we are speaking to is sufficiently attuned to us, succeed in conveying to them what it is like to be us. We even succeed, as Nagel argues, in gaining a certain kind of understanding of experiences which we have not had ourselves, or perhaps could not have ourselves, as in the case of creatures which are entirely different in structure from us.[12] In a similar way, in literature, a good writer can use language to convey the uniqueness of a character or a situation. The language consists, as all language must, of general terms: which implies that it is not so much the presence or absence of concepts which counts, but the *use* which is made of those concepts. We could distinguish between a use of language for 'scientific', fact-stating purposes, in which the important thing was to secure a shared reference for terms by means of already accepted rules (Bergson's 'fixed concepts'), and a use of language for more expressive purposes, in which what was to be conveyed was what was unique about someone's experience, so that success in communication depended on the speaker's skill in finding appropriate expressions combined with the hearer's responsiveness to what the speaker had to say (Bergson's 'fluid concepts, capable of following reality in all its sinuosities').

We can now attempt, on this basis, to reconstruct Bergson's account of philosophical method, and of the role of intuition in it. (I must gratefully acknowledge here the influence of F. C. T. Moore's excellent book *Bergson: Thinking Backwards*.)[13] Metaphysics, for Bergson, is prior (which does not imply superior) to science and common sense, in that the latter is a derivative of the former. Science and common sense take for granted a view of the world as detached from our experience of it (and conversely of our experience as belonging to a detached, purely internal, world of subjectivity). But this view of the world is not reality, so much as an adaptation of reality to the interests of practice and the exigencies of social life. In this sense, it is derivative from 'real reality', which is given to intuition, and which can properly be described only by means of 'fluid concepts'. The proper method of metaphysics, as the study of 'real reality', must therefore be intuitive, rather than intellectual. Metaphysics must seek to describe reality as it is given to immediate intuition, in the form of an undivided continuity. It only goes astray when it tries to become a science, putting forward theories about a world of objects whose very existence presupposes an immediate experience in which subject and object are not yet clearly distinguished.

So the Bergsonian method in philosophy can be seen as having two sides. On the one hand, it has a negative, critical, aspect: it shows how the attempt to do metaphysics as if it were a science leads to difficulties, even to contradictions. These difficulties may even bring confusion into gen-uinely scientific theorising in the relevant areas: hence Bergson often cites empirical scientific findings and theories which do not fit well with the conceptual framework of traditional metaphysics. On the other hand, the more positive aspect of Bergson's account consists in the attempt simply to describe, in a theory-free way, what our actual experience is like in the rel-evant respects, in such a way as to imply its superiority, in both truth and usefulness, to the account offered by traditional metaphysics. Bergson applies this method to a wide range of metaphysical questions, above all, of course, to questions about biological life and evolution. In this essay, however, my main concern is with its application to the concept of a per-son and to the so-called 'mind–body' problem, as it appears in *Matter and Memory* in particular.

II

Cartesian dualism is the doctrine that a human being is made up of two distinct 'substances', where a 'substance' is defined as 'a thing which exists in such a way as to depend on no other thing for its existence'.[14] The two substances are 'mind', defined in terms of consciousness alone, and 'body', defined in terms of extension alone. So a person consists of a mind and a body which have no properties in common and which are each capable of existing without the other. In consequence of its very definition, therefore, there are certain very familiar difficulties arising out of this substantial dualism: namely, how can we account for the *unity* of the human person (which Descartes himself recognised as much as anyone), and for the *inter-action* between the mental and the physical which we experience every day? Bergson's claim was that he could retain dualism in the sense of an affirmation of 'the reality of spirit and the reality of matter', while doing so 'in such a way as, we hope, to lessen greatly, if not to overcome, the theo-retical difficulties which have always beset dualism'.[15]

Since these 'theoretical difficulties' depend on the Cartesian account of mind and body as distinct *substances*, it is clear that Bergson's view will have to abandon that feature of Cartesian dualism. This is a case for the application of the critical part of the Bergsonian method sketched in Sec-tion I. The conception of mind and body as distinct and independent sub-stances will have to be shown to be part of that overall picture of reality, derived from an intellectual analysis in the service of social communica-tion and shared intervention, in which it is held to consist of distinct and independently existing entities. Given that picture, then, we have to see our relation to reality outside ourselves as one between distinct and independent objects. Taking, as seems right,[16] *perception* as paradigmatic for our understanding of that relationship between ourselves and external reality which we call 'experience', Bergson proceeds to show how this picture affects the account of perception which we give.

If perception is a relation between distinct and independent objects, ourselves as perceivers and the thing perceived, then it seems that it must be a one-way *causal* relation. We can perceive things only because they are there before us and causally impact upon our sense-organs. But to perceive something, of course, is more than to be affected by it in one's sense-organs: it is also to be *aware* or *conscious* of perceiving it. Thus, the causal relationship must be not just between the external object and the sense-organ, but also between what goes on in the sense-organ and one's consciousness: these two must be different causal relationships, because the former could exist without the latter. Hence, the body and its sense-organs must be a distinct entity from the consciousness or mind.

But not only distinct in the way one material object may be distinct from another: consciousness or mind must be a distinct *kind* of entity. For it has very special characteristics of its own, not shared or even shareable with any material object, even a human body or brain. Body is by definition extended, mind by definition unextended; body is quantity, mind quality; body is causally determined, mind free; the material world transcends mind in that it extends far beyond what our mind can conceive of it, but mind transcends the material world in that it can in imagination conceive of the transformation of matter. So, starting from the intellectual vision of reality, we arrive at Cartesian dualism, the doctrine that mind and matter are distinct 'substances' which, by reason of their essential natures, must be capable of existence independently of each other.

Something must, however, have gone wrong somewhere along the way which led to this conclusion. For if substantial dualism were right, then our whole relationship to reality in perception would become rationally unintelligible, that is, a mystery. If the relationship between what we perceive and our perception of it is taken, as seems natural on a simple realist view, to be a causal one, then realism, on Cartesian assumptions, makes the possibility of perception inexplicable. For if matter and consciousness are ontologically distinct kinds of entity, how can matter causally determine consciousness? 'All realism', Bergson says, 'is thus bound to make perception an accident, and, consequently, a mystery.'[17]

Now some philosophers who have broadly accepted Cartesian assumptions have thought that the mystery of how matter might cause perception in consciousness could be avoided simply by denying that the relations between matter and consciousness are causal. They have maintained that the correspondence between what goes on in 'matter' and what goes on in 'consciousness' is either simply a parallelism or is the result of divine intervention, as in Malebranchean 'occasionalism' or Leibniz's theory of pre-established harmony. In either case, Bergson argues, it will again become rationally unintelligible that our perceptions should reveal the nature of an objective world. 'You will have to bring back this order by conjuring up in your turn a *deus ex machina*', he says; 'I mean that you will have to assume, by an arbitrary hypothesis, some sort of pre-established harmony between things and mind, or, at least (to use Kant's terms) between sense and understanding. It is science now that will become an accident, and its success a mystery.'[18]

That is, in the Leibnizian or Malebranchean case, a scientific account of the material world will be possible only if we assume that a benevolent God has happened to arrange that our perceptions should correspond to the independent reality of matter, which makes science into something which is only *accidentally* true. The other possibility which Bergson refers to here is that of a Kantian transcendental idealism, according to which our experience is such that it involves a 'pre-established harmony' between sense and understanding, resulting in what we call 'objective reality'. In that case, scientific knowledge will not be of the world of independent reality at all, of 'things as they are in themselves', but only of things as they *appear* to beings constituted as we are. So, on either a realist or an idealist view, the success of perception in giving us access to an independent material world, and so the success of science itself, becomes a mystery, and that is, to say the least, counter-intuitive.

These problems do not arise when we confine ourselves to the world with which intellectual analysis is *fitted* to deal, the world of social communication and practical intervention in material reality. For there what is important are the straightforward and perfectly intelligible causal relations between material objects and human sense-organs: even the individual variations in perception, such as colour-blindness, are objective variations between the sensory equipment of different human beings. The problems arise only when we try to include within that framework of causal explanation those features which make perception part of our *experience* of a world, rather than simply one item in the world that we experience. These features are, as said earlier, that perception as experience is subjective, qualitative, perspectival, and an expression, to some degree at least, of freedom. Treating these features as Descartes does, as properties of a certain kind of object called a 'mind', is part of treating experience as something to be explained within a quasi-scientific framework, rather than as a presupposition of the very possibility of that framework itself. More generally, it is the result of treating metaphysics as if it were a science,

125

whose role is to offer explanatory theories, rather than as a description of what reality and the experience of it are actually like.

III

Instead of trying in this way to *explain* our relationship to an 'external world' in perception, then, Bergson's method, in its positive phase, is to try to show what being a perceiver is actually like. We then see, he argues, that 'while introspection reveals to us the distinction between matter and spirit, it also bears witness to their union'.[19] The mind–body problem, as we actually experience it, is not that of attempting to explain the possibility of interaction between two distinct substances, but that of '[defining] the function of the body in the life of the spirit'[20] (which he says is the whole purpose of 'this work', *Matter and Memory*). We experience ourselves, not as a composite of two substances, but as a unity of spirit and body, and the problem is only to set out their respective roles in our interaction with the world around us.

The view we necessarily form, Bergson argues, if we start by considering simply the experience we have, without seeking to analyse or explain that experience, is one which makes no ontological distinction between 'mind' and 'body'. His neutral word for experiences, implying no prior assumptions about the character of those experiences, is 'images'. If I simply consider the images I have, he argues, I shall naturally isolate the image of my own body from others as the one which is *always* there and which is the *centre* of my experience: and on that basis will make a distinction between what is 'inside' me and what 'outside'.

> But if, on the contrary, all images are posited at the outset, my body will necessarily end by standing out in the midst of them as a distinct thing, since they change unceasingly, and it does not vary. The distinction between the inside and the outside will then be only a distinction between the part and the whole. There is, first of all, the aggregate of images; and then, in this aggregate, there are 'centers of action', from which the interesting images appear to be reflected: thus perceptions are born and actions made ready. *My body* is that which stands out as the center of these perceptions; *my personality* is the being to which these actions must be referred.[21]

The last sentence of that quotation is particularly important, for it reveals how far Bergson was from Cartesian dualism. My body is not, for him, something distinct from me, from 'my personality': it *is* me, to the extent that I am an active being. The actions of which my body is the 'centre' are 'referred to' my personality, they are *my* actions. And although, in virtue of the reality of human spirit, I am more than my body (more than the possibility of action), it remains true that it is central to how I actually experience myself that I experience myself as embodied, and so as active. Inasmuch as my body is one of those 'images' which we call 'material objects', that implies that I experience myself as in part at least material, as that kind of material thing called a living organism.

Even my experience of myself as 'spirit' is, Bergson contends, ultimately inseparable from my experience of myself as a material living organism. For he argues that it can be deduced *a priori* from the very definition of living bodies that the primary function of consciousness in relation to external perception is to make action possible by integrating the present with the past. 'For though the function of these bodies is to receive stimulations in order to elaborate them into unforeseen reactions, still the choice of the reaction cannot be the work of chance. The choice is likely to be inspired by past experience ... memory is thus the reverberation, in the sphere of consciousness, of the indetermination of our will.'[22] Perception and memory, he goes on to claim, 'always interpenetrate each other':[23] they are distinct, but not, as for Descartes, different *substances* capable of independent existence.

> But if, in fact, the humblest function of spirit is to bind together the successive moments of the duration of things, if it is by this that it comes into contact with matter and by this also that it is first of all distinguished from matter, we can conceive an infinite number of degrees between matter and fully developed spirit – a spirit capable of action which is not only undetermined, but also reasonable and reflective.[24]

The distinction between matter and spirit, then, is one of *degree*, not one of ontological *kind*.

The claim that spirit and matter interpenetrate each other is not only supported by phenomenology, according to Bergson, but also fits well with what we know of the evolution of human brain function. If living bodies are by definition centres of action, and if action by definition requires the possibility of choice between responses to perceived stimuli on the basis of memories of past perceptions, then one would expect human beings to differ in these respects only in degree from those living organisms from which they have evolved. And this, Bergson contends, is what we seem to find:

> The progress of living matter consists in a differentiation of function which leads first to the production and then to the increasing complication of a nervous system capable of canalizing excitations and of organizing actions: the more the higher centers develop, the more numerous become the motor paths among which the same excitation allows the living being to choose, in order that it may act.

Along with this increasing nervous complexity, he continues, goes 'the growing and accompanying tension of consciousness', which 'becomes more capable of creating acts of which the inner indetermination ... will pass the more easily through the meshes of necessity'.[25]

This is not materialism: Bergson never *reduces* spirit to matter, never ceases to insist that spirit is distinct from matter. And there is surely no contradiction between this insistence and the view of spirit as evolving in parallel with the evolution of the brain and nervous system. Bergson is a dualist precisely in the sense that he is not a materialist reductionist: but he is not a Cartesian dualist, because his view implies an intelligible connection between spirit, or at least its manifestations, and the bodily structures required for those manifestations.

Spirit, in the form of memory, comes into existence in the first instance as an adjunct to bodily action: in this sense, memory 'is just the intersection of mind and matter'.[26] But once it has come into existence, it makes it possible for human beings to transcend their existence as purely biological organisms. For to recall the past is to step back from direct involvement with the present in action. So to have the ability to recall the past is to have the possibility of an existence which is not totally 'in the world'. Even though memories may be recalled primarily with a view to present action, they are not in themselves part of present action: they are representations of a past existence, a past self. And their recollection makes of the present action something more than a reflex response to a current stimulus, something more like a chosen expression of one's self as it has developed so far. In other words, it individualises one's existence.

IV

Bergson's negative argument is thus that Cartesian dualism (and indeed materialism) is the result of taking the intellectual picture of the world as if it represented ultimate reality. According to this picture, matter, including my own body, must be something distinct from me, as spirit. But this picture itself presupposes, according to Bergson, a deeper reality, given to intuition, in which I experience myself as an active being, and so an embodied being, and the world as intimately related to me, because it is what I act upon. When we describe that immediate experience of myself as an active and embodied being, we get a picture of what it is to be a person who recognises the reality of mind and of spirit, but who is nevertheless not a Cartesian dualist. To experience oneself as a person, for Bergson, is to experience oneself both as a being active in the world and as a being who must be capable of standing back from active involvement with the world.

The nearer we come to that pole of human existence in which we are purely engaged in active relations with the things and people around us (if you like, the more we operate at the surface of our existence), the nearer we are to being pure 'matter'; the further from such involvement we get (the more we operate in the depths of our being), the nearer we become to being pure 'spirit'. But no human being ever does, or ever can, actually reach either of those poles (at least while alive). For bodily activity, for human beings at least, requires some involvement of spirit, and spirit naturally presses towards involvement with bodily activity, as we shall now see.

To act at all requires embodiment, since it requires the possibility of physical interaction between the agent and the things acted upon. To act in the typically human fashion requires a particular sort of body, above all, a particular sort of brain and nervous system, in which, as described earlier, more than one possible pathway of response to a stimulus exists. For human activity is typically more than a mere automatic, reflex or instinctive, response to a stimulus: it is *chosen* by the agent as the movement which seems to him or her the best response in these circumstances. Such a power of choice makes possible and indeed requires the development of a sense of *oneself* as a continuing being, with desires and purposes of one's own, that is, the development of memory or consciousness, which is the principle element, for Bergson, of what he calls 'spirit'. Choice makes self-consciousness *possible* in that it enables a degree of detachment from one's involvement with the surrounding milieu which is not possible for an animal which simply responds automatically to external stimuli. And it *requires* self-consciousness, in that to choose implies a weighting of alternatives in terms of some scheme of values which is experienced as the agent's own.

At the same time, this account makes it possible to see, at least in outline, how it might be possible to overcome the principal theoretical difficulty in Cartesian dualism – that of making it intelligible how matter and spirit can be radically distinct in nature yet intimately connected with each other. Spirit manifests itself in human beings, as we have seen, in the indetermination of our will, which allows to our activity a greater degree of independence of matter than is possible in lower animals. But Bergson emphasises that this particularly human manifestation of spirit is matched by a correspondingly greater degree of complexity in our nervous system than is found in those of the same lower animals. It is true that he describes this neurophysiological development as 'only a symbol' of the inner (presumably spiritual) energy.[27] But even to say this is to imply an intelligible relationship (the relation of 'symbolising') between the biological evolution of the human organism and the spiritual possibilities open to human beings.

Thus, for Bergson, human spiritual activity differs in degree rather than kind from the neurophysiologically more limited reactions of simpler animals. It is in the first instance a (considerably) more sophisticated way of responding to practical needs by appropriate actions. But to say that human memory has evolved in the service of action is quite compatible with saying that, having evolved, it can become to some degree at least *detached* from action. And we do indeed experience such possibilities of detachment, for instance (though these are certainly not the *only* instances) in dreams and insanity, which, he says, appear to be little else than what results when attention becomes detached from life, that is, from action.[28]

The greater complexity of human action makes possible a sharper distinction between *oneself* (what is 'inside') and *objects* (what is 'outside'). The more instinctive reactions of simpler organisms do not lead to what could be called a 'personal experience' in the sense in which human free choice does. To have to *choose* to act in one way or another, however, necessarily introduces a sense of this distinction. To be conscious of oneself as choosing is, first, to be conscious of a *point of view* which is one's own, of a place which one occupies within the world of objects, but which is yet not the position of another object. It is, so to speak, a *qualitative place*, defined in terms of the meaningful relations of objects to oneself, rather than a *spatial location*, determinable by its quantitative relations with other points in space. Second, it is to be conscious of having a *duration in time*, of a relation between what one is perceiving and doing now and what one has done in the past. And this duration is, again, experienced *qualitatively* and *inwardly*, rather than *quantitatively* and *spatially*: the relations to one's own past are not experienced as causal relations between distinct objects, but as relations of meaning, in virtue of the fact that both past and present are *one's own*, elements in oneself. That is why Bergson does not accept that memories can be 'stored' in the brain: not so much because the brain plays no part in our ability to remember, but because memories are not objects or things which might be 'stored' anywhere. Pure memory, he says,[29] consists in a 'virtual state', a state of preparedness for action, in other words, as a disposition rather than a thing.

V

So in what way does all this make Bergson a non-Cartesian dualist? He is a dualist in emphasising that human beings are both matter and spirit, and in his claim that, as spirits, human beings are more than merely biological organisms. But he is far from Cartesian in his conception of what is meant by the terms 'matter' and 'spirit', and so of the relations between the material and the spiritual. The key to understanding what Bergson says about matter and spirit is to take account of the centrality of *action* in his view of human beings. He says that 'the orientation of our consciousness toward action appears to be the fundamental law of our psychical life'.[30] Action involves both material and spiritual elements, inseparably. The bodily movements which are the material elements constitute an action only because they are chosen by a person, whose perception of the surrounding environment is interpreted in the light of his or her memories of past experience, which are the spiritual elements. At the same time, as in the passage just cited, this consciousness, or spiritual element, is fundamentally orientated towards action.

If we try, following the methodology sketched in an earlier section, simply to describe what it is like to be such a being in a world, then we see 'matter', whether in the form of our own bodies or in the form of external objects, not as a thing or substance separate both in its existence and its nature from ourselves, but as a moment in our own being in the world. Our own body 'has for its essential function to limit, with a view to action, the life of the spirit'.[31] And other things, though certainly distinct from us, are not marked off from us by sharp boundaries: 'the separation between a thing and its environment cannot be absolutely definite and clear-cut; there is a passage by insensible gradations from the one to the other'.[32] External objects are seen from this point of view as possible items on which we can act, and become more and more separate from us the further away they get from being actual objects of action. The whole world of our experience, seen in this way from the 'inside', from the point of view of 'intuition', is within the scope of duration, of the onward flow of experienced time in which there are no clear-cut divisions, no homogeneous units, and so no room for quantitative measurement or for causal determinism. Spirit and matter are thus not distinguishable, except in degree, in terms of intensity/extensity, quality/quantity, subjectivity/objectivity or freedom/determinism.

Why then does Cartesian dualism seem so plausible? It is precisely because we are active beings, and because we have a tendency to confuse action and speculation. The needs of our activity require us to divide up the world which we actually experience as continuous, indivisible and qualitatively variegated into a number of distinct, homogeneous units, arranged in a homogeneous space and time. But if we then forget the essentially active nature of our involvement with the world, we confuse this instrumentally useful picture with a speculatively true account of what things are like in themselves. My own body then ceases to be specifically *my* body, the centre of *my* experience of the world, and becomes just one object among others. 'Matter' becomes the name for the totality of the homogeneous units, and extension, in the sense of *partes extra partes*, becomes its defining feature; space becomes quantitative, and time, even inner duration, becomes spatialised.

To repeat, this view of the world and our place in it is perfectly in order, if properly understood, as a necessary assumption for the purposes of action. It becomes a source of confusion only when it is taken as a metaphysically or theoretically true description of how things are in themselves. If we take it in that way, we simply create unnecessary puzzlement for ourselves by misunderstanding the nature of what we are saying: 'our understanding,' Bergson says, 'of which the function is to set up logical distinctions, and, consequently, clean-cut oppositions … sets up, at one extremity, an infinitely divisible extension and, at the other, sensations which are absolutely inextensive. And it creates thereby the opposition which it afterwards contemplates amazed.'[33] The metaphysics of mind and body, as traditionally understood, is a vain attempt to grapple with problems which we have thrown up for ourselves.

VI

In my introductory remarks, I said that Bergson's treatment of the 'mind–body problem' has much to contribute to our contemporary discussions in philosophy. I should like to conclude by indicating some of the ways in which that might be so, though for reasons of space I can do no more than list them as possibilities for future research.

To begin with, Bergson's version of dualism seems to open up the possibility that we could accommodate two equally plausible beliefs: first, that any account of human consciousness or spirit must establish an intelligible relationship between the phenomena of consciousness and what we know scientifically about human mental life; and second, that any account of consciousness must include an account of subjectivity, intentionality and quality. These two beliefs are often held to be incompatible, or at least difficult to combine. The first belief seems more important to contemporary materialists: Dennett, for instance, has emphasised the need to give an *evolutionary* account of consciousness,[34] while Paul Churchland, among many others (including Dennett again), has tried to give an account in terms of neurophysiology.[35] The second belief has seemed more important to opponents of (at least simple) materialism, such as Nagel and Searle.[36]

Bergson's own account, as we have seen, offers a way of understanding the close connection between the special ways in which spirit manifests itself in human life and our complex and highly evolved neurophysiology; but at the same time, unlike materialists, he does not *identify* spirit with any neurophysiological structure, since spirit, for him, is not a thing or object, in the way in which brain cells are, but a function of the unified human person. And he can then allow that the operation of that function can take on certain features (subjectivity, intentionality and so on) which are not to be found in the operations of simpler material structures and thus create an important distinction between creatures such as ourselves and those others which have not evolved such complex brains. The neurophysiology of Bergson's time was, of course, much less advanced than that of the present day, but his account appears to offer the possibility at least of combining scientific plausibility with a sense of the uniqueness of human mentality.

The other contemporary philosophical debate to which Bergson's account could make a useful contribution is that concerning personal identity. Most philosophers writing about personal identity have a certain conception of the problem, according to which it is essentially the same as any other problem of identity: that is, it is the problem of finding criteria of identification and re-identification of an entity as the same over time. Given this conception of the problem, then, the answer must be either what one might call 'essentialist' or 'conventionalist'. That is, either a 'person' is a particular kind of entity which has a continuing essence which enables it to be identified and re-identified as the same entity at different times, or the term 'person' is one which has only a conventional use, so that it is a matter for decision whether someone is or is not the same person. The essentialists, such as Joseph Butler, must face the difficulty of finding a plausible candidate for the 'essence' of an individual person, in view of the sheer changeability of people, physically and psychologically.[37] The conventionalists, such as Parfit,[38] avoid that difficulty, but then come up against the moral and emotional counter-intuitiveness of a view of who someone is which makes it dependent *only* on decision.

Bergson's view of a person as unified, not by a continuing essence, but by a developing life-*history* seems, at least at first sight, to offer the possibility of a view of personal identity which could accommodate the changeability just spoken of while retaining the idea, so important to us morally and emotionally, that a person remains the same throughout his or her life. It is in ways like this that it seems to me that contemporary philosophical discussion is impoverished by the neglect of Bergson, who may not always have got it right (who does?), but at least usually has something to say which is worth considering.

Notes

1 MM p. xi/9; OE, p. 161; emphasis added.
2 See Thomas Nagel, *The View from Nowhere* (New York and Oxford, Oxford University Press, 1996).

3 CM, p. 161/190; OE, p. 1395. I am using the translation of 'Introduction to Metaphysics' by T. E. Hulme (London, Macmillan and Co. Ltd, 1913), though references will cite the corresponding pagination in CM and OE.

4 Eric Matthews, *Twentieth-Century French Philosophy* (Oxford, Oxford University Press, 1996), pp. 16–18.

5 See Thomas Nagel, 'What is it Like to be a Bat?', in his *Mortal Questions*, Canto edition (Cambridge, Cambridge University Press, 1979), pp. 165–80.

6 MM, pp. 239–40/183; OE, p. 319.

7 MM, p. 282/212; OE, p. 346.

8 CM, p. 162/191; OE, p. 1396.

9 CM, p. 192/227; OE, p. 1424.

10 CM, p. 192/227; OE, p. 1424.

11 CM, p. 190/225; OE, p. 1422.

12 See Nagel, *The View from Nowhere*, pp. 22–5.

13 F. C. T. Moore, *Bergson: Thinking Backwards* (Cambridge, Cambridge University Press, 1996).

14 René Descartes, *The Philosophical Writings of Descartes*, trans. John Cottingham, Robert Stoothoff and Dugald Murdoch (Cambridge, Cambridge University Press, 1984), vol. 2, p. 114.

15 MM, p. xi/9; OE, p. 161.

16 See Maurice Merleau-Ponty, *Phenomenology of Perception*, trans. Colin Smith (London, Routledge and Kegan Paul, 1962).

17 MM, p. 16/27; OE, p. 178.

18 MM, p. 16/28; OE, pp. 178–9.

19 MM, p. 235/180; OE, p. 317.

20 MM, p. 235/180; OE, p. 317.

21 MM, p. 44/47; OE, p. 196.

22 MM, pp. 69–70/65; OE, pp. 212–13.

23 MM, p. 72/67; OE, p. 214.

24 MM, pp. 295–6/221; OE, p. 355.

25 MM, pp. 332/248 f.; OE, pp. 377 f.

26 MM, p. xvi/13; OE, p. 164.

27 MM, p. 296/222; OE, p. 355.

28 MM, p. 228/174; OE, pp. 312–13.

29 MM, p. 319/240; OE, p. 369.

30 MM, p. 234/180; OE, p. 317.

31 MM, p. 233/179; OE, p. 316.

32 MM, p. 278/209; OE, p. 344.

33 MM, p. 327/245; OE, p. 374.

34 See Daniel Dennett, *Consciousness Explained* (London, Allen Lane, The Penguin Press, 1991), especially chapter seven.

35 See, for example, Paul Churchland, *The Engine of Reason, the Seat of the Soul* (Cambridge, Mass. and London, MIT Press, 1995), especially chapter eight.

36 Nagel, 'What is it Like to be a Bat?'; John Searle, *The Rediscovery of the Mind* (Cambridge, Mass. and London, MIT Press, 1992).

37 See Joseph Butler, 'Of Personal Identity', Appendix 1 to *The Analogy of Religion*, in J. Butler, *Works*, ed. W. E. Gladstone (Oxford, Oxford University Press [1736], 1896).

38 Derek Parfit, *Reasons and Persons* (Oxford, Oxford University Press, 1984).

f. c. t. moore

MAGIC

Magic is often represented as something *exotic*, that is, as belonging to a remote and foreign place or time. It is practised in 'primitive societies' or by medieval alchemists, by Persian magi or Chinese geomancers. It is at a distance from us, especially those of us who are devoted to rational enquiry. And its occurrence calls for explanation. Now Bergson disagreed with the most famous of his near contemporaries, such as Durkheim, Mauss, Lévy-Bruhl and James Frazer, who did offer explanations of the occurrence of magic and religion. This essay offers a brief demonstration that Bergson's treatment of magic is of continuing interest. But first, we should set the scene.[1]

An aberration?

Magic, or superstition, is sometimes contrasted with religion on the one hand and science on the other.[2] On one simple version of this view, magic is a human *aberration*, a way in which things go wrong, which would therefore have, at best, piecemeal and varying explanations from time to time and from place to place. This seems somewhat unsatisfying, given the prevalence of such practices and beliefs in human life.

For instance, the Royal Society is programmatically viewed as the vehicle of the advance of experimental science in seventeenth-century England, a model of the progress of rational empirical enquiry. It, surely, is not 'exotic'. However, in fact, some of its members moved in and sympathised with the millenarian circles of the time, and Newton himself took a serious, active and continuing interest in alchemy.[3] This suggests that the programmatic picture of the work of the Royal Society may be historically misleading. Closer study may reveal a configuration of such ideas and practices which had its own unity. Later thinkers, however, wish to discard religious or magical elements in the thought of the period in order to preserve the model which they value. Such processes are frequent in the history of thought, and they are motivated. In the case of philosophy, Bergson described them in this way: 'The work by which philosophy appears to assimilate the results of positive science, and likewise the procedure by which a philosophy seems to gather together in itself fragments of previous philosophies, is not a synthesis but an analysis.'[4] I take it that Bergson's point is that when we wish to *make use of*, for example, the thought of this period, we analyse it perforce according to our needs and interests. This analysis isolates certain 'scientific' practices, themes and developments which can be seen as precursors and treated as models, while what it isolates as magical or religious will be left aside. Clearly, such analytic processes may lead to a historically false or misleading view of the thought of an earlier period, which other scholars, with different needs and interests, will hasten to correct. But it is not our task here to correct such interpretations. For a more general question remains. Is there any reason, say of a psychological or sociological kind, which could explain, not the details, but the fact, of human magical or superstitious practices and beliefs, whenever and wherever they occur?

Evolutionary explanations

One attempt at this arises from the varieties of evolutionary or genetic explanation which dominated so many disciplines in the nineteenth century. This is a second way in which magic is contrasted with science. The story goes that there is a 'pre-logical' mentality which existed in more 'primitive' stages of human development. People thought quite differently then. Meanwhile our mental abilities have developed, though there are remnants of the old way of thinking here and there, which ought to be eliminated.[5]

A more gentlemanly version of this story makes magic a primitive *form* of science, rather than something to be contrasted with it. It has the same objectives of describing and explaining the world around us, in a way which is intended to enable us to manipulate that world, but it performs this task with inferior tools which do not work at all, or do not work well.

Such explanations, though more systematic, are very unsatisfying for a number of reasons, but in particular since they fail to address adequately the question why the 'survivals' of the 'old' way of thinking do survive, even, for instance, in the very citadels of the rise of modern science. For this reason, we shall set aside evolutionary explanations of magic as at best insufficient.

Functionalist explanations

A different approach is to account for the existence and persistence of such beliefs and practices by showing that they perform a social function. This is not the place for a general assessment of functionalist accounts of human societies. Let us just make a strategic point. Functionalist accounts of some biological phenomena do seem tempting and useful, including, for instance, their application to the hymenopterans. But humans are precisely not hymenopterans. Human social organisation, unlike hymenopteran, leaves a wide margin for individual action.[6] This makes it clear in advance that any systematic application of a functionalist theory to human communities will require a great deal of costly reinterpretation of individual actions which are ordinarily and perhaps properly understood in what seems a more direct and uncomplicated way. This provides a reason for avoiding this path, if we can.

If there is a general explanation of the phenomenon of magic, it should perhaps come from our understanding of the human mind in general, whether this comes from data of observation, or from phenomenological data, or both.

Cognitive explanations: magic as a by-product

In *Rethinking Symbolism*,[7] Dan Sperber postulated and gave a schematic account of a 'symbolic mechanism' in the human mind. Its survival value at the level of our species, and its developmental value to individual human beings, is that it enables them to retain, rather than simply throw out, propositions that are not, or not yet, fully understood, as well as to remember things by associative rather than inferential means. (Parallel claims might be made about practices, as well as propositions.) Some of these beliefs and practices will, and others will not, be incorporated over time in a fully determinate and instrumental way in our lives. We could then view the occurrence of magical beliefs and practices as a sort of natural by-product of the operation of the symbolic mechanism.

Bergson: never mind the word 'magic'

I shall not pursue Sperber's arguments further at this point, since I want to go to some ideas of Bergson, which provide a certain complement to them.

For Bergson, it is not exactly that magic is a *by-product* of useful cognitive capacities. Rather, there are kinds of action and experience which themselves invite, prefigure or require the magical. Like Sperber, he considers that we need to look to a 'mental function'. Unlike Sperber, he wants to find this by starting from the phenomenology of action, and also thinks that we need to be suspicious of the role of language. This is because our languages may divide up reality in a questionable way.

Bergson develops this methodological point in a passage which deserves commentary (given in italics):[8]

> Philosophers usually study something which common sense has already designated by a word.

The word 'magic' itself and its roughly similar equivalents in at least some other languages seem to give us a rough taxonomy of what we may experience. We have already asked at the beginning of this essay whether there could be a general explanation of this phenomenon. Yet can we be sure that there really is 'a phenomenon' to be explained? After all,

> this thing may only have been glimpsed; it may have been badly seen; it may have been muddled together with other things from which it ought to be isolated. It may even have been cut out from reality as a whole solely as a matter of linguistic convenience without actually constituting a thing capable of independent study.

So is 'magic' a sort of linguistic accident, rather than a phenomenon? And can we, in philosophy, risk leaving this possibility unaddressed?

> Here is the great inferiority of philosophy compared to mathematics and even to the natural sciences. It has to start from the dismemberment of reality which has been carried out by language, and which is perhaps entirely relative to social needs: too often it forgets this origin, and carries on like a geographer referring to the frontiers established by treaties in order to delimit the various regions of the globe and indicate the physical relations between them.

The example of geography is quite serious. I recently read a piece by a philosopher who asked what would happen in societies in Africa in the event of 'a change in the African climate'. But the continent of Africa houses many different climates. From the point of view of climate, 'Africa' is a 'false dismemberment of reality'.

> In our study, we have guarded against this danger by at once turning away from the word 'religion', and from what it covers in virtue of what may be an artificial dismemberment of things, to a certain mental function which can be observed directly without concerning ourselves with the division of reality into concepts corresponding to words.

A similar point may be made about 'magic'. Never mind the word itself. Let us instead attend to some of the phenomena to which we apply the word, but then try to find in our immediate and everyday experience some mental functions which may be related to such phenomena.

Bergson's straight lunge

I shall concentrate on three of Bergson's examples. The first takes the case of fencing. This is one of those physical arts acquired by training which take us beyond the ordinary physical skills and abilities, such as walking, which most humans acquire at an early stage of their lives. *How* such trained abilities are or can be acquired is already very interesting, but *what* is acquired is even more so. According to Bergson,[9]

> The swordsman knows perfectly well that it is the movement of the button which has pulled the épée, the épée which has taken the arm along with it, and the arm which has stretched the body as it itself is stretched: one cannot lunge properly or make a straight lunge except after feeling things in that way.

We may imagine that the trainer says to the novice 'Don't push; let the button pull your arm', rather as a voice-trainer may say to the singer 'sing through your forehead'. But, according to Bergson, the novice in fencing who acquires the technique then knows that it is the button pulling the arm. Paradoxical though this may seem, it nevertheless corresponds to the experienced structure of the acquired technique. Similar points were later to be made by Sartre about someone who has learned to write, and is now halfway through writing the word 'independent'.[10] Phenomenologically, he suggests, it is the word due to appear which is guiding the hand, and its specific movements of penning letters and parts of letters. Presumably, such experiences have a neurological correlate also. We cannot properly understand such a capacity by treating it as a simple accumulation of individual instrumental events.

> To put them in the inverse order is to reconstruct, and thus to philosophize; anyway, it is to make explicit what is implicit, instead of restricting oneself to the demands of pure action, to what is immediately given and truly primitive.

Thus, for Bergson, the 'demands of pure action' in fencing make us know that the button is pulling our arm. Yet, in a different way, we want to say that we know that the button is not really doing any pulling. One would not speak of superstition here, nor accuse the fencer or the trainer of talking nonsense; yet there is a puzzle. More importantly, from our present point of view, this description of the lunge (or again, Sartre's description of writing a word) have the form or structure of magical descriptions: by what incantation do we make the button pull our arm?

Bergson at the casino

The second example is different.[11]

> Place a sum of money on a number at roulette, and wait till the ball has
> nearly stopped rolling: at the moment when it may land ... on the number
> of your choice, your hand moves to push it and then stop it.

Here too we have a familiar kind of everyday experience. The gambler
wants the ball to drop into his slot, and is watching intently. He knows perfectly well that no amount of urging on by him will affect the outcome, yet
he does urge on, he does gesticulate. So the gesture which is rightly construed by an onlooker as the gambler 'encouraging the ball into the right
slot' is a sort of 'make-believe' action: however natural it may be as the
appropriate expression of a real wish, it is not efficacious, nor even under-
taken in the belief that it is efficacious.

Expressive behaviour

It is worth noting that expressive gestures of this sort are typical of the
emotions in general. Banging the table in anger (often) accomplishes little.
Observing this feature of emotional behaviour, Sartre was led to view the
emotions as states of mind in which the world is transformed into something ruled by magic,[12] and to a puritanical condemnation of them as
manifestations of 'bad faith'.[13] Yet there can be no general reason to dis-
count expressive behaviour in this way. Table-banging is an effective
symbolic expression of anger, since the resistance of the table to the fist
neatly mimics the resistance of the world to one's will: something has
happened which you reject, yet you cannot really reject it, since it has
already taken place. Furthermore, mere expression need not be its only
point. Indeed, there is reason to think that expressive behaviour *does* have
some tendency to produce relevant effects overall.

Now if we construe expressive behaviour as behaviour aimed notion-
ally at a goal which the agent does not believe that it will achieve,[14] the
response may be: 'Well then, so much the worse for expressive behaviour.
It's all irrational.' Yet this response seems highly unsatisfactory, for expressive behaviour seems to be universal. To say that it is irrational merely
avoids explanation by treating it as an aberration.

The best explanation, I believe, lies in the fact that the boundary
between instrumental and expressive behaviour is uncertain.[15] While
there are plenty of cases where we are confident in our ability to do something towards achieving a goal (such as opening a window to let air in), and
plenty where we are confident that we have no such ability (people don't

usually think that they can do anything which will help to bring about a fine day tomorrow), there are plenty more where we are not sure.

What can be a goal?

The question then arises what we can rationally treat as a goal. On a strict instrumental view, the answer would be that a goal is rational only if we believe that we can do something towards it. Yet taking this strict view would risk precluding the possibility, for instance, of acquiring new skills. We should weaken the requirement above, and say that a goal is rational provided that we do not believe that there is nothing we can do towards it.

This will allow us a larger range of possible actions, which may in turn extend our abilities to act in the world, even though it exposes us to a considerably greater risk of wasting our time. Thus the description of actions *in this margin* between what we believe to be within our power and what we believe not to be within our power will also turn out to have the form or structure of magical descriptions, since the agent is not in possession of any specific belief which makes the instrumental link between the action and its goal. Here is a second example of a birth of magic. As Bergson deftly put it, we see 'superstition arising from the will to success'.[16]

A third example

These two examples from Bergson involve the phenomenology of action, from the point of view of the agent. Bergson, however, also gives another sort of example, also phenomenological, in terms of our experience of agency which is not our own. Evidently, we experience other people's movements as intentional actions, and there are many interesting questions about how we do this. But sometimes we experience natural events also as though they were of the same sort. William James experienced an earthquake while staying in Stanford University, and wrote as follows:

> For 'science', when the tensions in the earth's crust reach the breaking-point, and strata fall into an altered equilibrium, earthquake is simply the collective *name* of all the cracks and shakings and disturbances that happen. They *are* the earthquake. But for me, *the* earthquake was the cause of the disturbances, and the perception of it as a living agent was irresistible.[17]

Bergson cites this passage,[18] in which James also comments:

> I realize now better than ever how inevitable were men's earlier mythologic versions of such catastrophes, and how artificial and against the grain of our spontaneous perceiving are the later habits into which science educates us.

It was simply impossible for untutored men to take earthquakes into their minds as anything but supernatural warnings and retributions.

James's comments here verge on the kind of evolutionary view which we earlier set aside. But we may pass over them for the time, and simply ask why we should have any tendency to treat natural events as having the structure of intentional action. Suppose, for instance, that a tree is falling. You may do well to react somewhat as you would to the descending club in the hand of an enemy.

Antinomies

The three examples from Bergson illustrate what I have called elsewhere the 'antinomies of intelligence'.[19] For, as instrumental creatures needing to act, we are led to treat the button in fencing as pulling our arm, even though we also want to say that it does not do so. This same instrumentality, when in danger of frustration, can overflow into expressive behaviour, which appears to be directed towards ends which it may not be able to achieve, or which it pretty definitely cannot achieve, as in the case of the gesture at the roulette-wheel. It may lead us also to perceive intentional action where it is not really present, as in the case of the earthquake.

These examples are, as Bergson put it, 'modest beginnings'.[20] What this means is that we do not need to look to distant and exotic places and times in considering how magical practices and beliefs arise: we have only to look to our own everyday experience. We are therefore obliged to reject the hypothesis of a 'pre-logical' or 'primitive' mentality mentioned at the outset of this essay, to recognise that magic is in no way exotic, and to search for the explanation of the occurrence of magical practices and beliefs in 'the general structure of the human mind'.[21] These examples and these remarks invite but do not constitute such an explanation.

Epidemiology

What form such an explanation might eventually take is beyond the scope of this essay, which is aimed mainly at what we can draw from Bergson's treatment of magic. But Sperber has advocated a research programme for the study of cultural phenomena based on the model of epidemiology.[22] Just as we can ask what accounts for the incidence of a given disease entity in given populations in given places at given times, so too with a cultural phenomenon like (for instance) the beliefs and practices which may be called 'magic'. And just as in epidemiology we cannot expect in advance a single kind of explanation, but rather a variety of mechanisms and factors, so too for culture. Sperber sees a risk in his proposal, given that the mechanisms of cultural transmission might prove to be remote from what common sense gives us access to: 'Should one take the chance of pulling the social sciences away from common-sense understanding?'[23] But Bergson's three examples are pointers to how there could be mechanisms for the contagion of magic, and they come, not from arcane scientific work, but directly from ordinary experience (if we are willing to listen to his elegant incantations, the few words of Bergson which somehow, like a spell, cause us to reconsider).

Notes

1 This essay is a development of parts of 'Magic and the Primitive: the Antinomies of Pure Intelligence' (chapter nine), in F. C. T. Moore, *Bergson: Thinking Backwards* (Modern European Philosophy) (Cambridge, Cambridge University Press, 1996), pp. 123–39. All translations from Bergson are the author's.

2 See J. G. Frazer, *The Golden Bough: a Study in Magic and Religion* (London, Macmillan, 1932–36), p. 307 (part VI, Vol. II): 'We may illustrate the course which thought has hitherto run by likening it to a web woven of three different threads – the black thread of magic, the red thread of religion, and the white thread of science.'

3 See the detailed treatment in Betty Jo Teeter Dobbs, *The Janus Faces of Genius: the Role of Alchemy in Newton's Thought* (Cambridge, Cambridge University Press, 1991).

4 CM, p. 125/148; OE, p. 1362.

5 For a discussion of such views, illustrated most clearly in the work of Lévy-Bruhl, see, for instance, Dan Sperber, 'Is Symbolic Thought Prerational?', in M. L. Foster and S. M. Brandes (eds), *Symbol and Sense: New Approaches to the Analysis of Meaning* (New York, Academic Press, 1980), pp. 25–44.

6 MR, p. 117; OE, pp. 1073–4.

7 Dan Sperber, *Rethinking Symbolism* (Cambridge Studies in Social Anthropology), trans. Alice L. Morton (Cambridge, Cambridge University Press, 1975), pp. 115–48.

8 MR, pp. 173–4; OE, pp. 1122–3.

9 MR, pp. 125–6; OE, p. 1081.

10 Jean-Paul Sartre, *Sketch for a Theory of the Emotions*, trans. Philip Mairet (London, Methuen, 1962), pp. 59 ff.

11 MR, pp. 140–1; OE, p. 1094.

12 Sartre, *Sketch*, pp. 56–91.

13 Jean-Paul Sartre, *Being and Nothingness: an Essay on Phenomenological Ontology*, trans. Hazel E. Barnes (London, Methuen, 1958), Part I, chapter two.

14 See F. C. T. Moore, *The Psychological Basis of Morality: an Essay on Value and Desire* (Library of Philosophy and Religion) (London, Macmillan, 1978), pp. 29–32.

15 See F. C. T. Moore, 'Thresholds of Coherence', inaugural lecture, *University of Hong Kong Gazette*, 27 (3) (1980).

16 MR, p. 140; OE, p. 1094.

17 William James, 'On Some Mental Effects of the Earthquake', in *Essays in Psychology* (Cambridge, Mass., Harvard University Press, 1983), pp. 331–3.

18 MR, pp. 155–6; OE, p. 1107.

19 Moore, *Bergson*, p. 139.

f. c. t. moore

20 MR, p. 125; OE, p. 1081.
21 MR, p. 104; OE, p. 1063.
22 Dan Sperber, *Explaining Culture: a Naturalistic Approach* (Oxford, Oxford University Press, 1996).
23 Sperber, *Explaining Culture*, p. 154.

IV

LIFE

keith ansell pearson

BERGSON AND CREATIVE EVOLUTION/INVOLUTION: EXPOSING THE TRANSCENDENTAL ILLUSION OF ORGANISMIC LIFE

Evolution is the outcome of the ultimate ascendancy of the trend toward increasing diversity and acceleration of the energy flow, counteracted and retarded by the individual species attempting to proceed in the direction of greater homogeneity and deceleration of the energy flow.[1]

If everything is alive, it is not because everything is organic or organized but, on the contrary, because the organism is a diversion of life. In short, the life in question is inorganic, germinal, and intensive, a powerful life without organs, a Body that is all the more alive for having no organs, everything that passes *between* organisms.[2]

Introduction

The problematic of 'creative evolution' is by no means a redundant or otiose one in the contemporary science of living systems. But given that it is a widely held view that the figure whose ideas could do a great deal to illuminate a whole host of problems belongs to a dead and buried tradition of vitalist thought, namely Bergson, it is perhaps not surprising that today questions of vitalism and finalism remain poorly thought out. In *Creative Evolution* Bergson endeavoured to steer a course beyond the opposition of mechanism (neo-Darwinism) and finalism (neo-Lamarckism), both of which reduce the past and future to calculable functions of the present, and developed a conception of evolution which placed the emphasis on the creation of forms and the continual elaboration of the 'absolutely new' through 'invention'.[3] The contentious issue of vitalism should not serve to downplay the continuing significance of Bergson's text.[4] Bergson's thinking on evolution and entropy has been defended against the many charges of mysticism levelled against it by Georgescu-Roegen.[5] Moreover, in that work Bergson is careful to distinguish his own work from illegitimate vitalisms and not to appeal to anything mysterious. After having noted that the inventive character of vitality resides in its tangential relationship to physical and chemical forces at any and every point, he acknowledges that while an appeal to a 'vital principle' may not explain much, it does at least serve to remind us of our ignorance, when mechanism simply invites us to ignore the ignorance.[6] Although the charge of mysticism may ultimately remain apposite in the case of Bergson, it is important to appreciate that there is much to his thinking about creative evolution that is apposite to continuing attempts within contemporary biophilosophy to define the nature of evolution.

Bergson follows Nietzsche in holding that no interesting account of evolution can be generated if it is simply conceived in linear, mechanistic terms as inner adaptation to external circumstances. Organisms cannot be treated as closed systems simply subjected to external forces and determinations; rather, they have to be understood in more dynamic terms as open systems that undergo continual flux. The process of 'adapting' involves, Bergson argues, not a mere 'repeating' but an active 'replying' (répliquer).[7] While adaptation may ably explain the 'sinuosities' of the movement of evolution it is unable to account for the movement itself.[8] In his classic study of individuation, Gilbert Simondon insisted that in order to articulate a truly dynamic model of complex adaptive systems it is necessary to modify the notion of an adaptive relation of the organism in connection to its milieu. We then learn that an organism does not build up a rapport with its environment, including knowledge of it, in abstraction from sensations, but rather 'through a problematic deriving from a primary tropistic unity, a coupling of sensation and tropism'.[9] A living system resolves its problems not simply by adapting itself through modifying its relationship to its milieu, but rather through a process of self-modification, in which it invents new structures which then serve to mediate and define its rapport with the environment.

On the model of natural selection it is the environment which simply selects the organism, exterminating the ill-fitted and selecting the fitter ones. On the model of co-evolution, however, it is equally the case that an organism 'selects' its environment. The biologist Brian Goodwin has argued, for example, that organisms have the potential for effecting appropriate responses to their environment, with the result that the variation available for evolutionary change and adaptation cannot be seen as simply arising from random genetic mutation, but rather 'from the intrinsically regulative and plastic responses of the organism to the environment during its life-cycle'[10] (this plasticity might include genetic response in the form of adaptive changes within the genome). Organisms for Goodwin are agents of 'immanent, self-generating, or creative power' which participate actively in 'a flowing unity, a creative river of life'.[11] George Kampis, another contemporary complexity theorist, expands upon this insight, arguing that if one adopts a co-evolutionary view, in which the relationship between an organism and an environment is seen to rest on a series of feedback loops, then it has to be recognised that the problems to be solved by evolutionary adaptation are themselves products of an evolutionary process (this is an essentially Bergsonian point about *creative* evolution). In other words, the process and its products are meaningful only with reference to one another.[12] As Kampis points out, neo-Darwinism remains wedded to the transformationalism of Darwin's theory of natural selection, in which evolution is conceived as the unfolding of subsequent stages that already exist, separately from the process, from the beginning on and always determined by an initial set of problems posed by an 'environment' once and for ever. In contrast, the new biology of complexity theory emphasises the fact that an environment cannot be separated from what organisms are and what they do. In the words of one of the most forceful advocates of this view: 'The environment is not a structure imposed on living beings from the outside but is in fact a creation of those beings. The environment is not an autonomous process but a reflection of the biology of the species.'[13] Francisco Varela, one of the leading thinkers of the school of autopoiesis, has argued that living beings and environments stand in relation to one another through the activity of 'mutual specification' and 'codetermination'.[14]

Bergson's stress on the 'creative capacities' of matter remains, therefore, apposite. A purely mechanistic biology conflates the passive adaptation of inert matter, submitting to environmental influence, with the active adaptation of an organism. Bergson gives the example of the eye, noting that to say that the eye 'makes use' of light is not only to declare that the eye is capable of seeing; rather, it is to refer to the exact relations between an organ and the apparatus of locomotion. Moreover, it would be absurd, he insists, to say that the influence of light has 'physically caused' the formation of those systems that are continuous with the apparatus of vision, such as a nervous system and an osseous system. Given the limitations of such a reductive view it becomes necessary to attribute to 'organized matter a certain capacity *sui generis* … of building up very complicated machines to utilize the simple excitation that it undergoes'.[15]

A 'Bergsonian' conception of creative evolution opens up the way for an innovative mapping of the biological domain, in which the concentration on organisms is rendered problematic. For while the organism is treated seriously by Bergson as an active participant in evolution, it is not regarded as the *telos* of the process; the process is without end and is its own becoming. Bergson is close to Schelling (as Deleuze recognised in his 1956 essay)[16] in construing a philosophy of nature or creative evolution in terms of a play between process and product.[17] While recent complexity theory has done much to expose the limitations of the neo-Darwinian model by pointing to the self-organising character of organismic life, it is still fixated, in a way that contemporary Darwinism is not, on the question of the organism. By situating Bergson in the context of recent trajectories of evolutionary theory, I hope to provide readers with a 'new' Bergson which is demonstrative of Deleuze's exemplary construal of the meaning of a 'return to Bergson'.[18]

Creative evolution

While parts of Bergson's argument appear to be well understood, there remains a tendency to simplify, and so distort, key aspects of his great text on evolution. It may help to rehearse some of the salient aspects of his thesis, in particular those facets which are important to the argument to be unfolded here. Evolution is invention, and invention involves duration. In terms reminiscent of Nietzsche, Bergson notes that an ego which does not change does not endure either, and he attacks the notion of a timeless substratum lying behind all reality: 'If our existence were composed of separate states with an impassive ego to unite them, for us there would be no duration.'[19] What is obtained by construing the flow of life in this way is an 'artificial limitation' of the internal life, a stasis which lends itself to the requirements of logic and language. For Bergson it is possible to think of movement without the support of an invariable substance underlying all becoming, while Nietzsche is insistent that logical–metaphysical postulates, such as the belief in substance, are the result of our habit of treating all our deeds as consequences of our will in which the ego does not vanish in the 'multiplicity of change'.[20]

Bergson seeks to move towards a more dynamic conception of life, a virtual and vital becoming which exists and subsists without being fixed into isolable or deterministic states. For Bergson the emphasis is on the virtual character of time, in particular of time's past which always 'grows without ceasing', meaning that there is no limit to its preservation (it possesses an infinite capacity for novel reinvention). It is in this context that he outlines his conception of memory, which is to be understood neither as a drawer for storing things away nor as a faculty. Whereas a faculty works only intermittently, switching on and off as it pleases, the reality of the past is a deep and productive unconscious that evolves automatically. We thus arrive at the definition that duration 'is the continuous progress of the past which gnaws into the future and which swells as it advances'.[21] It is irreversible, since 'consciousness cannot go through the same state twice. The circumstances may still be the same, but they will act no longer on the same person, since they find him at a new moment of his history.'[22] Even if states can be repeated and assume the character of being identical, this is merely an appearance, so we cannot live over and over again a single moment. The future, which is implicated in the past's becoming, is both irreversible and unforeseeable. Bergson speaks here of the person, but his analysis can readily be extended to systems.[23] The process is not only one of change but of invention, since the forms do not exist in advance; the process involves not a realisation of the possible but an actualisation of the virtual. Here one is no longer dealing with a linear evolutionism in which evolution's task is simply to bring to realisation something that already existed in a nascent state. The process of the virtual actualising itself is an inventive one in the sense that what gets actualised does not simply come to resemble the virtual. Where the process of the realisation of the possible involves rules of resemblance and limitation, the process of the actualisation of the virtual does not. The reality of the virtual never gets exhausted, but provides a 'reservoir' for evolution to reinvent perpetually its inventive character (the notion of the virtual is treated at length in chapter two of Bergson's *Matter and Memory* and is explicated at length in chapters three and five of Deleuze's *Bergsonism*).

Classical Newtonian physics calculates the position of any point of a system in space and seeks to identify the future forms of that system which are held to be theoretically visible in the present configuration. Bergson's emphasis throughout is on divergent lines of evolution and on the virtual as a vital power of differentiation. Life is not like geometry, in which things are given 'once and for all'. If time is a virtual reality then it makes no sense to break the movement into distinct instants, since there cannot be an instant which immediately precedes another instant any more than we can say that one mathematical point touches another.[24] It is only the confusion of space and time, and the assimilation of time into space, which generates the illusion that the whole is given in advance of its becoming.[25] The whole is neither given nor giveable 'because it is the Open' whose nature it is constantly to change and to give rise to the new.[26]

At one point in his argument Bergson insists that there is no universal biological law that can automatically be applied to every living thing. Rather, there are only directions from out of which are thrown only relative finalities and fixities. This is true of both life and death, or rather, of the processes of living and dying. This is the reason why Bergson holds that there is an unbroken continuity between the evolution of the embryo and the complete organism: 'The impetus which causes a living being to grow larger, to develop and to age, is the same that has caused it to pass through the phases of embryonic life.'[27] Development is nothing other than a perpetual change of form. Life is but a continuum, with death serving as an interruptive force. In the case of the organism, for example, do we say that it is growing old or that it is still the life of an embryo continuing to evolve? In the case of the human organism the crises of puberty and menopause are 'part and parcel of the process' of ageing, comparable to changes which occur in larval or embryonic life. This is to say that such events do not occur *ex abrupto* from without. Puberty is 'in course of preparation at every instant from birth'.[28] Thus, Bergson is able to claim that what is 'properly vital' in growth and ageing is nothing other than the 'insensible, infinitely graduated, continuance of the change of form'.[29] The phenomena of organic destruction are an integral feature of this evolution of the living being which, like that of the embryo, implies 'a continual recording of duration', that is, the persistence of the past in the present:[30]

> At a certain moment, in certain points of space, a visible current has taken rise; this current of life, traversing the bodies it has organised one after another, passing from generation to generation, has become divided amongst species and distributed amongst individuals without losing any of its force, rather intensifying in proportion to its advance.[31]

One source of intensity for Bergson is 'germinal life'. Here he discusses Weismann's famous distinction between soma and germ plasms, the significance of which was to divorce Darwinism from its entanglement in the Lamarckian doctrine of the inheritance of acquired characteristics. Lamarckism is a doctrine of finalism in that it explains evolution in terms of the process of adaptation being directed by the organism's own recognition and control of the changes required to effect this adaptation. Evolution becomes on this view a matter of directed somatic change, not the random genetic change associated with the triumphant neo-Darwinism of the twentieth century. On the Lamarckian model evolution gets reduced to a process of realisation. There is invention, but such invention involves the mere realisation of a plan or programme of adaptation. Although Bergson does not fully endorse Weismann's conception of the continuity of the germ-plasm (contained in the sperm and the egg),[32] he does want to advance the idea of there being a continuity of 'genetic energy' which involves the expenditure of energy at certain instants, just enough to give to embryonic life the requisite impulsion, which is then 'recouped' again in order to assure the creation of new sexual elements in which it 'bides its time'. When treated from this perspective, life can be construed as *like a current passing from germ to germ through the medium of a developed organism*'.[33] Life appears in the form of an organism as if the organism were only an 'excrescence, a bud caused to sprout by the former germ endeavouring to continue itself in a new germ'.[34] This genetic energy does not guarantee the production of the same, but is a source of novelty in which life perpetually reinvents the character of its own evolution or becoming. Bergson is close to Weismann, although he does not wish to locate the vital principle in something as concrete and determined as a germ-plasm, since this would reduce the scope within 'creative evolution' for invention and innovation. Of course, the problem with this conception of evolution is that it is in danger of falling into a mystical vitalism and spiritualism with evolution itself getting reified by being treated as a kind of transcendent spiritual force or mind-energy conceived independently of its contingent actualisation in and through duration.

In short, therefore, we can say that Bergson is making the major claim that time has not been taken seriously in previous science. It is his contention that both common sense and science deal with isolated systems, systems which realise themselves 'in the course of time'.[35] Time is reduced to a process of realisation on account of the fact that mechanical explanation treats both the past and the future as calculable functions of the present.[36] As a result time is deprived of efficacy and, in effect, reduced to nothing, having just as much reality for a living being as an hour-glass. This is true of both mechanism and finalism for Bergson; indeed, he contends that finalism is merely an inverted mechanism.[37] Our intellect is not designed to perceive creative evolution at work; for all sorts of practical needs and utilitarian calculations it needs to divide reality and time into instants and segments. In *Creative Evolution* Bergson will oscillate between identifying in matter itself a tendency to constitute isolable systems that can be treated geometrically, and locating such stratification solely and squarely within the reified consciousness of the intellect which is compelled to effect a spatialisation of time in order to procure the satisfaction of its practical needs. While the subdivision of matter into distinct bodies is relative to our perception, it is also true to claim for Bergson that nature itself has closed off and made separable the living body.[38]

Evolution is creative for Bergson because it is characterised by an unending conflict between the cessation of the flow of becoming – in the creation of fixed forms such as organisms and species – and the tendency of the flow of becoming to break out of ossification. For him, matter never goes 'to the end', with the result that the isolation of life 'is never complete' (this is one of the reasons why Bergson is such an interesting and complex finalist). Whatever remains excessive to an isolable system is untouched by science, since it regards the existence of this excess as negligible to its own monitoring of a system's activities. But it is this excess which is important to Bergson:

Our sun radiates heat and light beyond the farthest planet. And, on the other hand, it moves in a certain fixed direction, drawing with it the planets and their satellites. The thread attaching it to the rest of the universe is doubtless very tenuous. Nevertheless it is along this thread that is transmitted down to the smallest particle of the world in which we live the duration immanent to the whole of the universe.[39]

Individuality is a characteristic property of life even though it is difficult to determine precisely its boundaries and borders. As Bergson acknowledges, individuality admits of any number of degrees and is never fully realised anywhere, 'even in man'.[40] He gives the obvious example of plants, an example which has been the subject of a more recent treatment by the biologist Richard Dawkins.[41] The reason why individuality can never be fixed once and for all is owing precisely to the vital character of life. A perfect definition could only be intelligible in relation to a completed reality, but 'vital properties' are never such realities since they exist only as 'tendencies', never as 'states'. Contemporary biologists who work within a certain Kantian tradition of thought, and place the emphasis on the self-organising aspects of life, similarly locate the vital properties of life in the non-equilibrium conditions and specific kinetic pathways which inform the organisation of living systems such as cells and organisms.[42]

Bergson admits that his thinking of creative evolution necessarily partakes of a certain finalism. But he has little time for the view, best expressed in Leibniz's conception of monads as having no windows 'through which something can enter into or depart from them', that life is characterised by an 'internal finality'.[43] This is where Bergson's argument becomes especially novel and interesting. First, he points out that each of the elements which are said to make up the organism may be organisms themselves. Second, he contends that the notion of a finality that is always internal is a self-destructive notion, since it is incapable of accounting for a whole range of phenomena from phagocytes (which attack the organism that feeds them) to germinal cells (which exist independently alongside the somatic cells).[44] It is precisely because there exists neither internal finality nor absolutely distinct individuality that the position of vitalism is so intangible. For Bergson declares if there is finality in the world of life it can only refer to the 'whole of life in a single indivisible embrace'.

It should now be apparent that Bergson means something quite specific by 'evolution'. He wishes to privilege not the thing produced or evolved but the activity of evolution itself, that which is responsible for the generation of new forms. This is important since it allows him to distance himself from theories which posit evolution as a simple or straightforward passage from the homogeneous to the heterogeneous.[45] This is the Spencerian view recently resurrected all too casually in current complexity theory.[46] Bergson's point is that this is to assume a vantage-point from which one can appraise the movements and directions which characterise evolution, transforming it in the process into a linear descent and a story of perfection and progress. This betrays an anthropocentric conceit, namely, the view that that which is more complex is higher in the scale of nature, with man being posited as the ultimate object and goal of evolution. He is opposed to all such attempts.

What would the Bergsonian conception of creative evolution, which places the emphasis on evolution as an unforeseeable and unpredictable process of invention, make of contemporary accounts which seek to show that evolution can be characterised as a process of negentropic complexification? According to the mathematical physicist Frank Tipler, 'progress' is a valid notion that can be applied to evolution in order to interpret its programme.[47] Self-replicating robot intelligence is life's solution to the problem of entropy and final heat-death. If the human species and the biosphere are to survive they must eventually leave the Earth and colonise space, for 'the simple fact of the matter' is that planet Earth is doomed – its sun is destined to burn out and the Earth destined to vaporise. Fortunately, life has devised a plan (reason is so cunning!) to deal with this problem, and this resides in the process of increasing complexification that will establish once and for all the immateriality of matter. What increases and progresses over time is the complexity of information coded by the most complex species of a given genus, order or class. This means an increased ability to survive and to deal with environmental change because of more complexity in the nervous system. 'It is the complexity of the human nervous system that will enable life to escape the greatest environmental challenge of all, the destruction of the earth by the sun.'[48] The anthropocentric arrogance of this view is evident in Tipler's claim that in order to survive, intelligent life 'must use the chaos in the physical laws to force the evolution of the universe into one of a very restricted number of possible futures. Its very survival requires life to impose order on the universe.'[49]

It is not a question of doubting that life has invented means of defying the second law of thermodynamics – the most 'metaphysical' of the laws of physics, according to Bergson[50] – but simply of demonstrating that it is erroneous to ascribe a vitalist teleology to the movements of negentropy on planet Earth in which the apotheosis of complexity is equated with 'human' intelligence, an intelligence whose evolutionary task and *telos* is to 'save' the Universe. Vilmos Csanyi has argued that the energy flow passing through the Earth has allowed the living system formed on it to move away from thermodynamic equilibrium, to increase its inner complexity and order through a succession of stable steady states, and to develop dissipative structures – structures capable of maintaining a minimum energy production – which then allow for various kinds of 'organisations' to emerge, from cells to ecosystems.[51] The basic idea is that once you have got more complex adaptive systems they will tend to change in the direction of higher complexity because of simple thermodynamic considerations to do with open systems and spontaneous chemical processes. Similarly, Depew and Weber have suggested that a drive towards complexification can only have a chance of being conceivable if evolution is seen as co-evolution, and if that co-evolution is viewed as a process of partitioning a dynamic ecological system under thermodynamic imperatives, not simply as one involving only morphological and behavioural tinkering.[52] But note, there is nothing finalist in a spiritualist or humanist sense about this evolution of complex systems or alleged 'drive' towards complexification. Creative evolution on this model is about redemption and is reduced to what Bergson insisted it must not be reduced to if we are not to lose sight of its inventive character, namely, a process of manufacture and the realisation of a plan or a programme. His radically intransitive model of creative evolution – evolution is not *for* the benefit of anything – serves the useful purpose of reminding us of the anthropocentric character of all attempts to grant evolution some global or universal meaning in which it gets reduced to a simple manufacturing process of realisation. It is a principle of contingency that such a conception of evolution lacks and which lies at the heart of Bergson's notion.

Like finalism, Bergson's model of creative evolution is committed to a principle of harmony. This harmony, however, proceeds by way of discord and can never be pinpointed as such (its 'vitality' is virtual). The 'identity' of life is due to an 'identity of impulsion' rather than a 'common aspiration'.[53] It is in this context that he clearly states it is illegitimate to assign to life an 'end', since this is human, all too human. On the model of creative evolution the positing of an 'end' of evolution makes no sense, since this would be to reduce creation to the realisation of a pre-existing model. Only once the road has been travelled is the intellect able to mark its direction and judge that where it has got to is where it was going all along. But this is no more than a deception, since 'the road has been created *pari passu* with the act of travelling over it, being nothing but the direction of this act itself'.[54] Evolution is characterised by increasing complexification for Bergson not on account of any plan but simply owing to an original impulse that has divided into divergent lines of evolution: 'Something has grown, something has developed by a series of additions which have been so many creations.'[55] Bergson acknowledges that this particular event of evolution is contingent: evolution, for example, could have developed in terms of one dimension only. If finalism is true, how can we explain cases of convergent evolution, that is, different trajectories of evolution arriving at similar results? Bergson's answer is to appeal to the common impulsion 'at source', pointing out that on his model something of the (virtual) 'whole' must reside in the multifarious parts and divergent paths of evolution. Here the Darwinian notion of 'adaptation' proves inadequate, since it relies on a purely exogenous model of causality which is unable to account for the generation of form, reducing adaptation to mere mechanical adjustment (a point made by complexity theorists writing *contra* Darwinism, such as Goodwin, for example).

So, how should we interpret Bergson's claim that 'an internal push' has carried life 'by more and more complex forms' to 'higher and higher destinies'?[56] Is he proposing that evolution does indeed have a purpose, and is that purpose man? The difficulty stems from the fact that while he rejects both mechanism and finalism, Bergson wishes to take seriously the inventions thrown up by the movement of evolution. His position is complex, but the salient features are: (a) There is progress if we mean by it no more than a 'continual advance in the general direction determined by a first impulsion';[57] (b) Evolution is not simply or only a moving forward. There is also a marking-time, a deviation and a turning back. As much as there is progress there is also 'increasing disorder'; (c) So, 'Before the evolution of life ... the portals of the future remain wide open.'[58] Evolution is too inventive to be governed by the restrictions of a plan. In spite of these important qualifications, often overlooked by commentators, I would contend that the internal push which is forever compelling evolution to 'higher and higher destinies' remains a notion which needs to be jettisoned because of its residual anthropocentrism. Bergson's belief that the movement of life displays a prolific unity and infinite richness to the extent that it rules out its comprehension by the intellect, which is merely one of its aspects, remains unconvincing and, moreover, encases the creativity of evolution in mystery, in a position that is prohibitive and unnecessarily limiting.

Creative evolution for Bergson involves a play between order and disorder, between consciousness and inert matter, between tension and extension, within which contingency plays a major role. This contingency applies both to the forms adopted and invented and to the obstacles that are encountered at any given moment and in any given place. The only two things required for evolution to 'evolve' are, first, an accumulation of energy, and, second, an 'elastic canalization of this energy in variable and indeterminable directions'.[59] This is certainly how life and death have evolved on Earth, but, as Bergson correctly points out, it was not necessary for life to assume a carbonic form. He is prepared to go so far as to assert that it was not even necessary for life to become concentrated in organisms as such, that is, in definite bodies which provide energy flows with ready-made and elastic canals.[60] As we shall see shortly, this is where

Bergson's speculations open out on to the field of non-organic life. One could quite easily argue that to privilege the organism is simply to fall prey to a certain transcendental illusion, namely, the illusion of organic and organismic life.

Bergson reaches the conclusion that there has never been any project or plan of evolution.[61] The animal 'man' is neither prefigured in evolution, nor can it be deemed to be the outcome of the whole of evolution. It is the divergent character of evolution, the fact that it has taken place on many diverse lines, that is decisive. It is only in a special sense that man can be considered to be the 'end' of evolution. Here Bergson seems to be suggesting that although man is an entirely contingent product of the inventive, non-teleological process of evolution – there is no way that we can say that evolution has been searching for man[62] – it is in the case of man that the virtual becomes equal to the actual, so opening up the possibility of a general scrambling of the various codes of life.[63] The interesting question to be posed is why life has assumed the forms it has (plant, animal, vegetable). Bergson answers by suggesting that life is an accumulation of energy which then flows into flexible channels and performs various kinds of work. It is this activity of energy which the vital impulse would 'fain to do all at once', were it not for the fact that its power is limited: 'But the impetus is finite ... It cannot overcome all obstacles. The movement it starts is sometimes turned aside, sometimes divided, always opposed; and the evolution of the organised world is the unrolling of this conflict.'[64] It is as if the vital impulse is the ultimate death which invents forms of life as little death-machines for itself in order to perpetuate itself. This is why Bergson insists that all that is necessary for creative evolution/destruction (the generation of 'free acts') to take place is the accumulation of energy and the canalisation of this energy in variable and indeterminable directions. In the lecture on 'Life and Consciousness' which opens *Mind–Energy*, Bergson expresses it as follows: 'But life as a whole, whether we envisage it at the start or at the end of its evolution, is a double labour of slow accumulation and sudden discharge.'[65] Life-forms are the vehicles through which the vital impulse discharges its energy and reorganises itself for further invention and creation.

Creative involution

The great achievement of Bergson's construal of creative evolution resides in its emphasis on the *élan vital*, the germinal life-force, as an example of intransitive production, that is, the constant elaboration of novel forms without end. Even Darwinian conceptions of evolution remain wedded to transitive models, with 'adaptation' playing the role previously occupied by purpose and 'selection' playing the role formerly assigned to God.[66] In the case of Darwin this results in absurdities such as the view that natural selection works 'by and for the good of each being'.[67]

In spite of Bergson's achievement in thinking evolution intransitively, it remains the case that the vital impulse amounts to a mysterious conception of creative evolution, which is based ultimately on a hylomorphic model. This comes out even more clearly in the lectures which make up *The Creative Mind*, where the emphasis is on the spiritual character of the *élan vital*. Here Bergson speaks of an 'intuition of the vital' arising out of the recognition of the 'indivisible' and 'substantial continuity of the flow of the inner life'.[68] No matter how much science comes to understand more and more about the physico-chemical nature of organised matter, it will always be unable, owing to its Newtonian or mechanistic foundations, to penetrate the 'underlying cause' of this organisation, that is, the vital impulse. The intuition of pure change, therefore, must necessarily be a spiritual thing and 'impregnated with spirituality'.[69] Although the unity of life must always appear at the end of any search, such a unity will always be a rich and full 'unity of a continuity'.[70] On this hylomorphic model, matter is never so deterministic as to prohibit relaxation which then allows consciousness to install itself.[71] All invention in evolution, therefore, can be seen as the result of consciousness and spirit acting upon elastic matter. Matter is blind and dumb, 'subject to necessity, devoid of memory';[72] consciousness, on the other hand, is that alone which is capable of free, spontaneous action: 'continuity of a creation in a duration in which there is real growth'.[73] In spite of his commitment to the necessary involvement of matter and consciousness, Bergson remains wedded to a hylomorphic schema. This partly explains why Bergson remains an evolutionist and humanist.[74] If consciousness is action continually creating and enriching itself, and if matter is this action continually unmaking itself and using itself up, then it is possible to 'see in the whole evolution of life on our planet a crossing of matter by a creative consciousness, and effort to set free, by force of ingenuity and invention, something which in the animal still remains imprisoned and is only finally released when we reach man'.[75] Bergson's residual perfectionism is clearly in evidence in his belief that the vital impulse is such that it has driven life to greater and greater risks of complexification 'towards its goal of ever higher and higher efficiency'.[76] But he then goes on to recognise that the apparent teleological movement of the vital impulse is an illusion: there has not been the one single direction, there is not a main line of evolution (such as hominid life), and the different life-forms (species) do not represent so many stages along a single route that has been searching for its goal via obstacles, setbacks, subterranean passages and blind alleys.

Bergson grants primacy to movement over solidified forms. But is he in danger of taking the invention of the form of man too seriously? I have argued that his conception of 'creative evolution' remains informed by a residual perfectionism, to the extent that one might locate in his thesis a metaphysics of presence in which 'man' is the privileged life-form, an apotheosis of the entire movement of matter and spirit, because in the becoming of his being the virtual finds its actual.[77] However, there are resources in Bergson for a non-organismic mapping of evolution which will take us well beyond any residual perfectionism and anthropocentrism. In this final section of the essay I want to try to show this through linking up Bergson's subtle and sophisticated vitalism – where a principle of vitality does not reside in the organism but only in genetic energy – with, first, the work of Richard Dawkins, and, second, with the work of Gilles Deleuze and Félix Guattari.

Dawkins's innovation is to come up with the notion of the extended phenotype. He introduces the idea in the context of the classic Darwinian debate over the object of evolution by natural selection, and contends that if it is legitimate to speak of adaptations as being about benefits, then these accrue to germ-line replicators and not to individual organisms.[78] The most important replicator is the gene, or to be more precise, the gene-fragment or network. We need to bear in mind on this model that genes are not selected directly but by proxy, that is, by their phenotypic effects. It is only for reasons of convenience that we think of these effects as being packaged or contained in discrete bodies or entities, such as individual organisms. Dawkins, however, holds that the replicator should be thought of as having *extended* phenotypic effects which are made up of all its effects on the world, and not just on the individual body in which it happens to be sitting.[79] He is referring here to the phenomenon of 'genetic action at a distance'. All bodies are made up of parasites, symbionts which infiltrate the systems of the host.

Dawkins has expressed the central theorem of the extended phenotype as follows: '*An animal's behaviour tends to maximize the survival of the genes 'for' that behaviour, whether or not those genes happen to be in the body of the particular animal performing it.*'[80] In spite of its entanglement in some of the most dubious aspects of neo-Darwinism, such as the idea that evolution acts 'for' something (gene replication) and the view that evolution is simply about competitive reproductive success and survival, the extended phenotype comes very close to what Deleuze and Guattari mean by transversal communication, communication of matter and information across phyletic lineages without fidelity to relations of species and genus. On this Darwinian model there is clearly more going on than simply mechanistic adaptation. The walls of the organism may be real, but they are also porous, allowing for becomings in evolution:

These phenotypic consequences are conventionally thought of as being restricted to a small field around the replicator itself, its boundaries being defined by the body wall of the individual organism in whose cells the replicator sits. But the nature of the causal influence of gene on phenotype is such that it makes no sense to think of the field of influence as being limited to intracellular biochemistry. We must think of each replicator as the centre of a field of influence on the world at large. Causal influence radiates out from the replicator, but its power does not decay with distance according to any simple mathematical law. It travels wherever it can, far or near, along available avenues, avenues of intracellular biochemistry, of intercellular chemical and physical interaction, of gross bodily form and physiology. Through a variety of physical and chemical media it radiates out beyond the individual body to touch objects in the world outside, inanimate artefacts and even other living organisms.[81]

Dawkins situates the whole biosphere on the plane of this intricate network of fields of influence, speaking of a 'web of phenotypic power'.[82] The key insight is that interactions are taking place among not only different gene-pools, but also among different phyla and different kingdoms.[83] As to why germinal life assumes organismic form, the answer Dawkins provides is very close to Bergson, even though he expresses it in very different language: 'An organism is the physical unit associated with one single life cycle. Replicators that gang up in multicellular organisms achieve a regularly recycling life history, and complex adaptations to aid their preservation, as they progress through evolutionary time.'[84] The important insight, therefore, is that organisms need to be treated as 'complex assemblages'.[85]

The extended phenotype which communicates beyond the confines of the organism is a good way of capturing the significance of what Deleuze and Guattari call the *machinic* phylum in which evolution takes place via modes of symbiosis and contagion. A rhizomatic model of evolution places the emphasis on the importance of communication across phyletic lineages, in contrast to the widespread usage in evolutionary theory of genealogical tree models where evolution gets mapped out only in terms of relations of filiation and descent. A rhizome is an assemblage of heterogeneous components, a multiplicity which functions beyond the opposition of the one and the many. It is neither a One which becomes Two (which would be to presuppose evolution as involving little more than a linear accumulation), nor a multiple that is either derived from a One or to which One might be added: 'It is composed not of units but of dimensions, or rather directions in motion.'[86] The rhizome is 'anti-genealogy', since it operates not through filiation or descent but via 'variation, expansion, conquest, capture, offshoots'.[87] It is the rhizome that Deleuze and Guattari wish to privilege as the most inventive domain of 'creative evolution'.

It is in the plateau entitled 'Memories of a Bergsonian' (in *A Thousand Plateaus*) that Deleuze and Guattari introduce the notion of 'blocks of becoming' as a way of breaking out of the grip of evolutionism which configures natural history in terms of a grand mimology. Within germinal life there is a subterranean level of 'animal becomings' (such becomings refer to the domain of transversal communication which takes place on the level of ethological *affect*). As in the movement from the virtual to the actual, a process of becoming involves neither resemblance nor imitation. Becoming-animal does not involve the desire on the part of a subject 'to become' an animal as if one were attaining some realisable state or condition. Nor is it a question of playing or imitating an animal, since becoming 'produces nothing other than itself'.[88] In speaking of this reality that is specific to becoming, Deleuze and Guattari refer to Bergson's notion of the coexistence of different durations which subsist in communication.[89] This is to bring Bergsonism – the emphasis on virtual times, on multiplicities and so on – into play with the non-evolutionist field of transversal communication. Becoming is of a different order than filiation, simply because it concerns alliances which cut across phyletic lineages: 'If evolution includes any veritable becomings, it is in the domain of *symbioses* that bring into play beings of totally different scales and kingdoms, with no possible filiation.'[90] Machinic evolution – 'originality in neoevolutionism' – is now mapped as creative involution. Involution is removed from its association with regression – regression always involves a movement in the direction of something less differentiated – and is conceived in terms of the formation of a block that creates abstract lines which allow for true passage beneath any assignable relations. The domain of involution can be considered to be 'creative' because its field of production is not differenciation (whether more or less), but the formation of blocks which create their own lines of invention and which allow for non-filiative becomings. Involution produces a dissolution of form and a freeing of times and speeds.[91] An animal can be defined not only in terms of characteristics of species and genus but also in terms of populations which vary from milieu to milieu and even within the same milieu (this would enrich any plausible account of the phenomenon of speciation). This is Dawkins's point too, namely, that evolution cannot be restricted to individual organisms, since at the molecular level one is dealing with populations of genetic material whose communication is not governed by fixed or deterministic organismic boundaries.

The mapping of multiplicity in *A Thousand Plateaus* refers back in a complicated manner to Deleuze's 1960s reading of Bergson. In his book on Bergson, Deleuze notes that it is the failure to distinguish between two types of multiplicity which generates false notions of intensity. The two types he is referring to are a multiplicity of space and one of pure duration, where the former is quantitative (one of exteriority, juxtaposition, order, and discrete) and the latter is qualitative (based on fusion, heterogeneity, organisation, and continuous).[92] The multiple is not opposed to the 'one', therefore; instead a distinction is to be made between types of multiplicity. However, this is no simple opposition that is to be or to become the subject of a dialectical *Aufhebung*. Even in *Bergsonism* Deleuze is insistent that Bergson's philosophical project was to effect a 'double progression': not only to complicate time in duration, but equally to conceive space as other than simply a form of exteriority ('a sort of screen that denatures duration'). To effect this transformation it will be necessary in any mapping of space to situate space intensively, 'based in things, in relations between things and between durations'.[93] This reading of Bergson is taken up again and continued in *A Thousand Plateaus*.[94]

It is on this question of multiplicities that a rapprochement between Bergsonism and neo-Darwinism (population thinking) can be established. Deleuze and Guattari credit the latter with a 'double deepening' of biology consisting of, on the one hand, an attention to populations as multiplicities in the Bergsonian sense (species are nothing other than populations), and, on the other hand, an equally important attention to degrees of development in terms of speeds, rates, coefficients and differential relations.[95] Taken together, these contributions help to steer biology in the direction of a nomadology or 'science of multiplicities'. In the former case, it means that forms of life cannot be taken to pre-exist a population: 'The more a population assumes divergent forms, the more its multiplicity divides into multiplicities of different nature.'[96] In the case of substituting rates for degrees the effect is to show that the degrees of development are not pre-existing ones awaiting their perfection through a process of realisation (as in the doctrine of preformationism), but rather function as global and relative equilibriums within the context of the advantages they bestow on particular multiplicities operating with a particular variation in particular milieus. This means that 'degrees are no longer measured in terms of increasing perfection or a differenciation and increase in the complexity of the parts, but in terms of differential relations and coefficients, such as selective pressure, catalytic action, speed of propagation, rate of growth, evolution, mutation, etc.'[97]

It should be noted that in *Creative Evolution* the neo-Darwinism Bergson is engaging with is not that of population thinking, which comes later, but rather the neo-Darwinism effected by the Weismannian turn of the 1880s. The difference is important, since it explains how it is possible for Deleuze and Guattari to revise Bergson's original appraisal of Darwinism and to effect a novel link between Bergsonism and Darwinism. It will be recalled that Bergson's quarrel with Darwinism is based on his claim that while it can explain the 'sinuosities' of the movement of evolution, it cannot explain the movement itself. Deleuze and Guattari's utilisation of the modern synthesis and population thinking suggests an important revision of this claim.

Finally, on the question of Bergson and hylomorphism, one could contend that this question has to be situated as a moment within a wider and more originary problematic. This concerns nature or life as a 'plane of consistency' in which the univocal *is* the multiple (pluralism = monism). For in the end we need to appreciate that the distinctions we make between nature and artifice, between lower and higher, and differences in level or orders of magnitude, are arbitrary in relation to the transversal inventiveness of evolution/involution: there is only the 'silent dance' of the deterritorialised movement of the most disparate things.[98] This is the domain of vital 'machinic' becomings first opened up by Bergson in his original thinking on the matter of creative evolution, and the sphere where his ideas remain apposite to the concerns of an inventive philosophical biology.

Notes

1 L. Johnson, 'The Thermodynamic Origin of Ecosystems: a Tale of Broken Symmetry', in B. H. Weber, D. J. Depew and J. D. Smith, *Entropy, Information, and Evolution: New Perspectives on Physical and Biological Evolution* (Cambridge, Mass., MIT Press, 1988), pp. 75–105: p. 88.

2 G. Deleuze and F. Guattari, *A Thousand Plateaus*, trans. B. Massumi (London, Athlone Press, 1988), p. 499.

3 CE, p. 11/11; OE, p. 503.

4 On this point see G. Kampis, *Self-Modifying Systems in Biology and Cognitive Science* (Oxford, Pergamon Press, 1991).

5 N. Georgescu-Roegen, *The Entropy Law and the Economic Press* (Cambridge, Mass., Harvard University Press, 1971), p. 192; see also René Thom, *Structural Stability and Morphogenesis* (Reading, Mass., W. A. Benjamin Inc., 1975), pp. 158–9. Georgescu-Roegen attributes to Bergson the view that life is characterised by the struggle against the entropic degradation of matter, and acknowledges that this is true for local systems but not for the entire system (*The Entropy Law*, pp. 191–3).

6 CE, pp. 32–3/31, 44–5/42; OE, pp. 520–1, 530–1.

7 CE, p. 61/58; OE, p. 544.

8 CE, p. 107/102; OE, p. 582.

9 G. Simondon, *L'Individu et sa genèse physico-biologique* (Grenoble, Jérôme Millon, [1964] 1995), p. 28, trans. as 'Genesis of the Individual' (introduction only), in J. Crary and S. Kwinter (eds), *Incorporations* (New York, Zone Books, 1992), pp. 296–320: p. 309.

10 B. Goodwin, 'Organisms and Minds: the Dialectics of the Animal–Human Interface in Biology', in T. Ingold (ed.), *What is an Animal?* (London, Routledge, 1994), pp. 100–10: pp. 104–5.

11 *Ibid.*, p. 108.

12 Kampis, *Self-Modifying Systems*, p. 16.
13 R. C. Lewontin cited in F. Varela, E. Thompson and E. Rosch, *The Embodied Mind: Cognitive Science and Human Experience* (Cambridge, Mass., MIT Press, 1995), p. 198.
14 *Ibid.*
15 CE, p. 76/72; OE, p. 556.
16 Gilles Deleuze, 'La Conception de la différence chez Bergson', *Les Etudes Bergsoniennes*, 4 (1956), pp. 77–112 (translation above in this collection).
17 On this link see A. O. Lovejoy, *The Reason, the Understanding, and Time* (Baltimore, Johns Hopkins University Press, 1961), pp. 36–7, 162–83.
18 'A "return to Bergson" does not only mean a renewed admiration for a great philosopher but a renewal and extension of his project today, in relation to the transformations of life and society, in parallel with the transformations of science' (Gilles Deleuze, *Bergsonism*, trans. H. Tomlinson and B. Habberjam (New York, Zone Books, 1988), p. 115).
19 CE, p. 4/4; OE, p. 497.
20 F. Nietzsche, *The Will to Power*, trans. R. J. Hollingdale and W. Kaufmann (New York, Random House, 1968), section 488; see also sections 484–5, 515–16 and Nietzsche's *The Gay Science*, trans. W. Kaufmann (New York, Random House, 1974), section 354. Section 515 of Nietzsche's *The Will to Power* states clearly: 'Not "to know" but to schematize – to impose upon chaos as much regularity and form as our practical needs require.'
21 CE, p. 5/4; OE, p. 498.
22 CE, p. 6/5; OE, p. 499.
23 His argument is not one simply about psychological duration; see Deleuze, *Bergsonism*, pp. 48, 76.
24 CE, pp. 22–3/21; OE, p. 512.
25 Deleuze, *Bergsonism*, p. 104.
26 Gilles Deleuze, *Cinema 1: The Movement-Image*, trans. Hugh Tomlinson and Barbara Habberjam (London, Athlone Press, 1986), p. 9.
27 CE, p. 19/18; OE, pp. 509–10.
28 CE, p. 20/19; OE, p. 510.
29 *Ibid.*
30 *Ibid.*
31 CE, p. 27/26; OE, p. 516.
32 On Weismann (1834–1914) see F. Jacob, *The Logic of Living Systems*, trans. B. E. Spillman (London, Allen Lane, 1974), pp. 215–17 and D. J. Depew and B. H. Weber, *Darwinism Evolving: Systems Dynamics and the Genealogy of Natural Selection* (Cambridge, Mass., MIT Press, 1996), pp. 187–91. For Weismann reproduction is possible through the germ cells which differ in their function and structure from the somatic cells. The germ cells are not a product of the organism and the germ line forms 'the skeleton of the species, on which the individuals are attached like excrescences' (Jacob, *Logic*, p. 216). Weismann's work introduced into biology the famous 'barrier' by which changes in the phenotype in the lifetime of an individual have no effect on the genotype. His thesis was updated in work in molecular biology in the 1950s which sought to demonstrate that no information in the properties of somatic proteins can be transferred to the nucleic acids of DNA. For further insight into Weismann's influence on the philosophical discourse of modernity see Keith Ansell Pearson, *Germinal Life: The Difference and Repetition of Deleuze* (London, Routledge, 1999).

33 CE, p. 28/27; OE, p. 517.
34 CE, p. 20/19; OE, p. 510.
35 CE, p. 10/9; OE, p. 502.
36 CE, p. 39/37; OE, p. 526.
37 CE, p. 41/39; OE, p. 528.
38 CE, p. 13/12; OE, p. 504.
39 CE, pp. 11/10–11; OE, p. 503.
40 CE, p. 13/12; OE, p. 505.
41 R. Dawkins, *The Extended Phenotype* (Oxford, Oxford University Press, 1983), pp. 253–4.
42 Cf. J. S. Wicken, *Evolution, Thermodynamics, and Information: Extending the Darwinian Paradigm* (Oxford, Oxford University Press, 1987), pp. 30–1.
43 See G. W. Leibniz, *Monadology: an Edition for Students*, ed. N. Rescher (London, Routledge, 1991), pp. 58 ff.
44 CE, p. 44/41; OE, p. 530.
45 CE, p. 52/49; OE, pp. 536–7.
46 See R. Lewin, *Complexity* (London, Dent, 1993), pp. 147–9.
47 See F. Tipler, *The Physics of Immortality: Modern Cosmology, God and the Resurrection of the Dead* (London, Macmillan, 1995). At the start of his book Tipler states that his book is a description of the Omega Point Theory, establishing de Chardin's poetic articulation of it on a much more scientific basis, so offering a 'testable physical theory for an omnipresent, omniscient, omnipotent God who will one day in the far future resurrect every single one of us to live forever in an abode which is in all essentials the Judeo-Christian heaven'. In his recent *Fabric of Reality* (London, Allen Lane, 1997), David Deutsch has utilised Tipler's ideas but has sought – in vain, I believe – to separate the genuinely scientific core of the argument from its theological shell.
48 Tipler, *The Physics of Immortality*, p. 123.
49 *Ibid.*, p. xi.
50 CE, p. 256/243; OE, p. 701.
51 V. Csanyi, *Evolutionary Systems and Society: a General Theory of Life, Mind, and Culture* (Durham, NC and London, Duke University Press, 1989).
52 Depew and Weber, *Darwinism Evolving*, pp. 425–6.
53 CE, p. 54/51; OE, p. 538.
54 *Ibid.*
55 CE, p. 56/53; OE, p. 540.
56 CE, p. 107/102; OE, p. 581.
57 CE, p. 109/104; OE, p. 583.
58 CE, pp. 110/104–5; OE, p. 584.
59 CE, p. 269/255; OE, p. 711.
60 Bergson's notion of creative evolution relies heavily on a principle of contingency, to the extent that it is opposed to all conceptions of evolution which have recourse to a superhuman power which designs its course in advance: 'We hold … that in the domain of life the elements have no real and separate existence. They are manifold mental views of an indivisible process. And for that reason there is radical contingency in progress, incommensurability between what goes before and what follows – in short, duration' (CE, p. 30, n. 2/29, n. 1; OE, p. 519, n. 2).
61 CE, p. 280/265; OE, p. 720.
62 This is a view argued for by Kevin Kelly in his recent *Out of Control: the New Biology of Machines* (London, Fourth Estate, 1994). For a critique see Keith Ansell

Pearson, *Viroid Life: Perspectives on Nietzsche and the Transhuman Condition* (London, Routledge, 1997).

63 See also CE, pp. 192/182, 195/185; OE, pp. 649–50, 653, where Bergson posits the difference between animals and man as not one of degree but of kind.

64 CE, pp. 267–8/254; OE, p. 710.

65 ME, p. 19; OE, p. 825.

66 Admittedly, 'adaptation' is construed in Darwinism only in terms of an *apparent* universal purposiveness. Selection works by mysterious but ultimately mechanistic means. For a recent reinstatement of the classical view see D. C. Dennett, *Darwin's Dangerous Idea: Evolution and the Meanings of Life* (London, Allen Lane, 1995), J. S. Wicken, 'Thermodynamics, Evolution, and Emergence: Ingredients for a New Synthesis', in Weber, Depew and Smith, *Entropy, Information, and Evolution*, pp. 139–73: pp. 151 ff. and D. J. Depew and B. H. Weber, 'Consequences of Nonequilibrium Thermodynamics for the Darwinian Tradition', *ibid.*, pp. 317–54: p. 348.

67 C. Darwin, *The Origin of Species* (Harmondsworth, Penguin, 1985), p. 459.

68 CM, p. 32/35; OE, p. 1273.

69 CM, p. 33/37; OE, p. 1274.

70 CM, p. 31/35; OE, p. 1272.

71 ME, p. 18; OE, pp. 824–5.

72 ME, p. 22; OE, p. 828.

73 ME, p. 23; OE, p. 828.

74 For Bergson's humanism, which has much to commend it, see his fascinating account of joy in ME, pp. 29–30; OE, pp. 832–3, and this passage: 'Man, called on at every moment to lean on the totality of his past in order to bring his weight to bear more effectively on the future, is the great success of life' (ME, p. 32; OE, p. 834).

75 ME, p. 23; OE, p. 828.

76 ME, p. 24; OE, p. 829.

77 Constantin Boundas has sought to defend Bergson's philosophy of duration against the 'charge' of 'another philosophy of presence' (see 'Deleuze–Bergson: an Ontology of the Virtual', in P. Patton (ed.), *Deleuze: a Critical Reader* (Oxford, Basil Blackwell, 1996), pp. 81–107: pp. 100–1). This is a persuasive argument in regard to the matter of time in Bergson, but will not, I believe, rescue Bergson in the case of man.

78 Dawkins has noted the proximity of his theory of the 'selfish gene' to the neo-Darwinian turn of Weismann's doctrine of the continuity of the germ-plasm. See R. Dawkins, *The Selfish Gene* (Oxford, Oxford University Press, 1989), p. 11.

79 Dawkins, *The Selfish Gene*, p. 4. It should be noted that for Dawkins the extended phenotype is still subject to laws of natural selection: 'Evolution is the external and visible manifestation of the differential survival of alternative *replicators* … Genes are replicators; organisms and groups of organisms are best not regarded as replicators; they are *vehicles* in which replicators travel about' (Dawkins, *The Extended Phenotype*, p. 82).

80 Dawkins, *The Extended Phenotype*, p. 233.

81 *Ibid.*, pp. 237–8.

82 *Ibid.*, p. 238.

83 *Ibid.*, p. 245.

84 *Ibid.*, p. 259; it is precisely the matter of 'evolutionary time' which is not being thought out here, as in all biology.

85 *Ibid.*, p. 263.

86 Deleuze and Guattari, *A Thousand Plateaus*, p. 21.

87 *Ibid.*

88 *Ibid.*, p. 238.
89 *Ibid.*
90 *Ibid.*
91 *Ibid.*, p. 267.
92 Deleuze, *Bergsonism*, p. 38.
93 *Ibid.*, p. 49.
94 Deleuze and Guattari, *A Thousand Plateaus*, pp. 483–5.
95 *Ibid.*, p. 48.
96 *Ibid.*
97 *Ibid.*
98 *Ibid.*, p. 69.

p. a. y. gunter

BERGSON AND THE WAR AGAINST NATURE

Bergson's philosophy has not entered into contemporary discussions of man and his relationships to nature, discussions sometimes classified under headings like 'environmental ethics' or 'eco-philosophy'. Though one finds stray references to Bergson's implicit environmentalism in the literature, one thinks instead in this respect of figures like John Muir or Aldo Leopold, of Martin Heidegger or A. N. Whitehead.[1] This is understandable. Bergson does not condemn the environmental destructiveness of modern technology, the loss of wilderness or the fate of endangered species. His attention appears to be directed exclusively towards man and what he might become.

In spite of this emphasis, I will argue that Bergson's thought provides a strong basis for environmentalism. Bergson's ecological connections lie just beneath the surface of his thought, and could easily have been developed. The slightest shift in our view of his philosophy makes them explicit.

Several approaches might be used to illuminate the 'green' Bergson. This essay will employ three, examining in turn his theory of knowledge, which accepts modern science and technology but submits them to a sharp critique; his concept of evolution, which locates man squarely *in* nature and stresses man's kinship to all living creatures; and his social philosophy, which, in its reflections on warfare and its elimination, recapitulates – and perhaps adds to – contemporary attempts to eliminate war against nature. These three aspects of Bergsonism 'interpenetrate': they interlock and reinforce each other.

Epistemology

Though he is hardly the first philosopher to use the term 'intuition' – one thinks, for example, of Spinoza and Schelling among the moderns – Bergson certainly popularised it in twentieth-century philosophy. Intuition, he argues, is a very rich knowledge by acquaintance which allows us to get 'into' our world and recover its dynamic, qualitative character. To intuition he opposes 'analysis' (sometimes specified as 'intelligence' or 'intellect'), an abstract knowledge by description.

Intuition, he insists, does not come to us easily. *Primum vivere*: we are practical creatures who must be able to live before we can philosophise. If we analyse our world, it is in order to adapt to and control it. Patterns of analysis are second nature to human beings, which, he suggests, should be defined not as *Homo sapiens* (man the knower) but as *Homo faber* (man the maker). Between a profound knowledge and sheer pragmatism there is a tension: a kind of epistemic 'gap'.

In Bergson's earlier writings the tension between intuition and analysis is worked out in terms of our personal human experience. In his later writings it is extended to deal with biological, physical, cosmological and social phenomena. In each case a similar claim is made: analysis misconstrues a reality which intuition can recapture. Beyond analytical concepts lies a dynamic, profoundly interrelated phenomenon which philosophy attempts to regain.

What is it about analysis which, in his view, leads 'analytical' thought to misconstrue our world? Trying, in 'Introduction to Metaphysics' (1903), to describe the essential difference between analysis and intuition, Bergson states:

> That is to say, analysis operates on immobility, while intuition is located in mobility or, what amounts to the same thing, in duration. That is the very clear line of demarcation between intuition and analysis. One recognises the real, the actual, the concrete by the fact that it is variability itself. One recognises the element by the fact that it is invariable. And it is invariable by definition, being a schema, a simplified reconstruction, often a mere symbol, in any case, a view taken of the reality that flows.[2]

But it is impossible to create movement out of immobilities. To do so is, in effect, to commit the fallacy of composition.[3]

This analytical direction in our attitude towards things accounts, Bergson believes, not only for our use of static concepts, but for the way we view experience:

> I have isolated from the whole of the inner life that psychological entity which I call a simple sensation. So long as I study it I suppose it to remain what it is. If I were to find some change in it, I should say that it was not a simple sensation, but several successive sensations; and it is to each one of the succeeding sensations that I should then transfer the immutability at

first attributed to the whole sensation. In any case I shall, by carrying analysis far enough, be able to arrive at elements I shall hold to be immovable.[4]

The knowledge by acquaintance which he terms intuition would thus not
be limited to sensation, but would include a far broader, more fugitive
component of experience. This Bergson calls 'duration'. There will turn
out to be innumerable 'levels' and kinds of duration: that is, of process, of
becoming. The task of philosophy will be to explore them.

To do so, however, is inevitably to critique, and move beyond, what
Bergson takes to be both perceptual and conceptual prejudices. Thus,
speaking of associationist psychology's attempt to resolve the self into psychological 'atoms' constrained by quasi-mechanical laws, he argues:

> What I find beneath these clear-cut crystals and this superficial congelation
> is a continuity of flow comparable to no other flowing I have ever seen. It is
> a succession of states each of which announces what follows and contains
> what precedes. Strictly speaking they do not constitute multiple states until
> I have already got beyond them, and turn around to observe their trail.
> While I was experiencing them they were so solidly organised, so pro-
> foundly animated with a common life, that I could never have said where
> any one of them finished or the next one began. In reality, none of them do
> begin or end; they all dove-tail into one another.[5]

The self is not a series of discrete 'states' from moment to moment, nor at
any one moment is it made up of such states. Nor is it, therefore, constrained – except superficially – by mechanical or quasi-mechanical laws.
As Bergson will try to demonstrate, this will be true of many phenomena,
not only our psychological existence.

Underlying this sketch of fundamental features in Bergson's epistemology is an assumption which is all too easily overlooked. From the ordinary
standpoint, intuition appears to be fleeting, insubstantial, subjective. By
contrast, our analytical concepts – those of our contemporary technological and scientific paradigms – appear to be substantial, permanent, objective.

Bergson's acceptance of the practical function of human intelligence –
of analysis – is subversive of our confidence in the perfect objectivity and
imperishable truth of its conceptual schemes, however. The given, he
argues, is qualitative and dynamic, and always exhibits an element of continuity. Analysis, with its quest for 'simples' out of which reality will be
reconstructed, not only 'freezes' what it touches, it ignores continuity and
breaks up its object into isolated parts. What reason is there to believe that
conceptual schemes developed on the basis of this procedure portray reality with perfect objectivity, or that our conceptual schemes will not change
from time to time? The 'simples' from which we will attempt to recon-

struct reality may change, as might our ways of conceiving their interrelations. We have such faith in them not because they are perfect representations of reality but because they *work*. But this – their sheer effectiveness – is no proof of their perfect noetic status.

Given the limitations of our analytical schemes – even if these limitations are only partial – why not appeal to intuition, not as a perception by the mind of the 'self-evidence' of some sort of truth, but as a participation in the processes of things? One would then at least have the hope of escaping conceptual structures founded essentially on the need to control and reshape our world. One would have the possibility of access to real events. Hence Bergson's conviction that intuition is both objective and pacific:

> the scientist, obliged to take immobile views of movement and to gather repetitions along a path where nothing is repeated, intent also upon dividing reality conveniently on successive planes where it is deployed in order to submit it to the action of man, is obliged to use craft with nature, to adopt toward it the wary attitude of an adversary, the philosopher treats nature as a comrade. The rule of science is the one posited by Bacon: obey in order to command. The philosopher neither obeys or commands; he seeks to be at one with nature.[6]

It is easy to imagine a Thoreau or a Muir – or their multitudinous green descendants – nodding agreement. A philosophy that emphasises 'oneness' with nature and critiques our flawed practical approaches to it, clearly bears within it the seeds of an 'ecological consciousness'. So far, though it is an inescapable component of Bergson's thought, this component remains only a very general set of assumptions. To see its concrete consequences it will be necessary to explore the broadening and deepening of the concept of intuition in his later works, and to understand the philosophy of nature to which it gives rise.

Matter, consciousness and evolution

To enter the arguments and data of *Creative Evolution* is to inhabit, at least temporarily, a world far removed from contemporary discussions of DNA, RNA and amino acids, or of selfish genes, stereochemistry and the human genome project. Or so it would appear. The emergence of molecular biology in the second half of the twentieth century has effectively marginalised the more or less 'vitalistic' biologies popular in the century's first fifty years, including Bergson's. Very little appears to suggest that we will see their revival.

There is not space to enter into a discussion of this issue. The goal here, as stated above, is to see how Bergson situates man in evolution and in nature generally. I would like to suggest here, however, that the biology to be explored below takes on a certain plausibility from the recent development of non-linear approaches to biology. Not only the theory of dissipative structures developed by Ilya Prigogine and his colleagues, but the theory of deterministic chaos and the proposed 'science of complexity' suggest the possibility of a very real paradigm-shift away from reductionist accounts of life towards a concept of evolution as truly creative.[7] It is too early to pronounce definitively on the result of this conceptual ferment in the sciences. Should it succeed in fully establishing itself, however, Bergson's theory of evolution will certainly appear in a new light.

'Life', Bergson asserts, is 'consciousness launched into matter'.[8] This is a dark saying for most of us. It gains in intelligibility, however, if we examine, first, his concept of matter, and second, the close relations which on his terms matter has with consciousness. The mutual immanence of these two terms, and their opposition, is for him what gives rise to living organisms.

'Mind' can only be 'in' matter, or conversely, if the two have something fundamental in common. Since the seventeenth century this has been considered implausible, if not self-contradictory.

The ghost of the ill-fated Cartesian dualism hovers over all attempts coherently to interrelate contrasting modes of existence. René Descartes, the author of this dualism, rendered it insoluble by assuming that matter is purely geometrical and mechanical, while mind is unextended and capable of spontaneous action. One thus has two radically different sorts of substances, any interrelations between which are made incomprehensible. Most philosophers today – including those who are scientists – assume that this epistemic and metaphysical dead-end *is* dualism. Dualistic approaches of any other kind are thus rejected out of hand as futile.

Few, however, have thought to question the terms of this dualism: to reconsider their nature in order to see whether, when reconceived, they can be intelligently presumed to interrelate. This, however, was Bergson's originality: to reconceive mind and body not as radically different kinds of substances, but as different modes of duration.

If, for the common sense of our time, matter is assumed to be passive, inert physical 'stuff', for Bergson (as for A. N. Whitehead, to take only one example) this is a misleading appearance. The atoms of ancient atomism, the mass particles of Newtonian mechanics are, he argues, useful fictions, but they might be replaced by more dynamic, flexible concepts. Arguing from the ideas of Faraday and Kelvin and from his own concept of duration, he concludes as early as 1896 that matter is better understood as energy than as mass; that its 'parts' are more interrelated in their nature than can be accounted for by simple particulate (corpuscular) models; and that its successive moments are not series of instantaneous states, but are best conceived as pulses of energy, each of finite breadth.[9] He even suggests that physicists may find measurable indeterminism in the behaviour of matter. Matter thus becomes the lowest as well as the briefest level of duration.[10]

Clearly, nothing could be less Cartesian than this view of matter as temporalised energy, possibly embodying an element of spontaneity. Matter here ceases to be entirely geometrical. As a mode of duration, moreover, it also ceases to be wholly alien to mind, as Bergson understands mind. For Bergson matter, like mind, is comprised of rhythms of duration.[11]

This view of matter, first developed in *Matter and Memory*, is retained in *Creative Evolution*, but is generalised there through a reflection on the science which deals with the transformations of energy: thermodynamics. The first law of thermodynamics is a conservation law according to which no energy enters or leaves the system of nature. The second law, however, is described by Bergson as 'the most metaphysical of the laws of physics'.[12] In prosaic terms, it states that the energies of the physical world become increasingly unavailable to perform work. This means that 'potential energy' gradually decreases; but it means, more profoundly, that the world is gradually losing its structure, its mutability, its – to employ a more recent term – 'information'. The physical world is thus caught up in a continual descent towards increasing disorder. This descent stands in dramatic contrast with the process of biological evolution, which continues to produce organisms increasingly elaborate in structure.

At this point Bergson projects a full-scale cosmology – at once both scientific and philosophical – depicting physical nature as the result of a previous creation, and as detending[13] successively into space. Cosmology thus becomes cosmogony: physical nature is in the making, or rather '*unmaking*'.[14] Both in its parts and as a whole it is a process, a duration of durations.

It might be argued that life is simply an 'emergent' from the physical and chemical characteristics of this matter. But for Bergson the contradiction between the 'downward' descent of matter and the 'upward' ascent of life is too striking to permit such a solution. Another – an inverse – factor is called for if a satisfactory explanation is to be given. As is widely known, he adds to his theory of the nature of matter the postulate of a vital impetus or *élan vital*. Because the creativity of the *élan vital* is strongly contrasted by Bergson with the descent of matter, it is often assumed that it is *separate* from matter. Nothing can be further from the truth. The 'interruption'[15] which constitutes the creation of matter, he states, simultaneously constitutes the emergence of life. The two are literally born together,

and are 'mingled' – for lack of a better word. Life is on these terms, therefore, present wherever matter descends the 'incline' marked by increasing
entropy.[16] It is found *in* matter, as a contrasting mode of duration. Hence
Bergson's speculations on the 'diffuse' character life may have taken in the
universe prior to the emergence of solar systems and planets.[17]

For our purposes the salient point in all of this is that for Bergson life
and matter, though distinguishable, are not separate; though opposed in
important respects, these two modes of duration have a durational nature
in common. Man on these terms is, like all living things, in and participat-
ing in non-living nature.

But if this is true for non-living nature, it is still more true for the biosphere. Man, and all living things, Bergson asserts, 'hold together'.[18] They
are parts of a whole, no members of which can be understood as existing
in splendid isolation from the others. Man, from his own vantage-point, is
not alien to the other creatures, or they to him. He possesses a capacity for
profound sympathy with everything that lives.

To explain this interrelatedness, and the possibility of sympathy, however, it will be necessary to follow the creative advance of evolution as
Bergson describes it. If for him life perpetually diverges from a common
beginning, the sheer plethora of organisms created by this divergence
shows a fundamental threefold pattern: the plants and, among the animals,
the arthropods and vertebrates. Each of these contains characteristics
common to the others. In spite of the 'antagonism'[19] between species, a kinship remains, as do mutually supportive relations.

Bergson is aware of further articulations in the evolutionary tree than
these. The plants are divided by him between soil bacteria and the more
complex plants that depend on them for nourishment. (He suggests that
the fungi be segregated as a distinct group.)[20] Animal evolution is fourfold,
consisting of echinoderms and molluscs as well as arthropods and vertebrates.[21] The major difference between the latter and the former pairs is
behavioural. Encased in armour, molluscs and echinoderms have rela-
tively limited behavioural repertoires. In comparison, arthropods and vertebrates both emphasise mobility. Complex behavioural repertoires
involve choices (at any rate, multiple possibilities), and these, Bergson
believes, involve more intense consciousness.

The arthropods (of which the most completely developed members are
found, he argues, among the social insects) emphasise instinct; the vertebrates (of which the most advanced members are the higher primates,
including man) emphasise intelligence. Instinct involves the use of tools
which are part of the body; intelligence involves the use of tools distinct
from the body. Instinct involves a knowledge – an unlearned awareness –
of living things. Intelligence, by contrast, involves the capacity to shape

non-living matter.[22] If instinct is a capacity to enter into life, intelligence is turned outwards towards the physical world.

Much has been said, *pro* and *contra*, about Bergson's concept of instinct. For our purposes, two points must be made about it. The first is that for him if instinct is emphasised by arthropods, it is also present in vertebrates, including man; intelligence in turn is present in arthropods, though not emphasised by them. The second is that while Bergson compares instinct with intuition, the two cannot simply be identified. Intuition for him is instinct that is 'disinterested, self-conscious, capable of reflecting'.[23] This is in striking contrast with instinct *per se*, which begins with awareness but, he holds, is quickly diverted into unconscious behaviour.[24]

By thus reinterpreting intuition in a biological context, Bergson hopes to enlarge his theory of knowledge and make it understandable in the light of biological evolution. In doing so, he opens the door to the possibility that man has, and can develop, a sympathy for all forms of life. Jung's theory of human 'racial unconscious' is widely known. Bergson proposes that man has not a racial but a biological unconscious: a reminiscence of all the 'vague potentialities' inherent in life. If this could be revived and made reflective, it would provide the basis for a sympathy with all living things.

Holistic life and atomistic intelligence: carving the continuum

If for the author of *Creative Evolution* there is a basis for human sympathy with life – a basis which at least potentially could be revived and made effective – on his terms this could only be achieved by a profound and determined effort. Man, in the common run of affairs, he argues, is inherently a cutter of the continuum of life, a congenitally less than perceptive shatterer of subtle biotic relations. In establishing his epistemology in a biological context he reasserts the tension between intuition and intelligence in a manner which finds its echoes among contemporary environmental philosophers.

Most environmentalists would argue three points: 1) Organisms in nature are profoundly interrelated and interdependent; 2) These interrelations are thoroughly dynamic; 3) Man is one of these organisms and must be conceived as a part of, and not apart from, nature. They would also add that 4) Man, as part of nature, is not the only creature having value; and 5) The complex of ideas developed in Western thought – particularly since the seventeenth century – is not very good at comprehending natural interrelations. All of these assumptions appear in *Creative Evolution*.

That Bergson insists on the profound interrelatedness of evolution and of life should come as no surprise. Insistence on the wholeness of life is probably the most persistent theme of *Creative Evolution*. The various branches of the evolutionary tree, though 'antagonistic' are also 'comple-mentary'.[25] Each of the main directions life has taken, he reiterates, con-tains aspects of the others. Nor is it the case that first one 'branch' grows, followed by the next. From the joint genesis of life and matter to the joint development of plant and animal, arthropod and vertebrate, one finds co-evolution.

If the course of evolution involves co-evolution through continuing interrelation, the biosphere (the result of evolution) exhibits powerful sus-taining interrelations, on Bergson's description. Nitrogen-fixing bacteria supply nutrition to higher-order plants. Ferments and fungi function sim-ilarly, breaking down complex organic substances utilised by plants. Plants in turn furnish nourishment for animals. Plants make oxygen, needed by animals; animals produce nitrogen, needed by plants. Life is a whole,[26] not only because each aspect, like a hologram, contains aspects of all others, but because each aspect depends upon, and often supports, others.

All of this clearly leads to the conclusion that man is a part of, and not *apart from* nature. Man's kinship with, and implication in, the world is threefold: kinship by descent from a common origin, by mutual involve-ment in the web of life, and kinship in value. On Bergson's view con-sciousness is widespread among living things – not concentrated human awareness, but vague sentience and even 'unconsciousness', a dull aware-ness in which reflection is completely neutralised.[27] Hence here, as in the philosophy of A. N. Whitehead, intrinsic value is everywhere in nature: even, as with Whitehead also, in non-living matter.

But if intrinsic value exists by degree in all living things, on Bergson's terms man will be loath to realise it, just as he will be likely to misconstrue the complex web of interdependencies which make up the world of living things. His critiques of 'analysis', 'intelligence', 'intellect' have the same ultimate consequence. *Homo faber* approaches nature as he approaches humankind: with blunt weapons. The human penchant for geometrism and oversimplification operates in a world of profound, often subtle inter-relationships, where boundaries are often not sharp and where change is throughout. It is no wonder that Bergson should have pleaded for more flexible, adaptable, subtle concepts capable of following the 'sinuosities of the real'[28] and should have lamented that the human intellect is charac-terised by a kind of misleading hereditary bias when it comes to concep-tualise living things.[29]

Such assumptions are often voiced by environmentalists, though not in exactly these words. They are sometimes countered by insistence that without good analytic scientific knowledge we can know neither the true causes of our environmental problems nor the manner of their possible cures. I believe that this protest on behalf of science (and usually, technology), though well-founded, can be met on Bergsonian terms. Here, however, it is necessary to move on to a fuller consideration of Bergson's concept of evolution – ultimately his view of man's social evolution. Man's inveterate conceptual attitude and its weaknesses no doubt account for much environmental destruction. But if our conceptual arsenals tend to be faulty, there are still deeper biological and socio-biological factors to be taken account of. These are in no simple sense 'conceptual'.

If life is in principle one, the fact remains that it is divided into a multitude of species. Each of these, Bergson observes, behaves as if it alone existed. The openness of evolution (paradoxically?) creates closed societies. Each particular species is 'a kind of circle':[30] 'Absorbed in the form it is about to take, each species falls into a partial sleep, in which it ignores almost all the rest of life; it fashions itself so as to take the greatest possible advantage of its immediate environment with the least possible trouble.'[31] Instinct, as we have seen, precisely bears out this contention, focusing on life, but only in terms of specific species and specific aspects of these species. Intelligence, Bergson argues, is not a transcendental faculty; it is the coping mechanism and *modus vivendi* of certain sorts of creatures on this planet. We should not be surprised, then, if man, the culmination of intelligence, should behave inveterately as a sort of human racist. If Bergson is right, we are born with a 'species bias'. The question becomes one of how – confronted with the disasters to which this leads – we can overcome it.

Socio-biology and the greening of humankind

The contrast between the openness of evolution and the closure or quasi-closure of its products (species, subspecies) is picked up and developed significantly in Bergson's last major work, *The Two Sources of Morality and Religion* (1932).[32] The most famous contrast stemming from this work is that of the 'Open' and the 'Closed' society: a distinction now as commonplace in sociology and political science as it is among politicians and media persons. Less recognised is the fact that the major practical preoccupation of this concluding work is the elimination of war. This section will deal with the surprising way in which Bergson, in attempting to suggest how wars between nations might be forestalled, always opens the way (we might say ways) to an elimination of the War Against Nature.

One of these 'ways' is practical and direct. If we do not deal with certain basic environmental problems, Bergson argues, there will be war. He is speaking in this context of problems of population, nutrition and luxury, and of the tangled social relations that surround them. Writing in the 1930s, he states: 'Europe is over-populated, the world will soon be in the same condition, and if the self-production of man is not "rationalized", as his labour is beginning to be, we shall have war.[33] The ancients were right. If Venus is allowed to have her way, Mars will follow.[34] Many other causes of war may play their roles: the neglect of agriculture,[35] the closing-off of markets,[36] the cutting-off of fuel and raw materials.[37] But population is the main problem.[38]

A close second to population increase in the causes of war is, Bergson argues, the desire for luxuries.[39] Conditions under which life may be lived reasonably well are considered by modern man to be insufficient; a higher standard of living must be sought – even if a high price must be paid. Nations may then decide to go ahead and *take* what they want from their neighbour or neighbours by force. If luxuries were not considered necessities, however, would wars be as likely to be fought?

Closely connected with the pursuit of luxury are the politics of the sexes. The possibility that woman can make herself man's equal – a possibility Bergson believes is a live option in our times – opens up the likelihood that woman would not require luxuries in order to be happy. That is, Bergson accepts the thesis that the subordination of woman in traditional society is compensated for by the providing of luxuries and, where possible, luxurious lifestyles. Whether this is considered a bribe or an effort to create a kind of justice, Bergson holds, it plays its part in the origination of war.

Finally, and most profoundly, there is the question of closure and openness. *Creative Evolution* portrays the development of life as impelled – and given a certain order – by a common 'impetus'. It is one of the frailties or failures of this process, as we have seen, that each species, born of a common origin and still carrying aspects of that origin within it, none the less lives for itself to the exclusion of others – even though it will certainly depend upon them, as on the entire web of life. Each species, to the extent possible, thus effects a kind of 'closure' in the midst of interdependence.

It is fascinating, in reading *The Two Sources of Morality and Religion*, to watch Bergson – thinking, as Charles Hartshorne notes, as a sociobiologist – reintegrate this fatality of biological evolution into the course of human history.[40] From the hunting–gathering group through the modern nation–state, Bergson argues, human societies have embodied – perhaps even parodied – the closure otherwise reserved for other species. Modern conditions have led to the potential overcoming of closure – indeed, have partially overcome it – in societies more or less open. But the move towards an open society is always threatened. (Writing in the 1930s under the shadow of Nazism, Bergson could hardly have been unaware of the contemporary threat. The extreme closure – the tribalism – of Nazism was an example of exactly the problem Bergson was trying to isolate and analyse.)[41]

Bergson was in favour of trying to overcome the dangers of closure in human societies by all means possible, from education to world government. But he was convinced that these are only stopgap measures, and that the ultimate problem is a function of ultimate concern. That is, the only possible decisive solution to the problem of the closed society and the threat of warfare that it carries with it is a religious one.

Here, as so often in this essay, it is not possible to go into detail. It is Bergson's contention that the open society – to the extent that we have such a society – is the product not of technological advance or national genius or Necessary Progress, but of the Judeo-Christian heritage, more especially of the Christian impulse as sustained and enriched by its saints and mystics (not, one gathers, by its scribes and scholastics, or even by its theologians, as theologians). Bergson does not deny that great religious leaders – profoundly inspired – have existed prior to the Christian era, or outside of it. He believes that certain recent Eastern figures live on as high a plane and with as great a dynamism as any Westerner. Still, he insists that Christianity embodies both a dynamism and a *caritas* which, fully developed, would break down the barriers between races, classes and nations.

All of these arguments are directed against the scourge of war – which, if it has been ruinous in the past, will become sheer disaster in the future with, Bergson hints, the emergence of atomic weapons.[42] It is fascinating to see contemporary environmentalists using exactly the same arguments as Bergson does in *The Two Sources of Morality and Religion*, not against war, but – as we have adumbrated above – against the war against nature.

To point out that environmentalists have insisted on the dangers of overpopulation for the environment is to raise understatement to new heights. From Paul Ehrlich's *The Population Bomb* (1968) to Garrett Hardin's *Naked Emperors* (1982) to the latest publications of the Worldwatch Institute, the threat of burgeoning world population is portrayed – correctly, I think, as casting a long, dark shadow. The shadow, interestingly, points as much to the possibility of war as to environmental disaster. Perhaps environmentalists should insist on the dual danger of war *and* environmental decay. In a planet teeming with hungry multitudes and beset with exhausted resources – and the plague of nuclear proliferation – the certainties of war and of ecological collapse are virtually the same.

Similarly for what might be called the 'auxiliary' problems which compete with overpopulation as sources of human ill. The problem of 'luxury' has gone through a semantic sea change since Bergson's time. Whether discussed under the heading of lifestyle or standard of living, however, it remains the same issue. When discussed – as it often is – in terms of the contrast between West and East (or North and South), it brings with it an aura of potential conflict between regions, if not nations. If Bergson urges his readers to simplify their lives and lifestyles, to counter the frenzy with which modern man has complicated his life while piling luxury upon luxury,[43] his plea finds itself echoed in innumerable contemporary environmental tracts.

In their *Ecofeminism*, Maria Mies and Vandana Shiva state, in the midst of a discussion of 'voluntary simplicity': 'Women's self-esteem in industrialised societies is closely linked to their outward appearance, but in spite of these efforts at compensatory consumption, this need can never be met by buying new clothes; they are pseudo-satisfiers. A deep human need cannot be fulfilled by buying a commodity.'[44] To change this, they argue, a new 'sexual division of labor' will have to be achieved. It is fascinating – even a bit disconcerting – to discover this argument of Bergson's decades later, independently, but directed in this case towards environmental 'peace'.

Finally, there is the religious issue. It can hardly be approached without sparking controversy. Many would urge that it not be approached at all. Still, one wonders what other impulse could lead us to simplify our lives, to overcome differences, to give up our compulsive quest for material goods and social status? The arguments of the philosophers are valuable. But can they ever bring us to effect the transformation of our society and ourselves necessary to protect the planet? Or to expunge the ancient lunacies of war?

Summing-up

This essay has seemed to its author to be as lengthy as it is insufficient. But it has been necessary to review, one after the other, the fundamental arguments-through-opposition of Bergson's philosophy. Intuition/analysis, intelligence/instinct, interpenetration/externality, disinterest/interest, open/closed, male/female … In working one's way through Bergson's antitheses one is haunted by the sense of an environmental awareness always implicit, rarely brought to the surface. It is only necessary to shift the focus slightly (the metaphor here could be a microscope or, better, a kaleidoscope) for the environmental import of Bergson's position to be clear.

Two points follow from this. The first is that Bergson's various arguments, related to nature, are *systematic*. All, from varying perspectives, point to a characteristic approach to the environment, one which values the world in its interconnectedness and critiques the pragmatic habits and concepts which break this interconnectedness and diminish or destroy value, along with the human racism which would prefer to ignore the damage done.

But there is something else to be learned from this systematic approach. How striking it is that the arguments Bergson used to protest against the devaluing and manipulation of people can be used to protest against the devaluing and manipulation of nature. Granted, this development of his thought would not be possible if Bergson did not already presume the existence of a real world containing real value. It is extremely revealing to see the extent to which the same arguments, by a turn of the conceptual kaleidoscope, can be deflected to the defence of nature. From the vantage-point of the history of ideas this is most instructive. Environmentalism does not begin *ex nihilo* in the history of recent thought.

Notes

1 One does, however, occasionally find a nod in this direction. A. R. Lacey concludes that were Bergson alive today, his vote might well go to the Greens (A. R. Lacey, *Bergson* (London, Routledge, 1989), p. 219). Bernard d'Espagnat, pointing out that the views of Bergson and similar thinkers are still 'intuitive and quite widespread in an implicit way', concludes that 'Most ecologists are latent Bergsonians' (Bernard d'Espagnat, *In Search of Reality* (New York, Springer-Verlag, 1983), p. 102). In her *Ecology in the 20th Century: a History* (New Haven, Yale University Press, 1989, pp. 54, 216–18), Anna Bramwell notes that in 1970 supporters of the Soil Association – the first effectively organised environmental pressure-group in Great Britain – cited Bergson's work as one of their inspirations.

2 CM, pp. 180/212–13; OE, pp. 1412–13.

3 CM, pp. 181/213, 189–90/223–4; OE, pp. 1413, 1421.

4 CM, p. 178/210–11; OE, p. 1411.

5 CM, p. 163/192; OE, p. 1397.

6 CM, pp. 126/148–9; OE, p. 1362.

7 Ilya Prigogine and Isabelle Stengers, *Order out of Chaos: Man's New Dialogue with Nature* (New York, Bantam Books, 1984), pp. 195–6, 207–9; Ilya Prigogine and Isabelle Stengers, *Entre le temps et l'éternité* (Paris, Fayard, 1988), pp. 19–22, 192–3; James Gleick, *Chaos: Making a New Science* (New York, Viking, 1988), pp. 308–14, 339; Stuart A. Kauffman, *The Origins of Order: Self-Organization and Selection in Evolution* (New York, Oxford University Press, 1993), p. 709. Cf. also P. A. Y. Gunter, 'Bergson on Non-linear Non-equilibrium Thermodynamics: an Application of Method', *Revue International de Philosophie*, 45 (177) (1991), pp. 108–21.

8 CE, p. 191/181; OE, p. 649.

9 MM, p. 278/208; OE, p. 343.

10 On this point see especially David A. Sipfle, 'Henri Bergson and the Epochal Theory of Time', in P. A. Y. Gunter (ed.), *Bergson and the Evolution of Physics* (Knoxville, University of Tennessee Press, 1969), pp. 275–94.

11 MM, pp. 266/201, 270/204; OE, pp. 337, 339.

12 CE, p. 256/243; OE, p. 701.

13 CE, p. 213/202; OE, p. 666.

14 CE, p. 258/245; OE, p. 703.

15 CE, p. 260/247; OE, p. 705.

16 CE, pp. 256–7/243; OE, p. 701.

17 CE, pp. 270–1/256–7; OE, p. 713.
18 CE, pp. 285–6/271; OE, pp. 724–5.
19 CE, pp. 135/129, 273/259; OE, pp. 604, 714–15.
20 CE, p. 112/107; OE, p. 586.
21 CE, pp. 136–9/130–2; OE, pp. 605–7.
22 CE, pp. 168–70/160–1; OE, pp. 630–1.
23 CE, p. 186/176; OE, p. 645.
24 CE, pp. 152–3/145; OE, p. 618.
25 CE, pp. 122–4/116–17; OE, pp. 594–5.
26 CE, pp. 39/37, 46/43; OE, pp. 526, 531.
27 CE, pp. 151/143–4; OE, pp. 616–17.
28 CE, pp. 107/102, 224/213; OE, pp. 582, 675.
29 CE, pp. 111–14/105–8; OE, pp. 585–7.
30 CE, p. 134/128; OE, p. 603.
31 CE, p. 135/129; OE, p. 604.
32 MR, p. 308; OE, pp. 1237–8.
33 MR, p. 290; OE, p. 1222.
34 Ibid.
35 MR, pp. 305–6; OE, pp. 1235–6.
36 MR, p. 289; OE, p. 1221.
37 Ibid.
38 MR, pp. 288–91; OE, pp. 1221–3.
39 MR, pp. 287, 289, 291, 297–8; OE, pp. 1221, 1223, 1228–9.
40 Charles Hartshorne, 'Bergson's Aesthetic Creationism Compared to Whitehead's', in Andrew Papanicolaou and P. A. Y. Gunter (eds), *Bergson and Modern Thought: Towards a Unified Science* (New York, Harwood Academic Publishers, 1987), p. 379.
41 Cf. Philippe Soulez, *Bergson politique* (Paris, Presses Universitaires de France, 1989), especially pp. 303–27.
42 MR, pp. 286–7, 312; OE, pp. 1219, 1241.
43 MR, pp. 296–8; OE, pp. 1228–9.
44 Maria Mies and Vandana Shiva, *Ecofeminism* (Atlantic Highlands, Zed Books, 1993), pp. 255–6.

V

ART

mark antliff

THE RHYTHMS OF DURATION: BERGSON AND THE ART OF MATISSE[1]

In a recently edited volume titled *The Rhetoric of the Frame* (1996), art historians have problematised the 'inside/outside' polar relation of artwork to frame, and in so doing have called into question notions of aesthetic autonomy crucial to the modernist project.[2] In analysing 'the role, function, or purpose of the frame in the construction of the artwork' the volume's contributors acknowledge their debt to Jacques Derrida's critique of theories of aesthetic autonomy, codified in his volume *The Truth in Painting* (1987). Taking as his starting-point Immanuel Kant's claim that frames are inessential or external 'supplements' to a work of art, Derrida argues that the parergon/frame, in marking a boundary, has an unstable life as part of two 'grounds' – that of the 'ergon' (work) and that of the 'milieu' or 'background'.[3] In this sense the frame refers not only to the physical boundaries circumscribing a painting, but, in the words of Christopher Norris, to 'an impermeable boundary between the artwork (ergon) and everything that belongs to its background, context, space of exhibition, *mise-en-scène* or whatever'.[4] Thus the essays included in *The Rhetoric of the Frame* focused on such non-physical boundaries as 'the institutional frame, the perceptual frame, the semiotic frame, or the gendered frame'.[5]

One such essay, devoted to the art of Matisse, shows how European conceptions of the 'Orient' may be said to frame Matisse's *Still Life with Aubergines* (1911) [1], even as the artist's use of Islamic motifs on the painting's border served to problematise the 'parergonal' dimension of his aesthetic.[6] The painting initially had a seven-inch-wide canvas border covered with the same floral motif permeating the painting itself, but in reversed colours, with dark violet on a light background.[7] In the words of Deepak Ananth:

The parergonal dimension is elided or at the very least rendered equivocal ... by virtue of the frame's provenance in the decorative art of Islam, an art that expressly privileges the ornamental, according it a significance of which Kantian aesthetics – with its distinction between the intrinsic and the extrinsic, the central and the marginal, form and matter – has no intimation.[8]

1] **Henri Matisse**, *Still Life with Aubergines*, 1911, distemper on canvas, 212 × 246 cm

In analysing Matisse's transgression of the parergonal dimension of the frame the present essay will consider not only the orientalism that informs his use of Islamic art, but the larger Bergsonian frame in which that use was initially couched. Art historians have long recognised the profound influence of Bergson's thought on Matisse from 1908 onwards – Matisse owned many of Bergson's books and made reference to *durée* in his 'Notes of a Painter' (1908) – but the role that discourse had in Matisse's *departure* from Kantian aesthetics and parergonal assumptions has yet to be analysed.[9] I would argue that many of Matisse's pre-war images – particularly those of his studio – were premised on notions of organic completion and aesthetic closure, but that his portraits were simultaneously based on a Bergsonian conception of *durée* as an unbounded flux which, in the words of Gilles Deleuze, remained 'irreducible and nonclosed', in a permanent state of 'coming into being'.[10] This condition pertained not so much to the structural properties of a painting but to its ability to instigate the beholder's creative faculties. As I have shown elsewhere, this Bergsonian problematic was shared by other artists of Matisse's generation, most notably Parisian Fauvists like J. D. Fergusson and Cubists such as Albert Gleizes and Raymond Duchamp-Villon, all of whom exhibited their work alongside Matisse's at the various avant-garde Salons.[11] Far from being alone in his interest in Bergson, Matisse should be seen as the most prominent artist among a cross-section of Parisian modernists who looked to Bergsonian theory to justify their aesthetic innovations. In contrast to Ananth, who would locate the motivation for Matisse's transgression of aesthetic closure in his embrace of a non-European, Islamic aesthetic, I would argue that Matisse's departure from Kantian assumptions resulted from his exposure to the alternative European 'frame' of process philosophy of which Bergson was an early representative.

Before turning to the theoretical dimension of this discourse we need to situate Matisse's Bergsonism in an historical context, namely the fusion of Bergsonian, Byzantine and Islamic aesthetics developed by Matisse's close friend Matthew Stewart Prichard (1865–1936) between the years 1909 and 1914.[12] Matisse's son-in law, Georges Duthuit, later recalled being introduced to Matisse by Prichard in 1910, noting that both the artist and the critic 'pursued in art directions more or less parallel to those which Bergson was tracing in philosophy'.[13] Prichard not only nurtured Matisse's interest in Bergson, in 1915 he interpreted his art from the standpoint of Catholic Modernism and contributed a preface to an exhibition of Matisse's art in New York, defending the artist in Bergsonian terms.[14] In short, any reading of Matisse's Bergsonism has to take into account the enduring influence of Prichard on the artist's aesthetic before 1914. In exploring that interaction I will reveal Prichard's awareness of what John Mullarkey has termed Bergson's 'method of multiplicity', and the extent to which that method was employed by both Prichard and Matisse in order to problematise notions of aesthetic closure.[15] That method resulted in three interrelated aesthetic strategies: a disavowal of Euclidean space in favour of a Bergsonian notion of extensity; an absorption of the frame within the 'organic' parameters of the painting itself; and the rhythmic structuring of the canvas with a view to initiating a reopening of aesthetic closure. As we shall see, that reopening was premised on a Bergsonian conception of the interrelation of artist to sitter, and beholder to the finished work of art.

Pictorial space

Like Bergson, Prichard not only condemned Kant's doctrine of transcendental idealism, he separated intuitive perception from an 'intellectual' experience of the world.[16] Bergson's 'position', states Prichard in a letter of December 1910, 'is that we obtain a wider knowledge by our feeling than by our reason, that intellectual knowledge and science serve only action, and that they only deal with that which is lifeless or is treated as if it were without life'. 'To understand life itself we must refer to the data of our feelings and trust our intuitions', Prichard concludes, before adding that Bergson 'puts reason, science, the concept on the lower plane, and feeling, art and intuition on the higher'.[17] In the realm of aesthetics Prichard's sharp distinction between intuition and intellect, art and a 'scientific' attitude informs his condemnation of the corporeal naturalism of classical Greek sculpture and his dismissal of perspectival illusionism in Western art. By 1913 Prichard declared the 'Byzantine and Islamic methods' utilised by Matisse to be 'intuitive' and therefore superior to the 'Greek–Renaissance–Academic position'.[18] Academic verisimilitude, combined with the placement of objects in a pictorial space ordered through Renaissance methods of proportional measurement, had resulted in an 'intellectual' rather than 'intuitive' experience of the world.

Prichard's linkage of Kantian aesthetics to the quantitative measurement of space in academic painting is indebted to the critique of Kant developed in *Time and Free Will*: according to Bergson, Kant's 'Transcendental Aesthetic' endowed space 'with an existence independent of its content', and made it an *a priori*, quantifiable and fixed entity into which bodies would then be placed.[19] Bergson by contrast argued that space as Kant and Euclid conceived of it was derivative of movement, that movement was fundamental to duration, and, in his later writings, that space was not unitary but multivalent, composed of differing 'degrees' of 'extensity', Bergson's term for the mixture of time and space found in concrete experience. Bergson labelled Euclidean space – the measurable, three-dimensional space Prichard associated with academic technique – homogeneous and immobile; duration by contrast was heterogeneous and mobile.[20] Movement in the Bergsonian sense encompassed other notions of change, including qualitative sensations of colour or sound and processes of ageing and psychological 'becoming'. Unable to recognise change, the intellect, like the Euclidean space it fabricated, substituted stasis for movement.[21] Euclidean space was an empty vessel independent of the invariable forms it contained; but since 'real movement is rather the transference of a state than a thing', no entity 'can change place without changing form'.[22] The intellect's homogeneous treatment of time and space, therefore, performed 'the double work of solidification and of division which we effect on the moving continuity of the real'.[23]

'That which is real', Bergson stated in *Matter and Memory*, 'is something intermediate between divided extension [abstract Euclidean space] and pure inextension [duration]. It is what we have termed the extensive.'[24] Prichard, having attended Bergson's London lectures in 1911, would have witnessed his critique of 'the confusion of concrete extension with mathematical space'.[25] In Bergson's durational cosmology, mind is in a continuum with matter, so that matter is simply the lowest state of mind and mind the highest state of matter.[26] To separate matter wholly from mind would be to deny that duration has extensity; to rob matter of mind would make it wholly homogeneous and discontinuous, in short, devoid of duration. The permeability of mind and matter, duration and extension, lies in the fact that duration has a rhythm, it is a synthesis of the temporal and spatial. Thus, in his 1911 lectures, Bergson could claim that there is an 'enormous difference between the rhythm of our own duration and the rhythm of the duration of matter', while in *Matter and Memory* he speculated that 'it is possible to imagine many different rhythms which, slower or faster, measure the degree of tension or relaxation of different kinds of consciousness'.[27] For this reason Bergson compares our consciousness to a 'melody'; similarly sensations such as colour are the 'qualitative' manifestations of the absorption of vibratory matter into the rhythmic tension of our duration. As the penultimate symbol of pure change, colour was a perceptual intermediary between the quantitative and qualitative, vibratory matter and the rhythmic pulse of our own consciousness. Colour as well as melody could signify rhythmic duration, for a state of intensity reportedly permeated our 'psychic elements, tingeing them, so to speak, with its own colour'.[28] To perceive such extensive rhythms required an effort of intuition, for the intellect could not discern such inner duration, but focused instead on an object's surface appearances, rather than plumbing its durational depths. If 'the faculty of *seeing* should be made to be one with the act of *willing*', wrote Bergson, our vision would transcend its habitual and utilitarian function and, through an effort of intuition, discern the melody of 'inner' duration.[29] For an artist it was this rhythm that served to bind the pattern of colours and shapes that make up a canvas into an integral, organic whole.[30]

Extensity and Matisse's pictorial technique

I would argue that Matisse and Prichard embraced this notion of rhythmic extensity, and associated it with Byzantine and Islamic art. Matisse integrated Prichard's Bergsonian critique of 'scientific' perspective with Bergson's qualitative conception of colour to arrive at a new definition of pictorial space. 'If I instinctively admired the Primitives in the Louvre and then Oriental art,' stated Matisse in a 1947 essay referring to the pre-1914

period, 'it is because I found in them a new confirmation. Persian miniatures, for example, showed me the full possibility of my sensations ... By
its properties this art suggests a larger, and truly plastic space.'[31] In the
same essay, Matisse added that his 1911 trip to Moscow and his exposure
there to 'Byzantine paintings' had confirmed the insights provided by Persian miniatures: 'revelation thus came to me from the Orient'. That revelation reinforced Matisse's desire to 'get away from imitation, even in
light', and to use colour to express 'emotion and not as a transcription of
nature'.[32] Like Bergson, Matisse associated colour with music. 'My choice
of colours does not rest on any scientific theory', wrote Matisse in his
'Notes of a Painter' (1908), for 'from the relationships I have found in all
the tones there must result a living harmony of colours, a harmony analogous to that of a musical composition'.[33] As the embodiment of spatial
extensity the quantitative dimension of colour in a canvas necessarily
influenced his choice of colours: referring to differences in colour in the
two versions of his mural painting *The Dance* (1933) Matisse claimed that
'the quantities being different, their quality also changes'.[34] Combining
both spatial (quantitative) and temporal (qualitative) properties, Fauvism's
colour harmonies assimilated the 'vibrato' of matter into the durational
consciousness of the artist.[35] As Richard Shiff has noted, the canvas thus
becomes 'a surface which (like colour itself) transforms the character and
emotional connotations' of the artistic motif.[36] In 1939 Matisse announced
his desire to create 'a luminous space', 'a perspective of feeling'.[37] His
extensive conception of colour was integral to the non-measurable nature
of 'plastic space'.

The rejection of the play of natural light across surfaces, the use of
chiaroscuro to model form, went hand in hand with the dismissal of quantitative systems of measurement associated with academic technique.
Matisse also rejected the academic technique of squaring for transfer,
wherein a composition is covered with a grid of horizontal and vertical
lines, and the contents of each square transferred to a grid of larger
squares on an expanded surface. Since Matisse regarded 'the entire
arrangement' of his pictures as 'expressive', he thought the form and content of a picture should be integral.[38] 'My drawing will have a necessary
relationship to its format', proclaims Matisse in 'Notes of a Painter' (1908):
'I would not repeat a drawing on another sheet of different proportions ...
Nor should I be satisfied with a mere enlargement, had I to transfer the
drawing to a sheet the same shape, but ten times larger'; 'An artist who
wants to transpose a composition from one canvas to another larger one
must conceive it anew in order to preserve its expression; he must alter its
character and not just square it up onto the larger canvas.'[39] The *durée* that
gave birth to a canvas meant that its form could not be subjected to

rational measurement, nor could its content be modified without affecting its form, for a painting's spatial dimensions cannot exist separately from its contents. There is no *a priori*, mathematical grid that would exist separately from the 'expressive' composition of Matisse's canvases.[40]

As Frereshteh Daftari has noted, Matisse's exposure to Islamic carpets and Persian miniatures showed him 'how to suggest three-dimensionality without imitating naturalistic space', for the miniatures, 'in spite of their flatness imply or create an illusion of depth'.[41] Indeed, Matisse's production before 1914 constitutes a pictorial meditation on the differences between European academic perspective and 'oriental' approaches to space. Ambiguous relations between foreground and background space, unmodulated planes of colour, disjunctions in scale, multiple viewpoints and lack of a compositional centre: all were pictorial devices adapted by Matisse from Persian miniatures.[42] A case in point is Matisse's *Harmony in Red* (1908), the durational qualities of which are clearly inscribed in the painting's title [**2**].

The rhythmic extensity in *Harmony in Red* has a disturbing effect upon our perception of spatial location. The first thing worth noting is that, with the exception of the items on the table, no single object, whether the window-sill, woman, chairs or table itself, is depicted in its entirety. The

2] Henri Matisse, *Harmony in Red*, 1908, oil on canvas, 180 × 220 cm

objects are not positioned on a visible floor, we cannot firmly ground them in three-dimensional space. The painting's narrative is disarmingly simple: a maid is preparing a table for dinner; but to what degree is the table identifiable as a solid object? Its shape is hidden under a red table-cloth, but the cloth, delineated by a pencil-thin line, is hardly distinguishable from the wall. In the bottom left-hand corner of the picture this line disappears, so that we can no longer separate the table-cloth from the wall behind it. On the side furthest away from us, where the table and the window-sill run parallel, Matisse periodically breaks the line, affecting a Cézannesque *passage* where spatial definition is needed most.

The most alarming feature in *Harmony in Red* is the manner in which the table-cloth's decoration of blue pots and vines seems to crawl over the table and wall. As part of the decorative table-cloth, these designs do not aid in defining the table as a three-dimensional object, nor do the still-life objects on the table, since they fail to cast shadows across its surface. Where there should be a clear distinction between the table's surface and the side facing us, there is only an unmodulated field of red. The effect of the surging field of red, combined with these partially delineated objects, is to push everything up to the foreground, transforming the space into a two-dimensional surface. The sense of play between foreground and background space is further enhanced by Matisse's adaptation of the Islamic technique of 'framing' an exterior view, for many of the Persian miniatures seen by Matisse contained window views in which the distant landscape appeared closer than the interior walls framing it.[43] *Harmony in Red* causes our attention to oscillate between volumetric depth and an unmodulated decorative surface, as if the fluctuating field of red introduced a rhythmic 'pulse' to our reading of the painting.

A red field of colour has a similar function in Matisse's *The Red Studio* of 1911 [**3**]. It is an image of 'an abstract, intangible, noetic space',[44] but even more importantly *The Red Studio* is a site of artistic creation, the spatial qualities of which register the rhythmic duration of the artist in a highly creative state of mind. As Jack Flam has noted, the painting bears a relation to duration, in so far as it is a pictorial record of his artistic production from 1906 to the time of painting.[45] As with *Harmony in Red*, Matisse has created spatial ambiguities: the unmodulated red invades every surface, with the result that the schematic, incomplete outlines of the floor and adjacent walls dissolve into a seamless spatial field. Matisse has reduced the materiality of the utilitarian objects inhabiting the room – the dresser and clock against the back wall, the chair and table in the foreground, the pedestals on which his sculptures stand – to a bare outline. By contrast, those objects identified with Matisse's creative powers – the decorated ceramic dish on the table, the adjacent box of crayons, the series of paint-

ings, frames, sculptures and unfinished plaster-cast lining the back wall –
all these, to quote Deepak Ananth, 'betoken the real, declaring themselves
in effect as markers of the only reality that counts for the artist'.[46]

3] Henri Matisse, *The Red Studio*, 1911, oil on canvas, 181 × 219 cm

Even more fundamental, I would argue, was the theme of contrasting
approaches to temporality that underpins *The Red Studio*. Indeed, at the
painting's central axis stands the very symbol of the temporality the
Bergsonian artist seeks to efface, that is, a free-standing clock. The clock
converts the rhythmic cadence of individual duration into an homogeneous, measured unit; the artist by contrast transposes that duration into a
creative act. Clock-time is the quantified, anonymous time of the scientist.
Real duration can only be grasped through intuition, it is part of a creative
process. To signal the suspension of the former experience of time in
favour of the latter, Matisse removed the hands from the clock and let it
stand as testimony to a concept of time he consciously rejected, and as a
foil to the durational experience and rhythmic extensity that gave shape to
the 'plastic space' of his canvases. This sensation of extensity is enhanced
by the ambiguous placement of the chair in the right foreground, which
undergoes a perspectival shift as one moves from the chair's top to bottom.

Framing concepts

'The four sides of a frame are among the most important parts of a picture', wrote Matisse in 1943; 'a painting or a drawing included in a given space ought, therefore, to be in perfect harmony with the frame just as a concert for chamber music will be interpreted differently according to the dimensions of the room in which it is to be heard.'[47] Deepak Ananth cites this passage as a prelude to her superlative analysis of Matisse's *Still Life with Aubergines* (1911) [1], a painting whose decorative floral pattern originally extended to encompass the now absent frame, as was revealed in a photograph of 1916.[48] Cut from the same cloth, this painted frame was not unlike the floral decoration embellishing the frame of the *Large Nude* of the same year; moreover, Persian miniatures and carpets again provided Matisse with a model for such decorative patterning. As Ananth observes, *Still Life with Aubergines* explicitly thematises the frame itself, 'for the painting is visualised as an array of frames and framing devices, a rhythmic play of borders and edges'.[49] Matisse again deploys spatial devices derived from Islamic art: the play between foreground and background initiated by the 'framed' window view, the effacement of a central vanishing-point by the planarity of a decorative screen, the collapsing of pictorial space into an unmodulated decorative pattern of blue flowers. Ananth argues that the cacophony of framed spaces – the two empty frames on the wall, the transient images framed by the left-hand mirror, right-hand window and open door between them – make this studio space akin to the enclosed, 'paradisal space' of Islamic carpets and Persian miniatures. The submergence of these enclosures in an abundance of floral and vegetal motifs ensured that any illusion of pictorial depth was countered by an all-encompassing surface design.[50]

Indeed, I would not only argue that the original frame circumscribing *Still Life with Aubergines* served this purpose, but that it stood in marked contrast to another version of the parergonal, namely the idea of a 'framing concept' as developed by Bergson and his followers Prichard and Edouard Le Roy. In critiquing the intellect for oversimplifying experience and denying its multiplicity, Bergson repeatedly referred to the 'theoretical frames' such thought produced; Prichard in turn applied this methodological critique to the function of the frame in Western art. I would argue that the decorative frame circumscribing *Still Life with Aubergines* was a conscious response to Prichard's critique, as was Matisse's later call for frames in 'perfect harmony' with what he recognised to be the rhythmic extensity of a painting.

'The intellectual faculty', states Bergson in *Creative Evolution*, 'possesses naturally only an external and empty knowledge; but it has thereby the advantage of supplying a frame in which an infinity of objects may find room in turn.' This empty frame, this 'formal knowledge is not limited to what is practically useful, although it is in view of practical utility that it has made its appearance in the world'.[51] Unaware of the intellect's utilitarian origins, we think it 'a faculty intended for pure speculation'; we take its 'general frames' for reality itself. To dispel this misconception Bergson and his disciple Le Roy analysed the intellect's utilitarian origins and perceptual biases. According to Le Roy in *The New Philosophy of Henri Bergson*, the intellect provides us with the 'pre-existing forms' and 'theoretical frames' through which the data of our consciousness 'is invariably interpreted, systematized'. Divorced from 'speculative interest' or the pursuit of 'pure knowledge', our perceptual faculties are thereby diminished. 'Concepts and abstract ideas', states Le Roy, are only 'distant and simplified views' of a durational reality, 'giving only a few summary features of their objects'. 'In this way we reach only the surface of things, the reciprocal contacts, mutual intersections, and parts common, but not the organic reality nor the inner essence.'[52] As Bergson states in *Creative Evolution*, 'organic reality' and 'inner essence' belong to a durational order typified by 'the form of tension, continuous creation, free activity', whereas the order envisioned by the intellect 'leads to extension, to the necessary reciprocal determination of elements exter-nalised each by relation to others, to geometrical mechanism'. Moreover, 'this first kind of order is that of the vital or of the willed', it is found in 'a free action or a work of art', and in 'life in its entirety, regarded as a creative evolution'.[53] Intuition, states Le Roy, alone allows us to grasp this order and develop it, for 'absolute revelation is only given to the man who passes into the object, flings himself upon its stream, and lives within its rhythm'.[54] The artist's *tableau* is an 'organic' product of the vital order animating the universe rather than the 'theoretical frames' developed by our intellect.

To Prichard's mind, museum curators and the collections they formed were governed by such 'framing' concepts. 'Modern life', Prichard wrote in a letter of February 1914,

> has been the history of the tendency to abstract. If you think of painting, you can trace this development very well. At first you have the Byzantine mosaic which is subordinated to the action of the church or room where it is placed. Next you find the altarpiece with its carving around the painting. It is only a step to make this a painting with a frame. Another step carries this picture from the church into the palace where it is looked at for itself but where it still functions as an effective element in the ensemble. The next step is to put the picture in the museum where there is no life and the surroundings them-selves are abstract. Another development brings us to the picture produced to hang in museums and galleries. The final step is to find the subject of the picture arbitrary and the subject becomes in turn abstract.[55]

As part of a liturgical programme, the Byzantine mosaic or altarpiece was subordinate to the act of worship; in the museum setting this religious experience – which Prichard describes as intuitive – is lost. 'No longer actuated by heightened sentiment', the museum-goer is 'in science, seeking identities and framing concepts'.[56] 'Framing concepts' initiate a process of psychological detachment, and the religious image no longer elicits an emotional response, no longer 'introduces rhythms' into our consciousness. Religious images, when removed from a church, become mere objects to be classified in a comparative manner according to style, date or pictorial school, yet originally 'they were not things, but unidentified parts of great unities'.[57] It is the curator who, like 'the man of science', destroys a unity Prichard identifies as 'living' and 'organic'. Removing paintings from a religious setting or the decorative ensemble of a palace interior, he 'cuts [this unity] all up into morsels and thinks that each of the pieces is a part of a whole; but he forgets that the whole has a life of its own, an existence he has destroyed in his operation'.[58] In response to such 'materialism' artists themselves had begun to produce paintings designed for museums, works devoid of the 'affective', with 'nothing related to an inner sense of reality'. Contemporary examples included the Cubist paintings of Picasso and the music of the composer Leo Ornstein. Ornstein's compositions, we are told, are 'arranged with an amazing sense of order', but convey 'nothing related to an inner sense of reality, only something to listen to consciously and accept with intelligence'.[59] In the spring of that year Matisse too dismissed Cubist technique for its 'materialism', claiming that the Cubists did not render their subjects with 'sufficient clearness and intensity' to enable the beholder to 'feel every element composing [a painting]'.[60] This materialist, intellectual order – like the 'framing concepts' of the museum curator – was antithetical to the organic, durational order resulting from an artist's intensive vision.

To overcome such materialism Prichard recommended that Matisse adjust his frames to his decorative aesthetic, to integrate them into the organic format of the paintings they enclosed.[61] We know that Matisse did indeed paint his frames to realise such decorative ends. Besides *Still Life with Aubergines*, the most notable examples are the grey frames surrounding the Moroccan paintings exhibited at the Bernheim-Jeune gallery in April 1913.[62] The colour of these frames, combined with their shallow depth, probably served to integrate them with the decorative precepts governing the paintings themselves. Matisse was following the example of the Impressionists, who maintained that their equally austere white or grey frames intensified the colours of their paintings; additionally the shallow depth of such frames served to integrate them into the decorative flatness of the painted surface.[63] This decorative integration was part and parcel of the avant-garde rejection of pictorial illusionism; given the pre-eminence of colour in Matisse's aesthetic we could conclude that grey frames served to extend the decorative harmony of the canvas to encompass the surrounding border. It was through colour that the grey, planar borders of Matisse's canvases were brought into 'perfect harmony' with the images they framed.

The multiple rhythms of duration

If we are to locate a context in which aesthetic closure – signified by the integral harmony of painting to frame – was transcended, it would be the wider durational frame of Matisse's initial relation to a sitter and the beholder's retrospective experience of his finished paintings. What Mullarkey has termed Bergson's 'multiplicity of abstract spaces' and the related concepts of 'tension' and 'intuition' have a direct bearing on this dimension of Matisse's aesthetic.[64] Bergson's extension of duration to the material realm in the guise of qualitative extensity was matched by an infiltration of space into mind so that the mind was no longer immaterial and its contents were regarded as spatial entities.[65] Bergson's process metaphysics, states Mullarkey, 'allows different layers of mind and matter to overlap at various levels and in varying degrees'.[66] Our states of mind, therefore, are characterised by varying degrees of rhythmic tension or relaxation roughly corresponding to the degree of freedom inherent in a given activity. The highest degree of psychic tension occurs through the effort of willed empathy Bergson refers to as intuition; this state of mind is both native for artists and a method of understanding for philosophers. It is 'by an effort of intuition', writes Bergson in his 'Introduction to Metaphysics', that we enter into the concrete flow of duration.[67] An effort of intuition is needed in order to reverse the mental habits imposed on us by pragmatic needs. It is by reversing such thought-patterns, through 'thinking backwards', to borrow F. C. T. Moore's phrase, that we are able to discern the multiple 'rhythms of durance' besides our own.[68] In following that rhythm to its lowest degree of tension, that is, its materiality, we would have to narrow our scope of attention, we would, to quote Moore, 'fragment it and go in the direction of simple items of experience possessing quantitative properties'.[69] Our state of psychological tension would be transformed into one of relaxation, intuitive consciousness would give way to the pragmatic designs of our intellect. As Bergson states in *Creative Evolution*: '*The more consciousness is intellectualized, the more matter is spatialized.*'[70] To move in the other direction, to intensify an intuition, requires us to 'expand our scope of attention' to 'concentrate ourselves on the rhythms of durance' and 'concede their solidarity, their lack of temporal limits'.[71] This is the direction chosen by Matisse in his attempt to intuit the duration of his sitters.

States of rhythmic tension are the object of intuitive consciousness; the artist's role is to translate this 'original harmony' into pictorial form so that it is 'the inner life of things that [the artist] sees appearing through their forms and colours'.[72] An artist, 'in breaking down, by an effort of intuition, the barrier that space puts between himself and his model', perceives 'the intention of life, the simple movement that runs through lines, that binds them together and gives them significance'.[73] Since such intuitive states entail a greater degree of freedom, their unfolding into pictorial form is necessarily unpredictable. 'The finished portrait is explained by the features of the model, by the nature of the artist, by the colours spread out on the palette,' states Bergson in *Creative Evolution*, 'but even with the knowledge of what explains it, no one, not even the artist, could have foreseen exactly what the portrait would be.' Just as the painter is transformed under the influence of the work he produces, 'so each of our states, at the moment of issue, modifies our personality, being indeed the new form that we are just assuming'.[74] In this heightened state of intuitive tension 'we have the more or less clear consciousness of motives and of impelling forces, and even, in rare moments, of the becoming by which they are organized into an act'.[75]

As Bergson argues in *Time and Free Will*, the beholder of a work of art can undergo a similar transformation. Speaking of the 'aesthetic feeling' induced by a work of art, Bergson notes that it is the 'rhythm and measure' of a work of art that is able to place us 'in the midst of this movement, the rhythm of which has taken complete possession of our thought and will'. This aesthetic feeling is nothing short of a 'qualitative process' composed of 'increasing intensities of feeling'; moreover, 'the successive intensities of the aesthetic feeling thus correspond to changes of state occurring in us.'[76] The painting therefore is both an integral, organic entity imbued with the rhythmic duration that created it, and an agent for creative development on the part of the beholder.

The state of psychic tension associated with aesthetic intuition; the intuition of the inner rhythmic tension of a sitter's duration; the effect of a work of art on a beholder's consciousness: all these elements are operative in Matisse's and Prichard's art theory. In a remarkable letter written in 1913 to Mabel Warren, Prichard described the manner in which Matisse put this perceptual theory into practice.[77] Referring to a series of drawings Matisse had made of Mabel Warren on 6 November 1913, Prichard noted 'the immense effort necessary for creation' that went into 'the little drawings made by Matisse of you yesterday afternoon'. That effort entailed a transformation of Matisse's perceptual faculties, for 'it was not a question

4] **Henri Matisse**, *Mrs Samuel Dennis Warren*, 6 November 1913, pencil drawing on white paper, 28.2 × 21.6 cm

of registering a perception', but 'another task, that of reading the depths of personality'. 'Listen for a moment how he prepared himself', added Prichard; 'when he first saw you Matisse felt that he wanted to make a drawing of you and when he heard on Monday that you assented, from then on until he had finished the work on Thursday he thought of nothing else, he consecrated himself to this end and purified himself for it just as if he had been an eastern craftsman.'

This psychic purification culminated in a two-hour drawing session with the sitter; having completed the third drawing [4], 'his service was at an end and the bow unstrung'. '"I couldn't do that every day," he said later, "I passed two hours of the intensest strain".'[78] This feeling of intensity pervaded other aesthetic experiences: speaking of Matisse's 'great portrait of his wife' in November 1913, Prichard noted that Matisse 'thinks he will be able to express in it a feeling he has already given utterance to but never to the point of conveying the full means of its intensity'.[79] Indeed, the effort that went into the *Portrait of Amélie Matisse* (1913) is legendary: it required over a hundred sittings, and the sitter reportedly wept over the disappearance of the naturalistic rendering that comprised its earlier state.[80] This transformative process affected other portraits as well; thus in speaking of Matisse's *Portrait of Yvonne Landsberg* (1914) – a friend of Prichard's and fellow Bergson enthusiast[81] – Prichard recalled its constant evolution over the period from the spring of 1914 to July of the same year. 'You think the picture is finished', he wrote 'and find next time a completely new one. Nothing is the same except the feeling; composition, colour, and drawing are all new.'[82]

The condition of psychic tension allowed Matisse to perceive the rhythmic duration of Mrs Warren. 'For some time I thought it too difficult,' said Matisse in recalling the drawing session; 'there was a constant movement of her will forwards and backwards, giving and withdrawing, opening and closing; my first drawing was nothing, but when, after hesitating, her being agreed to lend itself I was able to work.'[83] Mrs Warren's willed sympathy with the artist, her agreement to 'open' her 'being' to him, resulted in a vibratory sensation: 'There was no change in her features unless in the light of her eyes,' reported Matisse, 'but there was a constant vibration (Matisse indicated this by turning his hand rapidly on his wrist), it was like a rippling lake ... there was nothing whatever to seize and there was no point where it seemed possible for me to begin.'[84] But begin he did, and as with every creative endeavour, the final product proved surprising. 'No one is more surprised than I am at the results, for I can never tell what a work will reveal to me', he stated. Referring once more to the third drawing, Matisse described the end product:

> there is a vitality in it, something no photograph can give, there's movement in the eyes; it is very difficult to achieve that in a drawing ... It is a miracle. She is a flowing stream. She is just a flame, she hangs by a thread, no point is indicated where you can grasp her. In spite of that the drawing is a complete realisation of my vision.[85]

In locking on to those eyes – windows to the soul, in artistic parlance – Matisse claimed to have grasped her personality. 'There is a great sensitivity in the eyes and that sense of hesitation in relation to others ... which is characteristic of sensitive natures.'[86] In the earlier drawings Mrs Warren's physiognomy is cursorily rendered with a single pencil-stroke to indicate each feature, but by the third drawing her eyes are deep-set, her head and shoulders composed of a series of overlapping, tremulous lines. These shimmering lines, I would argue, set the precedent for the radiating lines emanating from the abstracted, pensive form of Yvonne Landsberg, both in Matisse's drawing of this sitter and in the monumental

5] Henri Matisse, *Portrait of Mlle Yvonne Landsberg*, 1914, oil on canvas, 147.3 × 97.5 cm

painting completed in July 1914 [**5**].[87] Matisse underscored the durational significance of these lines by comparing them to 'the overtones in music'; Yvonne's brother, who was present during her sitting and accompanied Prichard to Bergson's lectures, thought they represented 'something like the aura of a chrysalis – of a being who, for long, has been concentrating its steadily growing powers in secret'.[88] These rhythmic 'overtones' were pictorial signs for the developing personality of this 19-year-old woman; appropriately Matisse had begun his first sitting with Yvonne Landsberg by drawing magnolia-buds, claiming that their rapid growth to full maturity reminded him of his sitter.[89] 'Our personality shoots, grows and ripens without ceasing', stated Bergson in *Creative Evolution*;[90] Matisse's *Portrait of Yvonne Landsberg* translated that metaphor into pictorial form, drawing a generative association between Yvonne Landsberg's burgeoning sexuality, fecundity in nature, symbolised by the budding magnolia, and vibratory rhythm.[91]

Prichard also shared Bergson's belief that artists themselves were trans-formed as a result of this intuitive experience. 'Dear Mrs Warren, by being drawn you summoned strength from Matisse which was not in him before,' asserted Prichard, 'for according to the belief which I hold such an act of creation constitutes a deathless addition to consciousness.'[92] Prichard described the final drawing as 'a conduit by means of which a cer-tain tide of sentiment could be caused to flow in others', thus indicating that the beholder of Matisse's work could undergo a similar transforma-tion.[93] In his preface to the Montross Gallery exhibition of 1915 Prichard wrote that 'a great portrait will start our imagination at a certain rate on an emotional slope, downward we must go creatively in order to attain some-thing which the artist has not realised or foreseen but only forefelt'.[94] In portraying an individual, Matisse does not 'restrict his intuitions' to the 'mere details' of 'the body' but instead develops 'order in art – that is form or design'. 'Colour' or 'pattern' are an artist's abstract means of capturing a sitter's duration. Rather than indicating 'to our intelligence the features of a subject', Matisse's portraits capture something 'dynamic', 'the emotional tendency', 'the character or will of the person'. 'The scheme of an artistic composition', reportedly, 'starts in us a tendency of the character or will of the person' portrayed, so that 'the complete constitution of the portrait is in our living experience, gained under the guidance of the artist's work'. 'Mentally active and productive in a given direction', we are 'invited to create side by side with the artist'; moreover we experience 'the con-sciousness of an internal drive, a steady emotional pitch, higher than (or lower than – other than) our usual spiritual barometric pressure'. 'My response is the movement of my will,' Prichard asserts, 'which by pro-longing and developing the tension of my individuality, through feeling into consciousness, and projecting it into matter, as idea, constitutes my act of creation.' The 'fruition of extensive life', such acts indicated the role of painting in developing 'the spiritual path of creation'.[95]

Conclusion: Bergson *contra* Greenberg

This reopening of aesthetic closure to the rhythmic pulse of Bergsonian duration has larger implications when we consider the post-structuralist critique of modernism developed by the art historian Rosalind Krauss. In a variety of texts Krauss has argued that the aesthetic function of the beat or pulse in art stands in opposition to the 'abstracted' vision of 'pure instan-taneity' championed by modernism's American apologist, Clement Greenberg.[96] The visual model promoted by Greenberg in the 1960s was a disembodied one, pared down to a temporal experience of 'pure instantan-eity, into an abstract condition with no before or after'.[97] Greenberg's call for an art of 'pure presentness', or pure opticality, was reportedly premised on 'a modernist culture's ambition that each of its disciplines be rationalised by being grounded in its unique and separate domain of experience'. Greenberg therefore extracted vision from any corporeal dimension that would link it to other sensory realms – vision had to be treated 'abstractly'. Additionally this art of 'pure instantaneity' had a 'utopian' goal: each art form, through alignment with a particular sense, could be 'newly understood as discrete, as self-sufficient, as autonomous'.[98]

Krauss countered this version of modernism with an alternative notion of the 'optical unconscious', premised on Jean-François Lyotard's post-structuralist notion of the figure-matrix, developed in his book *Discours, figure* (1971), and the related function of 'rhythm, or beat, or pulse' in the art of Max Ernst and Marcel Duchamp.[99] According to Krauss this rhythmic pulse acted to disrupt the modernist moment of abstract instantaneity through an infusion of corporeal desire. The 'perceptual field of the dream' represented in Ernst's 1930 collage novel, *A Little Girl Dreams of Taking the Veil*, was premised on the 'beat' or 'pulse' of the mass-marketed zootrope, while Marcel Duchamp's *Rotoreliefs* – inspired by the revolving turntable of a record-player – enacted 'the slow throb of a spiral, contracting and expanding biorhythmically'.[100] Duchamp and Ernst thus take their place alongside a number of Surrealist-related artists of the 1920s and 1930s who 'corporealize the visual, restoring to the eye (against the disembodied opticality of modernist painting) that eye's condition as bodily organ, available like any other physical zone to the force of eroticization'.[101]

As this essay has demonstrated, Duchamp and Ernst were not alone in rejecting aesthetic 'instantaneity' in favour of the corporeal temporality of the 'pulse', 'rhythm' or 'beat'; nor is the post-structuralism of Lyotard the only model worth applying to this alternative form of modernism.[102] If we turn to the art of the early twentieth century, to the art and art criticism of the Cubists, Futurists and Fauvists, it is the thought of Henri Bergson – with its metaphysics of rhythmic duration – that is the foremost philosophical influence.[103] I would argue that any complete analysis of modernism's temporal dimension must take into account the reopening of aesthetic closure instituted by Bergsonian aesthetics and its philosophical legacy in the post-structuralist thought of Gilles Deleuze.[104] Indeed Deleuze's own celebration of the 'diastolic' and 'systolic' rhythms in the art of Francis Bacon deserves comparison to the precedent set by these modernists, whose own Bergsonian rhythms effectively undermined the Greenbergian notion of aesthetic autonomy Krauss would associate with the modernist project.[105]

Notes

1 My thanks go to Walter Cahn, Linda Henderson, Robert Herbert and Richard Shiff for their comments on an earlier version of this essay; also to Patricia Leighten and John Mullarkey for their reading of the present manuscript, which is part of a projected study on the issue of aesthetic closure and modernism. Richard Shiff deserves a special note of thanks for the thought-provoking seminar on modernism that resulted in my initial exploration of Matisse's relation to Bergson.

2 Paul Duro (ed.), *The Rhetoric of the Frame: Essays on the Boundaries of the Artwork* (Cambridge, Cambridge University Press, 1996).

3 See his essay on the 'parergon' in Jacques Derrida, *The Truth in Painting*, trans. Geoff Bennington and Ian McLeod (Chicago, University of Chicago Press, 1987).

4 Christopher Norris, 'Deconstruction, Post-Modernism and the Visual Arts', in Andrew Benjamin and Christopher Norris, *What is Deconstruction?* (London, Academy, 1987), pp. 7–31.

5 Paul Duro, 'Introduction', in Duro, *The Rhetoric of the Frame*, p. 1.

6 Deepak Ananth, 'Frames within Frames: on Matisse and the Orient', in Duro, *The Rhetoric of the Frame*, pp. 153–77.

7 For a reproduction and analysis of the painting as it existed in 1916, see Jack Flam, *Matisse: the Man and His Art, 1869–1918* (London, Cornell University Press, 1986), pp. 306–11.

8 Ananth, 'Frames within Frames', p. 175.

9 On the basis of historical evidence Matisse's first exposure to Bergson probably came from secondary sources in the field of literature. As a subscriber to the Symbolist journal *Vers et Prose* (1905–14) Matisse would have read the criticism of Bergson's major literary apologist, Tancrède de Visan. Art historian Jack Flam has argued that Matisse's Cézanne-oriented desire to 'penetrate apparent reality in order to arrive at an image of the deeper Reality' was premised on a Bergsonian notion of duration. Flam regards duration as 'the underlying and guiding metaphor of most of Matisse's painting after around 1905', which led Matisse to highlight the 'process of painting' in his art. As proof of this influence he points to Matisse's rejection, in his 'Notes of a Painter' (1908), of the Impressionist emphasis on momentary appearances in favour of an art that captured a subject's 'truer, more essential character'. Matisse was not alone in taking up this position. As I have shown elsewhere, the attack on Impressionism in the name of Bergsonian *durée* was common currency among the Parisian avant-garde by 1909. Art historians concur that Matisse's exposure to Bergsonian thought intensified following his contact with the aesthetician Matthew Stewart Prichard in 1909. Pierre Schneider has noted Matisse's ownership of books by Bergson, but does not mention the specific books Matisse owned or speculate on when he may have purchased them. See references to Bergson, Prichard and Matisse in the following volumes: Alfred Barr, *Matisse: his Art and his Public* (reprint, New York, Arno Press, 1966); Georges Duthuit, *The Fauve Painters* (New York, Wittenborn, Schultz, Inc., 1950); Flam, *Matisse*; and Pierre Schneider, *Matisse*, trans. Michael Taylor and Bridget Strevens Romer (New York, Rizzoli, 1984). For an historical analysis of the avant-garde's Bergsonian denigration of Impressionism, see Mark Antliff, *Inventing Bergson: Cultural Politics and the Parisian Avant-Garde* (Princeton, Princeton University Press, 1993).

10 Gilles Deleuze and Félix Guattari, *Anti-Oedipus: Capitalism and Schizophrenia*, trans. Robert Hurley, Helen R. Lane and Mark Seem (New York, Viking Press, 1977), pp. 95–6.

11 See Antliff, *Inventing Bergson* and Mark Antliff, 'Organicism against itself: Cubism, Duchamp-Villon and the contradictions of Modernism', *Word & Image*, 12 (4) (1996), pp. 366–88.

12 For a biographical overview of Prichard's life see Walter Muir Whitehill, 'Some Correspondence of Matthew Stewart Prichard and Isabella Stewart Gardner', *Fenway Court: Art Review of the Isabella Stewart Gardner Museum* (1974), pp. 14–29. For evidence of Prichard's enthusiastic endorsement of Matisse's art on Bergsonian grounds beginning in 1909, see M. S. Prichard to I. S. Gardner, 12 November 1909, Archives of American Art, Washington, DC (hereafter cited as the Gardner Papers, AAA). On 22 June 1909 Prichard informed Gardner that he was reading 'a great book on consciousness, next to take up discussion of *Matière et Mémoire*'; letter of M. S. Prichard to I. S. Gardner, 22 June 1909 (Gardner Papers, AAA). For references to Prichard's attendance of Bergson's lectures both in Paris and London see letters written on 18 December 1910 and 13 November 1911 (Gardner Papers, AAA). Prichard also accompanied Matisse to the 1910 Munich exhibition of Islamic art. See M. S. Prichard to I. S. Gardner, 22 November 1910 (Gardner Papers, AAA).

13 For Duthuit's reflections on Prichard's relationship to Matisse, see Georges Duthuit, *The Fauve Painters*, pp. 2, 9–10.

14 Matthew Stewart Prichard, 'Preface', *Henri Matisse Exhibition* (20 January to 27 February 1915), Montross Gallery, New York. Prichard's preface took the form of extracts from two letters to Frances Gordon Burton-Smith, written on 7 June and 6 July 1914. For information related to the exhibition, see Barr, *Matisse*, pp. 179–80; and Flam, *Matisse*, pp. 396–7. Thanks go to Allan Antliff for alerting me to Prichard's role in the exhibition. For evidence of Prichard's interest in the Catholic Modernism of the Bergsonian Edouard Le Roy see M. S. Prichard to I. S. Gardner, 4 November 1913 and 6 December 1913 (Gardner Papers, AAA). On Bergson, Le Roy, and neo-Catholicism see Paul Michael Cohen, 'Reason and Faith: the Bergsonian Catholic Youth of Pre-War France', *Historical Reflections*, 13 (2, 3) (1986), pp. 473–97.

15 John Mullarkey, 'Bergson's Method of Multiplicity', *Metaphilosophy*, 26 (3) (1995), pp. 230–59.

16 See Prichard's disparaging references to Kant in his 13 August 1911 letter to Gardner (Gardner Papers, AAA).

17 Letter of M. S. Prichard to I. S. Gardner, 18 December 1910 (Gardner Papers, AAA).

18 For Prichard's endorsement of the art of Matisse, Byzantium and Islam, see letters of M. S. Prichard to I. S. Gardner, 11 August 1909, 18 April 1912 and 24 April 1913 (Gardner Papers, AAA).

19 TFW, pp. 92–3; OE, p. 63.

20 TFW, pp. 236–40; OE, pp. 154–6; for a succinct analysis of Bergson's critique of Kant, see Mullarkey, 'Bergson's Method of Multiplicity', pp. 232–6.

21 Mullarkey, 'Bergson's Method of Multiplicity', p. 234.

22 See MM, p. 267/202; OE, p. 337; and CM, p. 147/173; OE, p. 1382.

23 MM, p. 280/211; OE, p. 345.

24 MM, p. 326/245; OE, p. 374.

25 M, p. 956.

26 See *ibid.*, pp. 956–7. Also see John Mullarkey's discussion of this issue in Mullarkey, 'Bergson's Method of Multiplicity', pp. 236–7.

27 M, p. 958; MM, p. 275/207; OE, p. 342.

28 TFW, p. 8; OE, p. 9.

29 CE, pp. 186–7/177, 250–1/237; OE, pp. 645, 696–7.

30 L, pp. 15–16/161; OE, pp. 461–2.
31 Henri Matisse, 'The Path of Colour' (1947), in *Matisse on Art*, trans. and ed. Jack Flam (Berkeley, University of California Press, 1995), p. 178.
32 *Ibid.*
33 Henri Matisse, 'Notes of a Painter' (1908), in *Matisse on Art*, pp. 40–1.
34 Henri Matisse, 'Letters to Alexander Romm, 1934', in *Matisse on Art*, p. 115.
35 Unlike Yve Alain-Bois, who claims that Matisse's treatment of colour was 'prior to the drawing/colour opposition', I would argue that colour in Matisse's painting served to define spatial extensity in a manner that was prior to any intellectual distinction between space and time. In contrast to Bois's model, which in his own words bears a 'superficial' relation to Derridean deconstruction, this notion of extensity can be firmly grounded in Matisse's familiarity with Bergson's metaphysics. For Bois's discussion of Matisse's use of colour and the related references to quantity and quality in Matisse's aesthetic, see Yve Alain-Bois, *Painting as Model* (Cambridge, Mass., MIT Press, 1993), pp. 22–3.
36 Richard Shiff, 'Imitation of Matisse', in Caroline Turner and Roger Benjamin (eds), *Matisse* (Brisbane, Queensland Art Gallery, 1995), p. 43.
37 Henri Matisse, 'Notes of a Painter on Drawing, 1939', in *Matisse on Art*, p. 131.
38 Henri Matisse, 'Notes of a Painter, 1908', in *Matisse on Art*, p. 38.
39 *Ibid.*
40 Matisse recognised that even a sketch and a finished work can never be the same, since the feeling that elicited an initial *esquisse* will inevitably develop over time. See Matisse's comments on the uniqueness of each *esquisse* in Henri Matisse, 'Interview with Clara T. Macchesney, 1912', in *Matisse on Art*, pp. 66–7. For a discussion of this aspect of Matisse's approach to the *esquisse*, see John Elderfield, 'Matisse in Morocco: an Interpretative Guide', in Jack Cowart with Pierre Schneider, John Elderfield, Albert Kostenevich and Laura Coyle, *Matisse in Morocco: Paintings and Drawings, 1912–13* (Washington, DC, National Gallery of Art), pp. 217–20.
41 For a comprehensive analysis of Matisse's familiarity with Persian art, see Frereshteh Daftari, *The Influence of Persian Art on Gauguin, Matisse and Kandinsky* (New York, Garland Publishing Inc., 1991), pp. 156–218.
42 See Daftari, *The Influence of Persian Art*, pp. 183–218 and Ananth, 'Frames within Frames', pp. 153–590.
43 See Daftari, *The Influence of Persian Art*, p. 166.
44 Ananth, 'Frames within Frames', p. 161.
45 Flam, *Matisse*, pp. 321–2.
46 Ananth, 'Frames within Frames', p. 161.
47 Henri Matisse, 'Témoignage, 1943', in Dominique Fourcade (ed.), *Ecrits et propos sur l'art* (Paris, Hermann, 1972), p. 196.
48 Jack Flam has reproduced this photograph, which dates from 1916. See Flam, *Matisse*, p. 311.
49 Ananth, 'Frames within Frames', p. 156.
50 *Ibid.*, p. 157.
51 CE, pp. 157/149–50; OE, p. 622.
52 Edouard Le Roy, *The New Philosophy of Henri Bergson*, trans. Vincent Benson (New York, Henry Holt and Co., 1913), pp. 30–40.
53 CE, pp. 236/223–4; OE, p. 685.
54 Le Roy, *The New Philosophy of Henri Bergson*, p. 40.
55 M. S. Prichard to I. S. Gardner, 9 February 1914 (Gardner Papers, AAA).

56 M. S. Prichard to I. S. Gardner, 26 November 1909 (Gardner Papers, AAA).

57 *Ibid.*

58 *Ibid.*

59 M. S. Prichard to I. S. Gardner, 9 February 1914 (Gardner Papers, AAA).

60 Walter Pach, *Queer Thing, Painting* (New York, Harper, 1938), p. 123.

61 In April 1913 Prichard claimed to have found a precedent for such decorative frames in the arabesque designs he saw at the exhibition of Islamic art in Munich. On 4 January 1913 Matisse wrote to Prichard of his 'total agreement' with Prichard's 'advice regarding the uselessness of frames for some works, and even of the bad influence of frames'. For Prichard's favourable evaluation of Islamic frames, see M. S. Prichard to I. S. Gardner, 24 April 1913 (Gardner Papers, AAA); for Matisse's reaction to Prichard's views, see Henri Matisse to M. S. Prichard, Hôtel Villa de France, Tangier, 4 January 1913 (Isabella Stewart Gardner Museum Archives, Boston, Mass.).

62 See the 19 April 1913 letter from Matisse to the Russian collector Ivan Morosov in which Matisse describes the painted frames. The Matisse–Morosov correspondence is reproduced in Cowart, Schneider, Elderfield, Kostenevich and Coyle, *Matisse in Morocco*, p. 264.

63 For a discussion of the function of frames in the art of the Impressionists, see Matthias Waschek, 'Camille Pissarro: from Impressionist Frame to Decorative Object', in Eva Mengden (ed.), *In Perfect Harmony: Pictures + Frame, 1850–1920* (Amsterdam, Van Gogh Museum, 1995), pp. 139–48.

64 The notion of a 'multiplicity of abstract spaces' alludes to Bergson's process metaphysics, wherein 'matter and mind are put in motion', and what serves to divide them 'is the type of movement they comprise'. See Mullarkey, 'Bergson's Method of Multiplicity', pp. 236–44.

65 MM, pp. 216/288; OE, p. 350; and CE, p. 214/202; OE, p. 667.

66 Mullarkey, 'Bergson's Method of Multiplicity', p. 237.

67 CM, p. 187/220–1; OE, pp. 1418–19.

68 'Durance' is Moore's rendering of 'durée' in place of the usual 'duration': see F. C. T. Moore, *Bergson: Thinking Backwards* (Cambridge, Cambridge University Press, 1996), pp. 58–9.

69 See Moore's analysis of Bergson's notion of 'tension' in Moore, *Bergson*, pp. 91–6.

70 CE, p. 199/189; OE, p. 656.

71 Moore, *Bergson*, pp. 95–6.

72 L, p. 155/161; OE, p. 461. For a fuller discussion of Bergson's theory of art, see Antliff, *Inventing Bergson*, pp. 45–66.

73 CE, p. 186/177; OE, p. 645.

74 CE, pp. 7/6–7; OE, pp. 499–500.

75 CE, pp. 251/237–8; OE, p. 697.

76 TFW, pp. 12–13, 18; OE, pp. 12–13, 16.

77 M. S. Prichard to M. Warren, Paris, 7 November 1913, in Philip Hofer, *Three Portrait Drawings with a Letter by M. S. Prichard Describing their Creation in 1913* (Boston, Mass., Meadow Press, 1974), n.p.

78 *Ibid.*

79 M. S. Prichard to I. S. Gardner, 4 November 1913 (Gardner Papers, AAA).

80 Flam, *Matisse*, p. 68.

81 Yvonne Landsberg's brother, Albert Clinton Landsberg, later recalled that both brother and sister had attended Bergson's lectures at the Collège de France in the company of Prichard. It was Prichard who introduced them to Matisse, and A. C. Landsberg who suggested to his mother that Matisse be commissioned to do the portrait. For a summation of Landsberg's recollections, which were recorded in letters of May–June 1951 to Alfred Barr, see Barr, *Matisse*, pp. 184–5.

82 M. S. Prichard to I. S. Gardner, 26 June 1914 (Gardner Papers, AAA).

83 M. S. Prichard to M. Warren, Paris, 7 November 1913, in Hofer, *Three Portrait Drawings*, n.p.

84 *Ibid.*

85 *Ibid.*

86 *Ibid.*

87 For a reproduction of the drawing that most closely resembles the finished painting, see Flam, *Matisse*, p. 388. I agree with Richard Shiff when he states that imitation for Matisse should be understood as 'the living through of another's actions, or the re-creation of the way of being of another physical being'. See Shiff, 'Imitation of Matisse', pp. 41–2.

88 Matisse compared the lines to 'overtones' in his correspondence with Frank Anderson Trapp. See Frank Anderson Trapp, 'The Paintings of Henri Matisse: Origins and Early Development, 1890–1917', Ph.D. dissertation, Harvard University, 1952, p. 211; and Flam, *Matisse*, p. 388. For A. C. Landsberg's statements regarding the portrait of his sister, see Alfred Barr's quotations from A. C. Landsberg's letters in Barr, *Matisse*, pp. 184–5, 541–2. Landsberg noted that Matisse scratched in these striations during the last sitting, for the whole canvas was repainted each session.

89 Flam, *Matisse*, p. 389.

90 CE, p. 6/6; OE, p. 499.

91 Alfred Barr and Jack Flam have made a similar point; in addition they conjecture that Matisse may have been influenced by the Bergsonian notion of force-lines expounded by the Italian Futurists. See Barr, *Matisse*, pp. 184–5 and Flam, *Matisse*, pp. 386–93. For an analysis of the Futurist concept of force-lines, see Antliff, *Inventing Bergson*, pp. 155–64.

92 M. S. Prichard to M. Warren, Paris, 7 November 1913, in Hofer, *Three Portrait Drawings*, n.p.

93 *Ibid.*

94 Prichard, 'Preface', *Henri Matisse Exhibition*, 1915.

95 *Ibid.*

96 Most important for the following argument is Rosalind Krauss, 'The Im/pulse to See', in Hal Foster (ed.), *Vision and Visuality* (Seattle, Bay Press, 1988), pp. 51–75. A revised version of the essay appeared in Rosalind Krauss, *The Optical Unconscious* (Cambridge, Mass., MIT Press, 1993), pp. 197–240.

97 Krauss, 'The Im/pulse to See', pp. 52–3.

98 *Ibid.*, pp. 52–4.

99 *Ibid.*, pp. 55–62.

100 *Ibid.*, p. 60.

101 *Ibid.*

102 Indeed Krauss, in conjunction with Yve Alain-Bois, has recently turned to George Bataille's concept of the *informe* for an alternative model. See Yve Alain-Bois and Rosalind Krauss, *Informe* (Paris, Centre Georges Pompidou, 1995).

103 Apart from Matisse, scholars have charted Bergson's influence on such modernists as Umberto Boccioni, Constantin Brancusi, Marcel Duchamp, Raymond Duchamp-Villon, František Kupka, Albert Gleizes, Fernand Léger, Wyndham Lewis and Kasimir Malevich. For an overview of Bergson's impact within Parisian avant-garde circles, see Antliff, *Inventing Bergson* and Antliff, 'Organicism against itself'.

104 I have made this argument in the concluding section of my article on Cubist organicism, where I consider existentialist and post-structuralist critiques of theories of
aesthetic 'closure'. See Antliff, 'Organicism against itself', pp. 385–8.

105 I intend to undertake such an analysis in a future study. For Deleuze's comments
on Bacon, see Gilles Deleuze, *Francis Bacon: logique de la sensation*, 2 vols (Paris,
Editions de la différence, 1981). Deleuze's notion of diastolic and systolic rhythms
is partially derived from the phenomenological reading of Cézanne found in Henri
Maldiney's *Regard parole espace* (Lausanne, Editions l'Age de l'Homme, 1973). For
an overview of Deleuze's aesthetic theory, see Ronald Bogue, 'Gilles Deleuze: the
Aesthetics of Force', in Paul Patton (ed.), *Deleuze: a Critical Reader* (Cambridge,
Mass., Blackwell Publishers, Inc., 1996), pp. 257–69.

paul douglass

BERGSON AND CINEMA: FRIENDS OR FOES?

All that we have to do, in fact, is to give up the cinematographical habits of our intellect.[1]

Even in his critique of the cinema Bergson was in agreement with it.[2]

There is no question that Henri Bergson's reaction against the film camera went to the core of his philosophical programme. In the final chapter of *Creative Evolution* (1907), he damned the 'cinematographical mechanism of thought' as the apotheosis of spatialisation, which must be overcome by 'revers[ing] the bent of our intellectual habits'.[3] This latter concept, which F. C. T. Moore has translated as 'thinking backwards', Bergson had already brought forward in 1901: 'The mind has to do violence to itself, has to reverse the direction of the operation by which it habitually thinks.'[4] That reversal of thinking meant to Bergson a struggle against the mind's 'cinematographical' tendencies. None the less, film criticism in the 1920s, especially in France, sought a theoretical framework in Bergsonian notions of time, memory and the self. In 1918, Marcel L'Herbier argued that Bergson's critique of the camera in no way undermined his profoundly cinematic conception of time and experience,[5] and Gilles Deleuze has repeated the argument that Bergson's critique of cinema was 'overhasty' and poses no obstacle to a marriage of Bergsonism and film semiotics.[6]

But is Bergson's work really in sympathy with cinema? The answer is not so simple as L'Herbier and Deleuze make out. Bergson's critique of cinematic technology cannot be quickly dismissed, even if Bergsonian 'durée' seems now to fall within film theory's ultimate grasp. Though Bergson acknowledged cinema's potential, his warnings about the character of cinematic representation remain an important legacy and can illuminate current discussions about film, perception and culture.

Bergson's discussion of the film camera is part of his general critique of the intellect, which begins with the primacy of movement and change. 'We change without ceasing', and life itself is 'nothing but change' and 'unceasing creation'.[7] Intellect compensates for the vertigo of flux: 'against this idea of the absolute originality and unforeseeability of forms our whole intellect rises in revolt'.[8] Bergson calls this the 'mechanistic instinct of the mind' that is 'stronger than reason, stronger than immediate experience'.[9] The intellect's role is to 'mark off the boundaries of bodies', creating 'a stable view which we call a form'. But really that 'body' is changing constantly,

> or rather, there is no form, since form is immobile and the reality is movement. What is real is the continual *change of* form: *form is only a snapshot view of a transition*. Therefore, here, again, our perception manages to solidify into discontinuous images the fluid continuity of the real.[10]

We suspend awareness of reality-as-mobility in order to function in the world: 'It is in *spatialised time* that we ordinarily place ourselves. We have no interest in listening to the uninterrupted humming of life's depths. And yet that is where real duration is.'[11]

Bergson explains what he means by 'spatialised time' by analogy with the paradoxes of Zeno of Elea. Zeno's paradoxes depend upon our dissecting movement into cinema-like 'frames'. For an arrow to strike a target, it must travel half the distance, half of half the distance and so on. For Achilles to overtake the tortoise, he must pass through an infinite number of places that the tortoise has just left.[12] Such 'pseudo-problems', as Bergson calls them elsewhere, expose the error in our mode of thinking and, incidentally, in the entire project of Western metaphysics. This failure of analysis to approach the Absolute is his recurring theme in all his major works, including his 'Introduction to Metaphysics': 'Were all the photographs of a town, taken from all possible points of view, to go on indefinitely completing one another, they would never be equivalent to the solid town in which we walk about.'[13] We can never understand reality-as-mobility through a cinematographic analysis, since 'rests placed beside rests will never be equivalent to a movement'.[14] Such is Bergson's critique. Certainly, as he claims, the film camera records a sequence of still shots, or 'immobile' images. Just as obviously, cinema's illusion of movement evolved and became hypnotically fluid. We will deal with this second aspect of the problem in a moment, including Bergson's contribution to film theory. First, let us probe his basic argument.

Bergson considers the film camera antithetical to the intuitive perception of life because it makes a mechanical transcription of perception. Since such transcriptions are pragmatic – meant to aid understanding and control – they embody a kind of intellectual imperialism. It is important to note that Bergson was reacting to the use of film technology to gain insights into motion. Stop- and slow-motion cinematography were revealing some astonishing things. But these were, he insisted, limited insights. Bergson's critique of the film camera must be understood as part of his reaction against Spencer and late-nineteenth-century progressivism. Heavily influenced by Spencer, Bergson envisioned the *élan vital* and 'the whole of humanity, in space and in time [as] one immense army'.[15] Perhaps this was why he chose a military regiment to illustrate his discussion of film's inadequacies, for it emblematises the march of progress, and this helps him point out the limitations of the cinematographical method:

> Suppose we wish to portray on a screen a living picture, such as the marching past of a regiment. There is one way in which it might first occur to us to do it. That would be to cut out jointed figures representing the soldiers, to give each of them the movement of marching, a movement varying from individual to individual although common to the human species, and to throw the whole on the screen. We should need to spend on this little game an enormous amount of work, and even then we should obtain but a very poor result: how could it, at its best, reproduce the suppleness and variety of life?[16]

Oddly enough, Bergson's example of cutting out 'jointed figures' perfectly describes the method of re-creating movement used in digital computer modelling. In the early 1990s, the Perrier bottled water company commissioned a computer-animated commercial from Industrial Light and Magic that featured seventy French Foreign Legion toy-soldiers marching in unison. The computer was first programmed with a single walk cycle. Then the cycle was attached to the figure of each soldier. The beginning of the cycle was then offset slightly for every soldier, and shadows were composited on to the 'live action'.[17] But in 1907, obviously, such a solution seemed unachievable, if not unimaginable. A better effect, Bergson argued, would be attained by taking snapshots of the passing regiment and projecting 'these instantaneous views on the screen, so that they replace each other very rapidly'. In other words, the best approximation would be provided by the film camera.

In order to evoke the illusion of movement, however, there had to be movement somewhere. 'The movement does indeed exist here', says Bergson, 'in the apparatus.' The film projector extracts

> from all the movements peculiar to all the figures an impersonal movement abstract and simple, *movement in general*, so to speak: we put this into the

apparatus, and we reconstitute the individuality of each particular movement by combining this nameless movement with the personal attitudes [of
each figure]. Such is the contrivance of the cinematograph. And such is also
that of our knowledge. Instead of attaching ourselves to the inner becoming
of things, we place ourselves outside of them in order to recompose their
becoming artificially. We take snapshots, as it were, of the passing reality,
and, as these are characteristics of the reality, we have only to string them on
a becoming abstract, uniform and invisible, situated at the back of the apparatus of knowledge, in order to imitate what there is that is characteristic in
this becoming itself.[18]

Bergson's critique of the cinema is based, then, upon the indivisibility of
motion. For the cinema, as for physics, motion cannot be projected unless
there is real movement somewhere. The illusion is dependent upon this
irreducible reality. At the same time, he warns of the usual dangers that
inhere in all such re-creations. No matter how effective the illusion of
movement it creates, the snapshots cinema animates remain immobile
'views'. He remains adamant that from movement one can pass to immo-
bility, but not vice versa.[19] The world cannot be apprehended without
resort to an intuitive 'grasp' of what is flowing by. No matter how good the
simulacrum our analytical tools create, it will be lacking without this
dimension of understanding.

Physics itself he predicts will be sterile, 'restricted as it is to the cinematographical method'.[20] We may shoot 24 instead of 16 frames per second. We may use a high-speed camera and shoot 48 or 60 or even 500
frames per second, if we want. There will always be a gap between each
frame which we must fill if we wish to achieve a true representation of the
fluidity of movement. We thus become stuck in a loop of 'perpetual recom-
mencement', in which our minds restlessly seek to resolve the immobile
images into a fluid whole. We may even imagine that our restless dissatis-
faction is the very movement we seek to reconstitute. But though we may
strain our minds 'to the point of giddiness' and create an 'illusion of mobility', we have never advanced towards our goal, for 'In order to advance
with the moving reality, you must replace yourself within it', and this we
have not done.[21] Snapshots, models and other aids to understanding are
like sieves. They capture things. But they do not capture essences.

In 1934 Bergson repeated the argument that, no matter how we try to
overcome the problem, the cinematographic method fails to capture the
essential reality:

> the film could be run ten, a hundred, even a thousand times faster without
> the slightest modification in what was being shown; if its speed were
> increased to infinity, if the unrolling (this time away from the apparatus)
> became instantaneous, the pictures would still be the same. Succession thus

understood, therefore, adds nothing; on the contrary, it takes something away; it marks a deficit; it reveals a weakness in our perception, which is forced by this weakness to divide up the film image by image instead of grasping it in the aggregate.[22]

And this lack reflected in the cinematographic method is once again charged to the failure of the tradition of Western metaphysics:

> In short, time thus considered is no more than a space in idea where one imagines to be set out in line all past, present, and future events, and in addition, something which prevents them from appearing in a single perception: the unrolling in duration would be this very incompletion, the addition of a negative quantity.[23]

That is what is wrong with previous philosophies, Bergson says, for none of them has 'sought positive attributes in time'. Instead, they have treated 'succession as a co-existence which has failed to be achieved', and time as 'non-eternity'.[24]

Bergson maintained this position well into the 1930s (he died in 1941 in his eighty-second year), when film had advanced dramatically in creating an effective illusion of movement. To the end, the cinematic analogy was one that threw into sharp relief for him the difference between spatialising intellection and *intuition philosophique*:

> It is true that alongside the states of consciousness which live this unshrinkable and inextensible duration, there are material systems which time merely glides over. Of the phenomena which follow from them one can really say that they are the unfurling of a fan, or better still, the unrolling of a cinematographic film.[25]

Bergson distinguishes 'between an evolution and an unfurling, between the radically new and a rearrangement of the pre-existing'.[26] A cinematic representation is an unfurling, not an evolution, a camouflage that 'glides over' the reality underneath. It allows us to function, but at a price.

There are some problems with Bergson's critique of the so-called 'cinematic method', from a late-twentieth-century perspective. It may be true that one cannot reconstitute movement from still shots. Still, when I view film, I do not find myself 'straining ... to the point of giddiness' merely to gain the 'illusion of mobility'. At 24 frames per second, film projection is so convincing that most viewers fall immediately under its spell. I acknowledge that film conventions to which I have been habituated since my childhood play a role in my response. None the less, if I find the evocation of movement *believable*, then what does it matter exactly how the mechanism works? Bergson may insist on his analogy all he wishes, but its intuitive rightness evaporates.

According to Gilles Deleuze, Bergson may be excused for failing to see that film embodies exactly that intuitive grasp of mobile reality that he denied it. Deleuze argues that Bergson had reacted against the crude, fixed-viewpoint illusions of Lumière, Edison and Méliès: 'We can … define a primitive state of the cinema where the image is in movement rather than being movement–image. It was at this primitive state that Bergsonian criticism was directed.'[27] Early film created an imitation of motion not all that far removed from the flip-book, typified by Méliès's inventive but crude *Trip to the Moon* (1902) or *Paris to Monte Carlo* (1903).

None the less, film-makers refined their art. We can observe this process occurring in Expressionist films such as *The Cabinet of Dr Caligari* (1919). The camera now captures objects in more complex movement – a roundabout in the background of a milling crowd scene, for example. And by the early 1920s, camera pans and tracking shots – which had already been pioneered by D.W. Griffith in *Birth of a Nation* (1915) and *Intolerance* (1916) – appear regularly in commercially released films, such as Murnau's *Nosferatu* (1922). Perhaps Bergson's continued scepticism was reinforced by the advent of cinematic sound-tracks. They were of low quality, and the noise of the camera necessitated its isolation in a sound-proofed booth on a set for synchronous sound, hindering the advent of the mobile camera.[28]

Laura Marks has said that Deleuze believed cinema did not 'attain its typical form' until after Bergson's death in 1941, and that this explains Bergson's continuing criticism of the film camera. But this would make the breakthrough to Deleuze's 'time-image' simultaneous with cinema's reaching its maturity as a simple representation of 'mobility'.[29] This is not Deleuze's view, nor can it be ours. Cocteau's *Le sang d'un poète* was released in 1930. Did Bergson see it? Did he see *All Quiet on the Western Front* (1930), with its mobile camera, excellent sound, deep-focus shots and its indictment of the machines of killing? Film was maturing rapidly. By 1931, all studios were using Mitchell news cameras in blimps, and the camera-booth virtually disappeared overnight.[30] But in this period Bergson was an ailing man preoccupied with finishing his last book, *The Two Sources of Morality and Religion* (1932). Perhaps he simply never encountered the innovations that might have changed his mind.

But assuming he knew something of cinema's development, what might be his reasons? Even today effects persist that reveal film's artificiality – who can forget seeing the film jam and melt in a projector? More to the point, who can forget watching a car or wagon on the movie-screen drive forwards while the spinning spokes of its wheels appear to be moving in reverse?[31] In extreme telephoto shots, people moving towards or away from the camera appear to walk or ride without progressing, like pantomimists. Such artefacts remind us that there truly are misrepresentations inherent in the film mechanism. The more one looks, the more there are. Film and television actors and directors know the screen adds weight. Actors must diet to gauntness in order to appear 'normal' on screen. This effect is an obvious consequence of spatialisation; the reduction of the figure to two dimensions at certain focal lengths makes it appear 'fatter' or 'thinner'. Bergson did not discuss this. He restricts his specific criticism to the problem of the 'gap'. In vain would we argue that in a film shot and projected at 500 frames per second anything remotely resembling a cinematic flicker has disappeared, and the effect of backward-spinning wheels disappears as well. In vain do we point out that Bergson's argument about the speed of film regards only its *projection*, not its shooting speed. Did he consider how anyone could possibly discriminate between two contiguous frames of a film shot at 500 fps? At such a speed, the evocation of fluidity has approximated so nearly to its target as effectively to blunt this prong of Bergson's argument.

In spite of this, his main thrust against the mechanistic nature of the film camera remains valid. The criticism of the 'gap', which accorded so well with his critique of Zeno's paradoxes, may fail to move us, but he is right that the cinematic image projected on the screen is not the exact replica of the world that it has come to be regarded as. In time, it will doubtless appear a perfect reflection of a peculiarly late-twentieth-century world-view. The film camera *is* an apparatus, and it does have important limitations and even ideological implications, and these are in harmony with Bergson's critique of spatialisation.

Jean-Louis Baudry and Jean Comolli were prime instigators of an ideological critique of the optics and mechanisms of the film camera that emerged in the 1970s. Baudry traced cinematic technology's roots to the theory of perception and the rules of painting promoted by da Vinci, Alberti and the Renaissance theorists of perspective.[32] Dudley Andrew and William Wees, among others, have clarified Baudry's argument that the lens of the camera obscura brings with it the mind of the Renaissance: 'The cinema thus inherits the desire of Renaissance culture for the centred representation of any visual field.'[33] It all began with Kepler and Descartes, who saw the eyeball as a 'mini-projection system with adjustable focus and a built-in rear-projection screen'.[34] The age of exploration demanded instruments for mapping the courses of ocean voyages, and the camera obscura led to the development of a monocular and mathematical theory of visual representation. Painters learned to think of their work as the production of a plane intersecting the rays of light emanating from the object in view. This led to the grid – now a commonplace of art classes – with which artists duplicated 'reality' more accurately. The Renaissance theorists of perspective 'conflated the perceptual and the purely optical aspects of perspective' and talked about the objects being represented 'as if they were explaining concepts in geometry and mathematics'.[35] Because this manner of proceeding eliminated so much that makes visual perception rich and deep, André Bazin condemned it polemically as 'the original sin of Western Painting' and José Arguelles charged that its goal was the 'mechanizing [of] vision, and thus mind'.[36] Painters can include more than one distance-point and therefore more than one implied point of view in a single painting.[37] And so can cinematographers, through the use of mattes and frame-division – that is to say, through the superimposition of images. This does not undermine the basic critique that cinematic images spatialise in an enlightenment-optics way. Lev Kuleshov, the legendary Soviet film director, whose career spanned the years 1917–43, described cinematic space as a 'metrical web' – like graph-paper in three dimensions.[38] As Wees explains, the twentieth-century film camera and projector

> incorporated the grids, eyepieces and other mechanical contrivances in the perspectivist's toolbox. From these rigid restrictions on seeing comes the typical cinematic image. Not only is it in 'natural perspective,' but the usual cinematic image shows a world that is focused, stable, and unambiguously lit. These additional norms are not required by the rules of perspective, but they have proved to be peculiarly suited to an image-making system based on mathematically precise calculations and geometrically exact proportions.[39]

The cinematic image has lost its oddity for us, and we rarely reflect on its severely limited range: little more than 2 degrees of the 200-degree angle of normal vision. The 'keyhole effect' of the very tight shot maximises awareness of this limitation, which does not disappear as the shot widens – rather, it becomes simply less occlusive, leaving us less *consciously* aware of our dependence upon the camera's movement to disclose what lies out of frame. The eye can move rapidly to assess a wide angle of vision, leaping in split-second saccades. Not so the camera.

Professional camera operators have always had to avoid excessive panning, zooming and tracking so that audiences do not get vertigo. A breakthrough has occurred in the development of a stabilised 'hand-held' camera that is strapped to the body of the operator and equipped with levers and pulleys, allowing the camera to communicate rapid movement in a more natural, body-connected way, but such innovations have only ameliorated, not fundamentally altered the restricted nature of the cinematic space. As Wees says, the peculiar thing is how desensitised audiences are to film's distortions: 'The situation has become so thoroughly institutionalised that the dominant cinema, its audiences, and most critics who write about it happily accept perspectivist norms.'[40] Anthropologists have reported that people with no experience of pictorial perspective find photographs nearly uninterpretable. But we have lost our sense of that strangeness.

Wees's critique, which emerges from that of Baudry, Comolli and Claude Baible, accords with Bergson's. The film camera is an extension of the spatialising, tool-making ability of the human race. A valuable innovation, it also covers over immediate experience, absorbing and transforming perception: 'We imagine perception to be a kind of photographic view of things', says Bergson, 'taken from a fixed point by that special apparatus which is called an organ of perception – a photograph which would then be developed in the brain by some unknown chemical process of elaboration.'[41] The problem is that 'the very mechanism by which we only meant at first to explain our conduct will end by also controlling it'.[42]

For film theoreticians like Baudry and Comolli, the invention of film technology has just such sinister implications. They observe film's supremacy with great misgivings. Comolli, especially, argued that the apparatus itself embodied a capitalistic ideology, not the 'scientific character' to which it pretended.[43] This argument seems overdone, and yet one need not be a Marxist to see that film technology is inseparable from the capitalistic enterprise system that gave birth to it in a mass market. Its conventions encourage each of us 'to desire and possess a consumable space from his or her own perspective', as Dudley Andrew has said. Further, 'The supposed scientific base of cinema guarantees the permanent rights of individuals to rule the world with their eyes just as science itself rules it with knowledge and a bourgeois class rules it with capital.'[44] Baudry argues that this effect is real and that it is repressed. Here we have passed from the biological (ocular) to the social-psychological aspect of perception, which has important ramifications for film theory.

For example, an interesting discussion of the way that sound effaced the artificiality of the cinematic image has been offered by Rick Altman. He argues that sound is the repressed, subconscious theatrical origin of film as we experience it: 'the major function of sound, considered from the standpoint of the image, is to convince the viewer that the image exists independently of the technology which would mark it as a fiction'.[45] This is an infrequently discussed but important aspect of Bergson's concern over spatialisation and mechanism in cinematic representation. Bergson said people must avoid covering over their inner, dynamic selves with a usurper. When we over-conceptualise life, 'our living and concrete self gets covered with an outer crust of clean-cut psychic states', a 'parasitical self' begins to encroach upon and destroy our lives, turning us into 'conscious automatons': 'Many live this kind of life and die without having known true freedom.'[46] Cinema has indeed had insidious, hypnotic, alienating effects, and if Altman is correct, sound itself participates in creating such effects in viewers.

In general, such worries over alienation have bothered viewer–critics ever since film's emergence as mass entertainment. T. S. Eliot, who attended Bergson's lectures in 1910–11, wrote a eulogy for the music-halls in 1923. Lamenting their passing, he noted that one goes now to the cinema to have one's 'mind lulled by continuous senseless music and continuous action too rapid for the brain to act upon', causing one to 'receive, without giving'.[47] Huge quantities of capital and labour have been expended in cinematising mass consciousness. The results have included the promotion of conventional ideas about how people and objects look and how they should be treated.[48] The cinematic experience usually ends in adjusting people to its functions, not vice versa.

But if the film camera hides a demon, does it not also capture 'lost time'? As we have noted, Bergson's critique of cinema did not dissuade its defenders from claiming him as their philosopher. He himself seems to have been drawn to cinema's possibilities, as is indicated in these remarks he made in 1914 upon the fourth chapter of *Creative Evolution*:

> As a witness to its beginnings, I realised [cinema] could suggest new things to a philosopher. It might be able to assist in the synthesis of memory, or even of the thinking process. If the circumference [of a circle] is composed of a series of points, memory is, like the cinema, composed of a series of images. Immobile, it is in a neutral state; in movement, it is life itself.[49]

This comparison of the film-experience with memory seems to have been precisely the aspect of Bergson to which film-makers, like literary artists, responded in the mid-1920s. Just before she began writing *The Waves* (1931), Virginia Woolf described film as an art of dream in which the past can be 'unrolled' and 'distances annihilated'. Like other early film critics, she predicted that cinema would find its own language and symbols.[50] Jean Epstein described this as a search for a 'cinematic grammar or rhetoric'.[51]

Emile Vuillermoz also responded strongly to Bergson's description of the flow of cinematic images as an evocation of 'life itself' and made use of Bergson's work in articles defending the cinema as a genuine art-form in *Le Temps* in 1916 and 1917. When Vuillermoz came under attack from Paul Souday, who argued that Bergsonism and the cinema did not mix, Marcel L'Herbier came to Vuillermoz's defence. In the course of a long article entitled 'Hermès et le silence', published in *Le Film* in 1918, L'Herbier wrote that Bergson's invidious comparison of 'conceptual thought to the mechanism of the cinema' hardly warranted the conclusion that the philosopher hated cinema. L'Herbier concluded that Souday was 'wandering in the cinegraphic wasteland', and that Vuillermoz had correctly understood cinema to be essentially Bergsonian.[52]

While sympathising with Vuillermoz and L'Herbier, I must none the less reassert that the cinematic analogy played an ambiguous part in Bergson's arguments. For example, 'Introduction to Metaphysics' tells us that life is like 'the unrolling of a coil', and also like a 'continual rolling up', but actually 'it is neither'.[53] Such cryptic formulations caused understandable annoyance in Bergson's critics. Even friends, like William James, confessed that there is a 'peculiarity of vision' in Bergson's work: 'I have to confess that Bergson's originality is so profuse that many of his ideas baffle me entirely.'[54]

What finally unifies his critique of the cinematographic method with his ideas of spatialisation, intuition and duration? It is the fact that his critique is part of an attack on Platonic idealism and Western metaphysics. It was in this context that James announced that Bergson had compelled him to *give up the logic*, fairly, squarely, and irrevocably'.[55] He believed Bergson had 'killed intellectualism' in its 'ancient platonizing role'.[56] Bergson's attack on the cinematic apparatus was part of this same battle. But if Bergson slew 'intellectualism', he also defined intuition as a mode of thinking.[57] As F. C. T. Moore has pointed out, the sneering slaps at Bergson's intuitionism from Russell and others are unfair, for Bergsonian intuition is clearly 'an exercise, often an arduous and densely argued exercise, of thinking'. In restricting human reason, 'Bergson's motive was not fear, but precision'.[58] His condemnation of the mechanisms of the cinema is identical, in that regard, to his critique of language. On the one hand, he says words 'can express the new only as a rearrangement of the old',[59] and claims that

> every language, whether elaborated or crude, leaves many more things to be understood than it is able to express. Essentially discontinuous, since it proceeds by juxtaposing words, speech can only indicate by a few guide-posts placed here and there the chief stages in the movement of thought ... I shall never be able to understand [your speech] if I start from the verbal images themselves, because between two consecutive verbal images there is a gulf which no amount of concrete representations can ever fill. For images can never be anything but things, and thought is a movement.[60]

This precisely repeats his critique of the film camera's 'gaps'. And yet, on the other hand, he also writes that intuition gave 'birth to poetry ... and converted into instruments of art words which, at first, were only signals'.[61]

Bergson's conception of cinema is also ambivalent. It partakes of the reciprocally interacting dualisms of his thought generally, in which flawed modes of thinking are never completely overcome, but do achieve self-consciousness and do progress. The struggle properly to represent experience always involves unsatisfactory methods and partial successes. 'Can time be adequately represented by space?', Bergson asks rhetorically. And the answer is, 'Yes, if you are dealing with time flown; No, if you speak of time flowing.'[62] So for classical metaphysics. So also for cinema: 'Yes' and 'No'. Flawed in its technological heart, film may never represent the indeterminacy of immediate experience. None the less, it can evoke the mechanisms of memory. Perhaps, as Deleuze claims, cinema has even proven capable of reflection and shown that it can 'do violence to itself' and 'reverse the direction of the operation by which it habitually thinks', as Bergson demanded.[63]

Such an outcome has indeed been the conscious goal of many avant-garde film-makers. Stan Brakhage wrote in the 1960s of 'deliberately spitting on the lens or wrecking its focal attention' to free the cinematic image from 'Western compositional perspective'.[64] Ernie Gehr's *Serene Velocity* (1970) is a direct assault on perspectivism. It shows a long corridor whose lines converge on a classic vanishing-point. By juxtaposing four-frame shots from an identical camera position taken with widely varying focal lengths (a zoom lens was used), Gehr makes the corridor pulse and stretch and appear to convulse itself, shattering the camera's illusion of three-dimensional space.[65] John Belton has described the zoom lens as 'a metaphor for the disintegration of space through time', because under its influence 'space is no longer defined in terms of perspective cues and parallax, but in terms of changing image size and time'.[66] Sidney Peterson's *The Lead Shoes* (1949) also undermines perspective by employing an anamorphic lens that elongates and foreshortens objects, estranging the viewer's eye from the illusion of three-dimensional accuracy. There have even been cameraless films, such as Brakhage's *Mothlight* (1963).

Bergson's critique of spatialisation in conceptual systems endorses such efforts to overcome film's technical limitations, and Deleuze asserts that the cinema is Bergsonian in precisely this way: it becomes self-aware. Deleuze cleverly exploits the 'terminological ambiguities' in Bergson's attack on cinematic illusion,[67] transferring the definition of Bergson's term 'cuttings' from the frame to the shot. He then argues that 'shots' are identical with the 'mobile sections' of reality described in *Matter and Memory*. Cinema progressed from its primitive state into sophistication with 'montage, the mobile camera', but most importantly for Deleuze, 'the emancipation of the viewpoint'.[68] Grasping, then, at threads trailing from this supposed terminological misunderstanding, Deleuze proceeds to claim that Bergson was 'startlingly ahead of his time' in defining the universe as 'cinema in itself, a metacinema'.[69]

Deleuze has done something wonderfully perverse here, as he admits.

Bergson never was ambiguous about 'cuttings'. For him, these always referred to film's individual frames, never to an editor's 'cuts' (or montage). Still, Deleuze's use of his concepts of memory and time in film are thought-provoking, and he makes us believe that perhaps he understood Bergson better than the philosopher understood himself.

Bergson described two kinds of memory: 'one, fixed in the organism, is nothing else but the complete set of intelligently constructed mechanisms which ensure the appropriate reply to the various possible demands'. This is an adaptive, habitual response: 'Habit rather than memory, it acts our past experience, but does not call up its image.' The other is pure memory, which 'retains and ranges alongside of each other all our states in the order in which they occur, leaving to each fact its place and consequently marking its date'.[70] If the past is like 'a register in which time is being inscribed',[71] then conscious remembering is like 'the focussing of a camera'.[72]

Deleuze believes that film images constitute a 'pre-verbal intelligible content (*pure semiotics*)' or 'direct time-image', in short, a representation of *durée* itself.[73] I see no reason to privilege film above other arts in this regard. All representation is partial and limited. But in the right hands, the film camera confronts those realities Bergson expected all human art to face. In its evocation of the flow of time, film has indeed approached Bergson's *durée* and embodied his construct of true and false selves. Since, above all, film deals with visual perception, its artificiality affords it that same sophistication to be found in the literary or plastic arts. The camera, too, can view objects subjectively – from the point of view of some definite character depicted, whether that character is established on screen or not. If seen subjectively, cinematic images of movement correspond to direct discourse in prose fiction. Alternatively, the moving image may be given from a point of view that cannot be established as belonging to a specific personage; it then corresponds to indirect discourse.

Like literature or painting, cinema can be self-reflexive. Novels may contain 'letters' or other texts, or even be composed of documents within documents, like Mary Shelley's *Frankenstein* or Vladimir Nabokov's *Lolita*. Film, too, can employ films or videos within films, as in the newsreel opening of *Citizen Kane* (1941). Directors now commonly use grainy television images to evoke 'realism'. Film also can grapple with its own mechanism through symbols of mechanised time. In Hitchcock's work such images are ubiquitous and self-reflexive. Take for example a sequence in *The Secret Agent* (1936), in which a young boy's journey to deliver booby-trapped film-cans is intercut with images of clocks and stop-lights, the montage building to a climax in which the bomb finally goes off.

Another Bergsonian aspect of cinema involves its evocation of a 'true self' to balance the 'parasitical' and alienated self discussed above. The most powerful unifying cinematic image is that of the human face. This was understood very early on, as established by the 'Kuleshov effect'. Around 1918, Kuleshov demonstrated that the insertion of a close-up of an expressionless human face at various points in a montage consisting of random objects (a bowl of soup, a child holding a teddy-bear, the body of a woman in a coffin, and so on) caused film-viewers to attribute emotions to the actor's expression. This led Deleuze to describe the image of the face as 'the recognition of self by self'.[74]

Great cinema thrives on the energy created by an oscillation of consciousness like that described by Bergson in his theory of memory and perception. Bergson's conception of the self is in a sense perfectly reflected in the cinema's floating consciousness: 'You may say that my body is matter, or that it is an image: the word is of no importance.'[75] And again: 'Itself an image, the body cannot store up images, since it forms a part of the images.'[76] The film projected on the screen creates a flow of images, like a consciousness that is constantly moving, attending alternately to memory and to life, aware of its internal power and its external entanglement in the world. For Bergson, conscious life means an awareness of this doubling, of two distinct selves,

> one of which, conscious of its liberty, erects itself into an independent spectator of a scene which the other seems to be playing in a mechanical way. But this duplication does not go through to the end. It is rather an oscillation between two standpoints from which one views oneself, a going and coming of the mind between perception which is only perception, and perception duplicated in memory.[77]

From this doubling of self we receive contradictory impressions: 'We act and yet "are acted". We feel that we choose and will, but that we are choosing what is imposed on us and willing the inevitable.' And because these selves are 'logically incompatible, reflective consciousness will represent them by a duplication of the self into two different personages, one of which appropriates freedom, the other necessity: the one, a free spectator, beholds the other automatically playing his part'.[78] The dreamlike experience of film-viewing is haunted by these competing personages, who are reflected in the objects to which the camera alternately attends.

The opening sequence of Hitchcock's *Number 17* (1932) exemplifies my point. A dolly-shot tracks leaves blowing down a street, focusing not on leaves in motion so much as motion itself. We follow as the camera picks up the dark figure of a man who retrieves his wind-blown hat and goes through the front door of a house. We peer over his shoulder, and the camera pans up to a neck-breaking view of the upper-floor balustrade – a view meant to be indistinguishable (for a moment) from that of the character himself. In rapid sequence we have gone from the free spirit of the wind to a breakneck view of a claustrophobic interior space. Such sequences, it has been proven statistically, typify Hitchcock's cinema.[79]

Not long after this film, Hitchcock had learned to use such camera movements to create an even subtler oscillation between first and third person. A famous sequence from *The Man Who Knew Too Much* (1936) shows his sophistication. Edna Best stars as Jill Lawrence in this drama of a woman who must decide whether to try to prevent an assassination, knowing that the assassins, led by Abbot (Peter Lorre), hold her daughter hostage. As Jill sits in a concert-hall, trying to pick out the probable victim of the crime, the camera pans across the upper balconies, hesitating and then returning to examine a moving curtain more closely, just as if we were seeing things through Jill's eyes. In a smooth pan, the camera then passes back over the balconies and across the audience. Jill herself appears in the shot; we are no longer looking through her eyes. This fluid shift from first to third person is then augmented by the introduction of an image that is either subjective or objective – or both. Jill suddenly realises who the assassin's target must be. Overcome by emotion, she stares down at the conductor, and we are shown her face, intercut with many perception-images of instruments and even of wires leading to a radio in the apart-ment of the conspirators. We see Jill's face, then the concert-hall through her eyes. The camera goes out of focus; her vision blurs until the screen goes white. A gun-barrel obtrudes in the white screen. The camera pulls back to reveal the curtain. We see Jill's face again, as she stares up at the balcony, horrified to see that the gun she imagined is real.

In that sequence Hitchcock creates an image in which interior and exterior realities become indistinguishable. Hitchcock's use of the white screen, whether in a fade to white or, as in the case of *Spellbound* (1945), a 'wipe' (Gregory Peck's vision is filled by the milk in the glass he is drain-ing), always represents a regression of both personality and consciousness. It thus seems directly connected to Bergson's diagram for his 'circuit' of 'reflective perception' in *Matter and Memory*.[80] In Bergson's view, there must be a minimum circuit in which perception occurs, a point at which the alternate flashing of the mental image and the stimulus that provokes it is so rapid that the difference is indistinguishable.

It is hard not to agree with Deleuze that in such movies Hitchcock has reproduced the 'very movement-image of the first chapter of *Matter and Memory*'[81] and that cinema went on to extend the mental image into a sophisticated editorial practice that presses the limits of the point of view (POV) – for example, in Welles's *The Trial* (1963) and especially in the con-clusion of *The Lady from Shanghai* (1948). Welles's use of deep-focus shots to trace complex strands of recollection in *Citizen Kane* seems to epitomise the cinema's power to evoke Bergsonian pure memory and the mechanisms by which memory is (or is not) effectively linked to the demands of action.

Bergsonian concepts offer the rudiments of a cinematic semiology, then, whether one agrees with Deleuze's handling of them or not. This is especially so because Bergson's view of cinema was ambivalent. I believe he would have agreed that, for better or worse, cinema has become a mode of expression demanding a semiological analysis. He would also have agreed that cinema has the same resources and limits as fiction or poetry. In his first book, *Time and Free Will*, Bergson wrote of the limited triumph art may achieve:

> Now, if some bold novelist, tearing aside the cleverly woven curtain of our conventional ego, shows us under this appearance of logic a fundamental absurdity, under this juxtaposition of simple states an infinite permeation of a thousand different impressions which have already ceased to exist the instant they are named, we commend him for having known us better than we knew ourselves. *This is not the case, however, and the very fact that he spreads out our feelings in a homogeneous time and expresses its elements by words, shows that he in his turn is only offering us its shadow: but he has arranged this shadow in such a way as to make us suspect the extraordinary and illogical nature of the object which projects it*; he has made us reflect by giving outward expression to something of that contradiction, that interpenetration, which is the very essence of the elements expressed. Encouraged by him, we have put aside for an instant the veil which we interposed between our consciousness and ourselves. He has brought us back into our own presence.[82]

Great art is, for Bergson, always self-reflexive, offering us striking 'perceptions' while also undermining our faith in their validity by exposing their artificiality. Like other forms of expression, cinema struggles for such breakthroughs to levels of reality that lie deep below the surfaces of which it is necessarily constructed. Deleuze is, then, correct in identifying Bergson as a philosopher of the cinema.

To recognise this is not, however, to overturn Bergson's distrust of the camera, despite what Deleuze has said. Film is a technological production. Its chief use at present is unfortunately to blind, to alienate and to numb us. Commercial cinema is dominated by stereotypes and sound-bites. Images are rapidly exhausted through overduplication. Digitisation to expedite commercial flow over cables and wires will only exacerbate these problems, of which we remain too uncritical.

'Nature', Bergson believed, endowed us with 'an essentially tool-making intelligence'. The cinema, too, is part of a vast expansion of human capabilities to invade, describe and control the world. But if our tools extend our reach, they do not simultaneously expand our grasp: 'The body, now larger, calls for a bigger soul', Bergson wrote towards the end of his long life.[83] His critique of the film camera looks thin and out of date from one point of view. But it becomes profound when viewed in the context of his fear that humanity will be crushed 'beneath the weight of its own progress' as machinery meant to liberate us instead bows our heads 'lower to the earth'.[84] Taken in this sense, his response to cinema engages the major issues with which we still struggle. His confrontation with cinema is ours.

Notes

1 CE, p. 329/312; OE, p. 759.
2 Gilles Deleuze, *Cinema 1: the Movement–Image*, trans. Hugh Tomlinson and Barbara Habberjam (Minneapolis, The Athlone Press and University of Minnesota Press, 1986), pp. 58–9.
3 CE, pp. 287/272, 331/314; OE, pp. 725, 760.
4 CM, p. 190/224; OE, pp. 1421–2. I am using the translation of 'Introduction to Metaphysics' by T. E. Hulme (London, Macmillan and Co. Ltd, 1913), though references will cite the corresponding pagination in CM and OE.
5 Richard Abel, ed. and trans., *French Film Theory and Criticism: a History/Anthology, 1907–1939*, 2 vols (Princeton, Princeton University Press, 1988), vol. 1, pp. 148–9.
6 Deleuze, *Cinema 1*, p. xiv.
7 CE, pp. 2/2, 24/23; OE, pp. 496, 513.
8 CE, p. 30/29; OE, p. 519.
9 CE, p. 18/17; OE, p. 508.
10 CE, pp. 318–19/302; OE, p. 750.
11 CM, pp. 149–50/176; OE, p. 1384.
12 CE, pp. 325–32/308–15; OE, pp. 755–60; CM, p. 17/16; OE, pp. 1258–9.
13 CM, pp. 160–1/189; OE, pp. 1394–5.
14 CE, p. 329/312; OE, p. 759.
15 CE, p. 286/271; OE, p. 725.
16 CE, pp. 321/304–5; OE, p. 752.
17 Christopher W. Baker, *How Did They Do It? Computer Illusion in Film and TV* (Indianapolis, Alpha Books, 1994), pp. 155–9.
18 CE, pp. 322/305–6; OE, p. 753.
19 CM, pp. 185–6/218–20; OE, pp. 1417–18.
20 CE, p. 361/342; OE, p. 784.
21 CE, pp. 324/307–8; OE, p. 755.
22 CM, p. 18/18; OE, pp. 1259–60.
23 CM, p. 18/18; OE, p. 1260.
24 *Ibid.*
25 CM, p. 20/20; OE, p. 1261; emphasis added.
26 CM, p. 21/21; OE, p. 1262.
27 Deleuze, *Cinema 1*, p. 24.
28 See, for example, the turgid cinematography of *Dracula* (1931).

29 Laura Marks, 'A Deleuzian Politics of Hybrid Cinema', *Screen* 35 (3) (1994), pp. 244–64: p. 246.

30 Barry Salt, 'Film Style and Technology in the Thirties', *Film Quarterly* 30 (1) (1976), pp. 19–32: p. 25.

31 The origin of this phenomenon is simple: if the number of revolutions per second of the wheel is greater than the number of frames per second (24 fps), then a retrograde movement of the spokes appears, speeding up as the spokes twirl faster.

32 Jean-Louis Baudry, 'The Ideological Effects of the Basic Cinematographic Apparatus', *Film Quarterly* 27 (2) (1974–75), pp. 39–47: pp. 43, 46.

33 Dudley Andrew, *Concepts in Film Theory* (Oxford, Oxford University Press, 1984), p. 23.

34 William Wees, *Light Moving in Time: Studies in the Visual Aesthetics of Avant-garde Film* (Berkeley, University of California Press, 1992), p. 34.

35 *Ibid.*, p. 38.

36 André Bazin, *What Is Cinema?* (Berkeley and Los Angeles, University of California Press, 1967), p. 12; José Arguelles, *The Transformative Vision* (Berkeley, Shambhala, 1975), p. 25.

37 Svetlana Alpers, *The Art of Describing: Dutch Art in the Seventeenth Century* (Chicago, University of Chicago Press, 1983), chapter two.

38 Lev Kuleshov, *Kuleshov on Film: Writings by Lev Kuleshov*, sel., trans. and ed. Ronald Levaco (Berkeley and Los Angeles, University of California Press, 1974), p. 10.

39 Wees, *Light Moving in Time*, p. 43.

40 *Ibid.*, p. 44.

41 MM, p. 31/38; OE, p. 188.

42 TFW, p. 237; OE, p. 155.

43 Jean-Louis Comolli, 'Technique and Ideology: Camera, Perspective, Depth of Field', *Film Reader* 2 (1977), pp. 128–40: pp. 128–30.

44 Andrew, *Concepts in Film Theory*, p. 23.

45 Rick Altman, 'Moving Lips: Cinema as Ventriloquism', *Yale French Studies* 60 (1980), pp. 67–79: pp. 69–70.

46 TFW, pp. 166–8; OE, pp. 110–11.

47 T. S. Eliot, 'In Memoriam: Marie Lloyd', *Criterion* 1 (1923), pp. 192–5: p. 194.

48 Andrew, *Concepts in Film Theory*, p. 24.

49 Georges-Michel, 'Henri Bergson nous parle au cinéma', *Le Journal* (20 February 1914), p. 7.

50 Virginia Woolf, 'The Movies and Reality', *The New Republic* 47 (609) (1926), pp. 308–10: pp. 309–10.

51 Abel, *French Film Theory and Criticism*, vol. 1, p. 207.

52 *Ibid.*, p. 149.

53 CM, p. 164/193; OE, p. 1397.

54 William James, *A Pluralistic Universe* (London, Macmillan, 1909), p. 226.

55 *Ibid.*, p. 212.

56 *Ibid.*, p. 215.

57 CM, pp. 33–5/37–9, 42/48; OE, pp. 1274–6, 1285.

58 F. C. T. Moore, *Bergson: Thinking Backwards* (Cambridge, Cambridge University Press, 1996), pp. 140–1.

59 CM, p. 82/96; OE, p. 1322.

60 MM, p. 125/159; OE, p. 269.

61 CM, pp. 80/94–5; OE, p. 1321.

62 TFW, p. 221; OE, p. 145.

63 CM, p. 190/224; OE, p. 1422.

64 Stan Brakhage, 'The Camera Eye', in P. Adams Sitney, ed., *Metaphors on Vision* (New York, Film Culture, 1963), n.p.

65 Wees, *Light Moving in Time*, pp. 50–4.

66 John Belton, 'The Bionic Eye: Zoom Esthetics', *Cinéaste* 11 (1) (1980/81), pp. 20–7: pp. 26–7.

67 Deleuze, *Cinema 1*, p. 59.

68 *Ibid.*, p. 3.

69 *Ibid.*, p. 59.

70 MM, p. 195/151; OE, p. 292.

71 CE, p. 17/16; OE, p. 508.

72 MM, p. 171/134; OE, p. 277. I find two, not three types of memory in Bergson, though some have argued that in addition to habitual and pure, there is also 'representational' memory. Bergson would acknowledge a projective function in memory that he calls 'representation', meaning the making of mental pictures (see translator's note in MM, p. 3, note/251, note). But he also specifically says: 'To *picture* is not to *remember*' (MM, p. 173/135; OE, p. 278). His memory theory seems to me thoroughly bipolar.

73 Deleuze, *Cinema 1*, pp. ix, 72.

74 *Ibid.*, p. 67.

75 MM, p. 5/20; OE, p. 171.

76 MM, p. 196/151; OE, p. 292.

77 ME, p. 169; OE, p. 920.

78 ME, pp. 169–70; OE, p. 920.

79 Salt, 'Film Style and Technology in the Thirties', p. 51.

80 MM, pp. 127–8/104–5; OE, p. 250.

81 Deleuze, *Cinema 1*, p. 3.

82 TFW, pp. 133–4; OE, pp. 88–9; emphasis added.

83 MR, pp. 309–10; OE, pp. 1238–9.

84 MR, pp. 317, 310; OE, pp. 1245, 1239.

INDEX